Colorful Impressions

Colorful Impressions

*The Printmaking Revolution
in Eighteenth-Century France*

Margaret Morgan Grasselli

WITH ESSAYS BY

Ivan E. Phillips

Kristel Smentek

Judith C. Walsh

National Gallery of Art, Washington

IN ASSOCIATION WITH

Lund Humphries

This exhibition was organized by the
National Gallery of Art, Washington.

EXHIBITION DATES
26 October 2003–16 February 2004

Produced by the Publishing Office,
National Gallery of Art, Washington
www.nga.gov

Editor in Chief, Judy Metro
Editor, Julie Warnement
Designer, Chris Vogel
Production assistant, Rio DeNaro
Typeset in Minion and Didot
Printed on PhoeniXmotion Xantur by
Graphicom in Verona, Italy

Beta-radiography
Lehua Fisher

LIBRARY OF CONGRESS
CATALOGING-IN-PUBLICATION DATA

National Gallery of Art (U.S.)
Colorful impressions : the printmaking revolution in
eighteenth-century France / Margaret Morgan Grasselli
with essays by Ivan E. Phillips, Kristel Smentek,
Judith C. Walsh.
    p. cm.
"This exhibition was organized by the National Gallery
of Art, Washington. Exhibition dates, 26 October 2003–
16 February 2004."
"In association with Lund Humphries."
Includes bibliographical references and index.
ISBN 0-89468-309-8 (pbk. : alk. paper)
ISBN 0-85331-892-1 (hardcover : alk. paper)
1. Color prints, French — 18th century — Exhibitions.
2. Prints — Washington (D.C.) — Exhibitions.
3. National Gallery of Art (U.S.) — Exhibitions.
I. Grasselli, Margaret Morgan, 1951– II. Title.
NE 647.2.N38 2003
769.944'09'033074753 — dc21

                              2003013301

BRITISH LIBRARY
CATALOGUING-IN-PUBLICATION DATA
A catalogue record for this book is available from
the British Library

First published in 2003 by
National Gallery of Art
Washington
www.nga.gov

Hardcover edition published in association with

Lund Humphries
Gower House
Croft Road
Aldershot
Hampshire GU11 3HR
UK

and

Suite 420
101 Cherry Street
Burlington
VT 05401-4405
USA
www.lundhumphries.com

Lund Humphries is part of Ashgate Publishing

10 9 8 7 6 5 4 3 2 1

Contents

Director's Foreword

Accustomed as we are today to seeing color in every conceivable medium, color in artists' prints seems normal to our twenty-first-century eyes. In the early years of the eighteenth century, however, color prints were the exception rather than the rule. Artists had long been searching for viable ways of making prints with realistic colors, but not until some years after Sir Isaac Newton published his theories on optics in 1704 did the breakthrough come: Enterprising printmakers finally realized they could create virtually the entire spectrum of color with just three basic hues of ink—blue, red, and yellow—printed one on top of the other from separate plates. In France, this discovery led to a remarkable period of invention and innovation that lasted only a few decades but resulted in the production of some of the most beautiful, complex, and intricately crafted color prints ever made.

The National Gallery of Art is fortunate to have a remarkably strong collection of eighteenth-century color prints, thanks largely to two of our earliest and most generous donors, Joseph E. Widener and Lessing J. Rosenwald. In recent years, a number of gifts and purchases have added further strength and scope to the collection. Since 1986 the leading donor in this area has been Ivan E. Phillips, who himself has been collecting eighteenth-century French color prints for more than thirty years. Of the 115 prints and related drawings presented here, 47 of them bear Ivan's name, 13 as a donor and 34 as a lender. His taste as a collector has thus had a considerable impact on the shape and substance of this show. Ivan has committed to supporting future purchases and to donating a substantial number of the works lent to the exhibition from his own collection. And for that we are very grateful.

The exhibition was also enthusiastically embraced by two other aficionados of French color prints, A. Thompson Ellwanger III and Gregory Mescha, charter members of the Gallery's Legacy Circle. Fascinated by the exquisite craftsmanship of French eighteenth-century color prints, they have acquired several fine impressions in recent years. A number of these have already been promised or given to the Gallery, and six of the most beautiful are included in the exhibition. Only two other works were borrowed for this show, one from Ruth Cole Kainen, one of the Gallery's most gracious and generous friends, and another from a kind donor who prefers to remain anonymous. Both of these prints have also been promised to the Gallery as future gifts.

Many talented members of the National Gallery's staff worked on this exhibition and the related catalogue with their customary skill and professionalism. Two deserve special mention here: Margaret Morgan Grasselli, curator of old master drawings, who led the project and wrote the catalogue; and Judith A. Walsh, senior paper conservator, who studied the techniques and papers used in the prints and wrote about them for the catalogue. We thank them for their dedication to this project and the new information they have provided about these beautiful works.

Earl A. Powell III

Acknowledgments

I was introduced to French eighteenth-century color prints as an undergraduate more than thirty years ago, and had always hoped I would someday find the time to get to know them better. They are closely linked, after all, with the drawings—of the same country and century— that I most love. It thus made sense that at some point I should spend some time learning about these prints and the print-making techniques that were invented in the eighteenth century specifically to replicate the appearance of drawings. I therefore welcomed the opportunity to work on this exhibition, and indeed, as I expected, the experience has proven to be both educational and challenging. Completing both the exhibition and the catalogue was not a solo effort, however. I depended very much on the invaluable and much needed assistance, advice, and support of a host of people from both inside and outside the National Gallery of Art.

My greatest pleasure in heading up this project has been working closely with some of my favorite donors and friends. Ivan Phillips and his wife Winnie offered their wholehearted support for this exhibition from its inception and warmly welcomed me on several memorable visits to their New York apartment, where we discussed the show and studied prints. Ivan also accompanied me on visits to Montreal to see and study the part of the collection that resides there with his former wife Lisa. She accepted the disruptions caused by our work with humor and understanding. Ivan was always a charming and entertaining companion on our many visits to museums and dealers in both the United States and France, and generously shared with me the knowledge he had gained from more than thirty years of studying and collecting French color prints. Hackneyed as the sentiment may be, this exhibition truly could not have taken place without his support. I have also enjoyed many hours poring over French color prints and discussing their merits with A. Thompson Ellwanger III and Gregory Mescha. Their warm affection for these works has added to my own pleasure in studying them, and their many questions about them have pushed me to probe ever

deeper for answers. I very much value their friendship and their keen interest in this exhibition. I am also grateful to Ruth Cole Kainen and an anonymous lender who both agreed to lend rare color prints to the show and then promised to give those works to the Gallery as future gifts. I must also thank my parents, Mr. and Mrs. Paul S. Morgan, for funding the purchase of a print that I very much wanted to include in the selection. I am delighted they were able to contribute to the exhibition in this way.

Several people made special efforts to make available the prints that I and my colleagues needed to see for our research and visual education. In Paris, we are indebted to Maxime Préaud and Giselle Lambert at the Bibliothèque nationale; Pascal Torres Guardiola and Anne-Marie Réol at the Collection Edmond de Rothschild in the Musée du Louvre; and staff members of the Bibliothèque de l'Arsénal. In New York, we were assisted by Perrin Stein and Colta Ives and the study room staff at The Metropolitan Museum of Art, and by Roberta Waddell and Elizabeth Wyckoff at the New York Public Library. On visits to the Worcester Art Museum and the Museum of Fine Arts, Boston, Ivan Phillips was helped by David Acton and Sue Reed. In London, Kristel Smentek was given invaluable assistance by Liz Miller and Katherine Donaldson at the Victoria and Albert Museum.

Within the rather small coterie of experts on French eighteenth-century color prints are a number of knowledge-able dealers. Several of them have contributed to the success of this exhibition by finding some remarkable impressions for both Ivan and the National Gallery to acquire, including quite a number just within the last couple of years. Ivan and I are especially indebted to the entire Prouté family, Hubert and Michèle and their daughters, Annie Martinez-Prouté and Sylvie Tocci-Prouté; David and Beth Tunick; André Candillier; Paul McCarron; Alan Stone and Leslie Hill; Emanuel von Baeyer; Françoise Michel-Arguillère; Daniela and Brigitte Laube; and Anne and Didier Martinez.

I am very grateful to Kristel Smentek, lecturer in the art department at Hobart and William Smith Colleges, and Judith A. Walsh, senior paper conservator at the National Gallery of Art, for agreeing to write essays for the catalogue.

I do not think either one of them realized how much work these contributions would require, but their efforts were clearly crowned with success. Both of them have come up with an abundance of new material—Kristel on the marketing of prints and Judith on their materials and manufacture—that will add significantly to our understanding of the special place held by color prints in eighteenth-century French art. Kristel is indebted to Jane Boyd, Rena Hoisington, Graham Larkin, Karen Sherry, John Shovlin, and Pamela Warner for their help with her work. Judith, for her part, offers special thanks to her colleagues in the paper conservation department at the National Gallery—Shelley Fletcher, Yoonjoo Strumfels, Constance McCabe, and Cyntia Karnes—for their advice and support. We are especially grateful to Lehua Fisher, conservation technician, for taking beta-radiographs of all the watermarks on the exhibited prints.

I am deeply indebted to Andrew Robison, Andrew W. Mellon Senior Curator of Prints and Drawings, for his encouragement and advice as work progressed on this project. He and Peter Parshall, curator of old master prints, read my introductory essay with great care, and their thoughtful critiques were enormously helpful. I am fortunate indeed to have the support of such generous colleagues. I must also thank Suzanne Boorsch, curator of prints, drawings, and photographs at Yale University Art Gallery, and Arthur Vershbow, a donor and highly knowledgeable collector of illustrated books, for kindly bringing to my attention some important examples of sixteenth-century color intaglio prints. Special thanks also go to Cristiana Garofalo of Florence—as an intern in my department in the summer of 2000, she laid the groundwork for my research by tirelessly copying and organizing bibliographic materials. In addition, invaluable assistance was offered on a daily basis by Sue Cook, Erin McSherry, and Stacey Sell in the department of prints and drawings.

I am grateful to Judy Metro in the publishing office and members of her team: Ira Bartfield, Sara Sanders-Buell, Amanda Mister Sparrow, and Mariah Shay. I must also thank Julie Warnement for editing the manuscripts with a light touch and great respect for the authors' individual voices and needs, and Chris Vogel for combining the authors' words and the printmakers' images into a thoughtfully designed and handsomely illustrated book. Four independent photographers made efforts to supply transparencies on short notice: Brian Merrett in Montreal; Christopher Erb, Robert Lorenzson, and Ross Sheehan in New York. I am also indebted to Larry Shar at Lowy in New York for preparing many of the Phillips collection prints for exhibition.

As always, my colleagues at the National Gallery who worked on this show made my job easier because they did theirs so well. I am grateful to D. Dodge Thompson, Ann B. Robertson, Elizabeth Middelkoop, and Jennifer Overton in the department of exhibitions; Sally Freitag, Theresa Beall, Lauren Mellon, and Dan Randall in the registrar's office; Deborah Ziska and Mary Jane McKinven in the press and public information department; Mark Leithauser and his talented staff in the department of design and installation, especially Deborah Clark-Kirkpatrick, Mari Forsell, and Barbara Keyes; the photographers Ric Blanc, Lorene Emerson, and Lee Ewing; the matters and framers Hugh Phibbs, Elaine Vamos, Laura Neal, and Shan Linde; and Genevra Higginson and her assistants in the office of special events.

Finally, all the authors would like to thank their families and partners for the understanding and support that has helped make this exhibition and catalogue a reality.

Margaret Morgan Grasselli

Color Printmaking before 1730

Margaret Morgan Grasselli

The history of color in prints goes back six centuries, to the very moment when the first woodcuts began to be printed on paper in about 1400. The woodcut technique itself was probably not new to Europe; it may have been used for years in the decoration of textiles. When paper started to become cheap and plentiful toward the end of the fourteenth century, woodcutters and artisans naturally explored the possibilities offered by this new support. Among the earliest works produced may have been playing cards, but devotional images dominated the subject matter. From the very beginning and for several decades thereafter, color played an integral role in every type of woodcut printed on paper (and also on vellum). In those early days, color was

always applied by hand—whether freehand or with the help of stencils—and with varying degrees of care and sophistication (fig. 1). Not only did color serve to fill in the forms and spaces created by the printed contours, but it also completed and enhanced the images. Indeed, without the addition of color, the simplified compositions of most fifteenth-century woodcuts (at least those dating from before the 1490s and the brilliant technical innovations of Albrecht Dürer) appear rather stark and empty.[1] It has recently been argued that some of these woodcuts may even presuppose the use of hand coloring to complete the meaning of the image.[2]

Unlike woodcuts, early intaglio prints—those printed from lines incised or etched into metal plates (usually copper)—were colored quite rarely. Engravings began to be printed on paper in the 1430s, but because the first engravers had trained in goldsmithing and fine metalwork, they quickly attained a high level of artistic merit and sophistication in the new engraving medium. Within a very short time engravers were producing richly worked, highly detailed black-and-white compositions that were complete in themselves. When color *was* used in engravings, it was usually applied more carefully and densely than the color in woodcuts, with the result that the prints were made to look like manuscript illuminations.[3]

Metalcuts, which came into being about 1450, were printed in the same manner as woodcuts, but from metal plates instead of woodblocks. They did not, however, resemble woodcuts in appearance, for cutting away large areas was much harder to do in metal than in wood. In addition, different tools—such as punches and awls—were used to create dotted and linear patterns on the plates. With a greater proportion of black ink to blank paper and the rich patterning of the compositions, metalcut images did not require the same enhancement with color that woodcuts did. Nevertheless, metalcuts were generally hand colored in the same manner as woodcuts, often to beautiful effect (fig. 2).[4]

As appreciation for the special qualities and aesthetic virtues of black-and-white prints developed, the demand for hand-colored prints began to wane at the beginning of the sixteenth century and thus fewer such works were produced

1. German 15th Century (Upper Rhine), *Christ on the Cross with Angels*, 1450/1470, hand-colored woodcut. National Gallery of Art, Rosenwald Collection 1943.3.541

thereafter.[5] Printed color, however, was already coming into regular use in relief prints. The earliest known woodcuts printed in color all occur in books: The first known examples are red and blue initial letters in the *Latin Psalter* published in Mainz by Fust and Schoeffer in 1457.[6] Twenty-five years later, Erhard Ratdolt, an Augsburg printer who lived and worked in Venice between 1476 and 1486, printed schematic diagrams in multiple colors for his 1482 editions of Sacrobusto's *Sphaera Mundi* and Hyginus' *Poetica Astronomica*. Then in 1487, shortly after his return to Augsburg, Ratdolt published the first color woodcut of a figurative image in his *Obsequiale Augustense*: a standing portrait of his patron, Bishop Friedrich von Hohenzollern, printed in black, red, yellow, and olive-green inks. Ratdolt continued to include color woodcuts in subsequent publications, most notably a handsome five-color woodcut (printed in black, red, ochre, light brown, and gray-blue) of the three patron saints of Passau in his 1494 *Missale Pataviense* (fig. 3). That print was almost certainly made by the young Hans Burgkmair I, who would go on to play an

even more important role in color printmaking in the first decade of the next century. All the color blocks used in the woodcuts published by Ratdolt were cut so that the printed colors were separated from each other by the black outlines; thus the prints look very much like woodcuts that had been hand colored with stencils.[7]

Only one example of a fifteenth-century engraving printed in color, that is, in a nonblack ink, is currently known: *The Madonna and Child in a Garden* of 1465/1467 by Master E.S., which was printed in white ink on paper prepared with black ink.[8] Just five impressions of this mysterious, rather ghostly print are known, all in the same combination of white ink and black-prepared paper. In the sixteenth century, the use of colored inks in intaglio prints is still very rare: Several engravings produced at Fontainebleau in France in the 1540s, for example, are known in red-ink impressions.[9] Additionally, in some copies of Raffaello Gualterotti's 1579 festival book, *Feste nelle nozze del serenissimo don Francesco Medici*, a number of the illustrations are printed in color.[10] Otherwise, finding color intaglio prints that were definitely published prior to the seventeenth century is remarkably difficult.

In the absence of colored printing inks, color was added to some intaglio prints by using papers prepared with colored washes. Toward the end of the 1490s, Mair von Landshut was the first to experiment with printing black line woodcuts and engravings on papers prepared by hand with colored washes. Prepared papers had already been used for many years for metalpoint drawings and more recently for virtuoso chiaroscuro (literally, light-dark) drawings.[11] Mair was therefore following a well-established drawing tradition when he adapted prepared papers for use in his prints. As in drawings of this type, the prepared paper served as an overall middle tone from which the artist worked to both dark and light to create the image. In drawings the artist used metalpoint, pen and ink, or brush and wash to draw the composition and to create the shadows, but in his prints Mair created the darks with printed lines. Like the draftsman, however, Mair then applied white gouache to his prints by hand to indicate the highlights. In *The Nativity* (fig. 4), dated 1499, Mair also added touches of gold to brighten the Virgin's halo. Since all the color in Mair's prints was applied by hand, the impressions do not properly qualify as having been printed in color. Nevertheless, they clearly pave the way for the first chiaroscuro woodcuts, which were published less than a decade later.[12]

4. Mair von Landshut, *The Nativity*, 1499, engraving on green prepared paper heightened with white and gold. National Gallery of Art, Rosenwald Collection 1943.3.9091

In its simplest form, a chiaroscuro woodcut consists of a black line block and one tone block that would serve both to print the background color and to create the highlights. Because woodcut is a relief technique, in which the ink is applied to the surface of the woodblock for printing, any part of the block that is not intended to be printed is cut away. For a chiaroscuro print, the areas that were intended to read as white in the final impression were carved out of the tone block. Thus, when that block was inked and printed, the parts of the block that had been removed and thus held no ink would leave the paper untouched and the white of the paper would serve as the highlights in the print. The first steps toward chiaroscuro woodcuts were made by Lucas Cranach the Elder and Hans Burgkmair I, who became notable rivals in this technique. Their first highly elaborate color prints, in 1507 and 1508, respectively, were equestrian subjects printed from two woodblocks on prepared paper.[13] In those prints the paper was washed with color and one of the blocks printed the whole composition in black. The second block served to introduce highlights, but in these first examples, the highlights were positively printed lines rather than blank paper and were gold or silver rather than white. Cranach seems to have "inked" the highlight block with a gluelike substance that was printed onto the image in the normal way. Then, while the printed "lines" were still wet, they were dusted with gold flocking. Burgkmair, by contrast, seems to have printed his

highlights with some form of liquid gold and silver. Both artists quickly took the next step of substituting a true tone block
that simulated the appearance of the prepared paper and at
the same time left parts of the white paper exposed to serve
as highlights. They then moved beyond the basic two-block
method to more complex examples that involved the addition
of a second color block. For example, in Burgkmair's *Lovers
Surprised by Death* of 1510 (fig. 5), the division of the colors is
already very sophisticated and the cutting of the three blocks
is so well integrated that each one contributes equally to the
creation of the image. Such works were the first to approximate effectively the appearance of drawings in printed form.

Perhaps the single most ambitious woodcut of the sixteenth century—certainly the most colorful—was Albrecht
Altdorfer's *The Beautiful Virgin of Regensburg* of 1519/1520,
printed in six colors (fig. 6). The print was uniquely complex
in its time, requiring the careful cutting and aligning of several separate woodblocks. The stencil-like separation of the
colors is somewhat old-fashioned, harking back to the use of

color in the woodcuts published by Ratdolt thirty years before.
Altdorfer's work is actually considerably more advanced, however. For the image of the Virgin and child at center (modeled
on a thirteenth-century icon that was one of the treasures
of Altdorfer's native Regensburg), Altdorfer cut highlights,
chiaroscuro-fashion, into each of the color blocks to give the
figures three-dimensional form. He then used the black line
block not just for the outlines, but also for the embroidered
decoration and swaying fringe on the Virgin's mantle. In the
framework he cut delicate white ornaments and patterns into
the color panels and used black lines to define the architec-
tural setting and to pick out ornamental details.

Within a short time of its invention in Germany, the
chiaroscuro woodcut technique began to be used by Ugo da
Carpi and a number of other Italian printmakers. The first
Italian chiaroscuro woodcuts were executed with only two
blocks, but the Italians, like the Germans, quickly progressed
to more complex works: multiple-block prints in which all the
blocks worked interdependently to form the image. One of
the most famous of all chiaroscuro woodcuts is the *Diogenes*
printed from four blocks by Ugo (fig. 7). Made in about 1528 to

7. Ugo da Carpi, *Diogenes*, c. 1528, chiaroscuro woodcut printed from four blocks. National Gallery of Art, Pepita Milmore Memorial Fund 1997.15.1

8. Augustin Hirschvogel, *Landscape with a Village Church*, 1545, etching on blue paper. National Gallery of Art, Andrew W. Mellon Fund 1980.60.1

reproduce a pen and wash drawing by Ugo's younger contemporary Parmigianino, the print conveys both the fluidity and the rich color variations of several layers of translucent washes.

The distinguished chiaroscuro woodcut tradition continued unabated through the end of the sixteenth century with the compelling works of Hendrik Goltzius and into the seventeenth century with the works of dedicated specialists like Ludolph Büsinck in France and Christoffel Jegher in the southern Netherlands.[14] In the eighteenth century, John Baptist Jackson in England and Anton Maria Zanetti in Italy gave the technique new life, but except for the works of some near contemporaries like John Skippe, very few chiaroscuro woodcuts were produced thereafter.[15]

Given the relatively widespread production of chiaroscuro woodcuts and the imitation of colored papers in these prints, it is somewhat surprising that paper made with colored pulp was used relatively rarely for prints prior to the eighteenth century. Manufactured blue papers existed as early as the late fourteenth century, but the earliest print on blue paper known to me is an Italian woodcut, *Saint Nicholas of Myra*, printed in about 1480.[16] It precedes by almost fifty years the next known figurative prints on blue paper, a group of Italian etchings from about 1527 to 1530 by Master F.P., all after drawings by Parmigianino.[17] North of the Alps, the earliest known print on blue paper is a unique impression of an etching, *Landscape with a Village Church*, dated 1545, by Augustin Hirschvogel (fig. 8). After that, northern prints on blue paper are exceedingly rare until Hendrik Goltzius' woodcuts, which were probably printed in the late 1580s or 1590s.[18] Until the eighteenth century, the total number of works printed on blue paper is relatively small.

About 1530, the painters Parmigianino and Domenico Beccafumi made chiaroscuro prints in a new technique that combined an intaglio line plate with one or two woodcut tone blocks. Parmigianino used this hybrid technique in only one work: a very handsome and quite subtle copy, printed in black and gray, of one of Raphael's tapestry designs, *Peter and John*

Healing the Lame Man at the Beautiful Gate.[19] Beccafumi, for his part, made several prints combining engraving and woodcut, using both together to reproduce with remarkable fidelity the appearance of his own drawings in pen and wash.[20] The thin, crisp engraved lines, in particular, captured the quality of pen lines in a way that woodcut line blocks could not. Similar combinations of woodcut tone blocks and engraved or etched line plates continued to be used by a few artists, including Crispin van den Broeck, Hubert Goltzius, Abraham Bloemaert, and his son Frederick.[21] The technique was revived in the 1720s by Nicolas Le Sueur and the comte de Caylus for a series of prints copying drawings in the collection of Pierre Crozat (fig. 9). Prior to the invention of the chalk-manner and aquatint techniques in the 1750s and 1760s, these works ranked among the best reproductions of drawings produced in France.[22]

About a century earlier, a different variation on the use of etching for chiaroscuro prints was invented by François Perrier: Like Beccafumi, Perrier first etched a black line plate, but instead of a tone block he used gray-brown paper for the middle tone. For the highlights, he etched a second plate that was printed in white ink. In 1633 and 1634, Perrier published several prints in this technique, including *Father Time Clipping the Wings of Love* and a series of six ancient statues.[23] This so-called cameo technique was also used by Abraham Bosse in 1636 for a set of prints illustrating the theological and cardinal virtues.[24] White ink does not appear to have been used again prior to J. C. Le Blon's color mezzotints of the 1730s (cat. 1).

One important printmaker who experimented with a number of ways of introducing color into his etchings was the Haarlem artist Hercules Seghers. He used colored papers and prepared papers, printed with a single colored ink, and added color by hand, with the result that each impression became a unique work in itself. Most of his prints exist in only a few impressions, but *The Enclosed Valley* is known in many examples, each one different from the last.[25] To connoisseurs of Dutch prints, Seghers was the first great experimental printmaker and his etchings rank among the most highly sought-after works of the seventeenth century.

Another inventive seventeenth-century Dutch printmaker was Jan van de Velde IV, who executed two-color intaglio prints about 1655. Working in the first true aquatint technique, Van de Velde used two plates, one inked in black and the other inked in red, to create a remarkable print after a drawing by Nicolas Lagneau, *Head of an Old Man*.[26] His efforts were surpassed by yet another Dutchman, Johann Teyler, who devised in the 1680s a new inking method known as *à la poupée* (literally, with the doll—the knob of fabric, usually muslin, that printers used to daub ink into just some of the lines of a copperplate and then to wipe the excess off the surface, leaving that color isolated in those selected areas). With *à la poupée*

9. Nicolas Le Sueur and the comte de Caylus, *The Assumption of the Virgin*, 1729, etching and two woodblocks printed in orange and green. Private collection

10. Johann Teyler, *Parrot*, c. 1695, color etching inked *à la poupée*. National Gallery of Art, Gift of A. Thompson Ellwanger III and Gregory E. Mescha in memory of Arthur R. Watson 2000.17.2

inking, two or more inks of different colors were applied to different parts of a single plate so that all the colors could be printed at once, in one pass through the press. Depending on how carefully the plate was wiped and how much ink was left on the surface, the inks, when printed, could create broad tonal areas of color as well as separate lines (fig. 10). Inking the plate could be quite a painstaking process, depending on how many colors were being used, and each impression was unique because of differences in the placement of the inks and the selection of the colors. How many prints Teyler himself made is not known, but about three hundred works inked "in the Teyler manner" have been identified, most of which were produced by his workshop.[27] The *à la poupée* inking technique became a staple of the printmaker's arsenal and is still in use today. It enjoyed a moment of heightened popularity toward the end of the eighteenth century in France (cats. 85, 86, 88–91) as complex multiple-plate color prints began to fall out of favor and *à la poupée* inking provided a cheaper way of producing the multicolored prints that were still in demand.

Perhaps the greatest prints made with this technique were a set of ten color aquatints produced by Mary Cassatt in Paris in the 1890s.[28]

Apart from the fifteenth century, when hand-colored woodcuts were produced by the tens of thousands, color played a relatively marginal role in the history of printmaking prior to the eighteenth century. From the sixteenth century onward, the only color print medium in regular use was chiaroscuro woodcut, but the number of artists who specialized in that technique was quite limited and the total number of works produced was comparatively small. Otherwise, the use of color in prints was largely experimental (when individual artists tried out new printing and inking techniques, for example) or exceptional (when a few individual impressions were printed on colored paper or in colored ink). Compared to the overwhelming number of black-and-white prints produced between 1500 and 1730, the total number of color prints produced during the same period is quite small. Toward the middle of the eighteenth century, however, and specifically in France, the production of and market for color prints surged dramatically. This new enthusiasm was fueled in large part by the invention of several new intaglio printmaking techniques, such as color mezzotint, chalk manner, pastel manner, aquatint, and wash manner, which were all specifically designed for color printing. Highly skilled and inventive printmakers happily exploited the new techniques and fed the new market for color prints with literally thousands of works, concentrating on charming, lighthearted images that catered unabashedly to the taste of the moment. The huge escalation in the production and market for color prints constituted nothing less than a revolution that transformed the role of color in printmaking, at least for a time.

Premiere Estampe aux trois Crayons d'après le deßein de M.ᵣ Boucher
premier Peintre du Roy. Gravé par Louis Bonnet le seul qui poßede le
secret d'Imprimer les blancs tire du Cabinet de M.ᵣ de la Garégade,

"An Exact Imitation Acquired at Little Expense"

Marketing Color Prints in Eighteenth-Century France

Kristel Smentek

In 1786, in his *Réflexions sur la peinture et la gravure* (Reflections on painting and printmaking), Charles-François Joullain described prints as objects that "compensate for the inequality of fortunes by satisfying amateurs of every sort. Sovereigns, grandees and opulent men possess paintings, and the public enjoys them in turn by way of an exact imitation acquired at little expense."[1] Joullain's comment is a particularly apt description of the new color print technologies developed in the eighteenth century. Whereas reproductive line engravers could only translate hue and tone into a visual language of black and white, color printmakers could use color mezzotint, chalk manner, and other multiple-plate color printing processes to facilitate the reproduction of color itself and thereby intensify the mimetic potential of printmaking. According to the color printmakers, a color mezzotint or a chalk-manner print was no longer a translation of a drawing or a painting, but rather a facsimile, a copy so exact as to deceive the eye of the most experienced artist or connoisseur. In this verisimilitude lay the novelty and utility of their prints. Easily multiplied color reproductions of artists' drawings and of naturalistically represented botanical specimens or human organs made exact replicas of such works of art and objects of knowledge accessible to all. The arts and sciences would be advanced and the public good served by the invention of color printing.

To stimulate demand for their new products, color printmakers and line engravers alike relied on journal advertisements. Whereas their catalogues simply listed works for sale, advertisements gave printmakers the opportunity to explain, often at length and with supporting editorial commentary, why their prints were desirable and how they could be used. Beginning in the 1730s and particularly after 1750, the number and variety of journals published increased exponentially, offering printmakers multiple venues in which to announce their new works to audiences in France and abroad.[2] In eighteenth-century France, advertising was considered a public service, and until the final decades of the century, it was free.[3] Advertisements advanced the common weal, journal editors asserted, by bringing producers and consumers together. They made new inventions known and thereby contributed to the well-being of the populace and of the entrepreneurs whose livelihood depended on publicity. Astute color printmaker-entrepreneurs such as Jacques-Fabien Gautier Dagoty and Louis-Marin Bonnet took full advantage of advertising, announcing their works repeatedly in almost all of the available journals. Such advertisements offer insights into how color printmakers envisioned the use of their prints and how they tailored their work in response to changing market demand. Journal announcements also suggest why color prints were desirable and how purchasers utilized the color prints they acquired.

In their advertisements, color printmakers appealed overtly to eighteenth-century ideals of utility and the advancement of useful knowledge. Color prints were beneficial, the printmakers and their apologists claimed, because they made inexpensive, coloristically exact reproductions of useful objects widely available. Future surgeons could familiarize themselves with anatomy by studying color mezzotints of the dissected human body (cats. 2, 3) just as aspiring artists could learn to draw by copying accurate chalk-manner prints after drawings (cats. 6, 29). At the same time, color printmakers catered more covertly to a desire for luxury goods that provided pleasure and signified good taste. Printmaker-entrepreneurs sought to furnish consumers with affordable alternatives to coveted but costly items. They advertised their wares as technically innovative, modestly priced facsimiles of paintings, drawings, and pastels for use in interior decoration. More unusual was their suggestion that color prints be used as substitute miniatures on fashion accessories such as snuffboxes, jewelry, and buttons. In the latter sense especially, eighteenth-century color prints resemble "populuxe" goods, a term used by Cissie Fairchilds to designate inexpensive copies of aristocratic luxury objects purchased by the middling classes in eighteenth-century France.[4] Thus if color printmakers engaged with the Enlightenment's cherished notions of progress and education, they also played a part in the emergence of a consumer society in France, one in which the signs of status, good taste, and fashionability could be purchased and enjoyed by those of a less exalted social station.

PRINTED PAINTINGS

In 1721, Jakob Christoffel Le Blon's invention of color mezzotint was announced to readers of the *Mercure de France*. Travelers recently returned from London, where Le Blon lived until 1735, reported that he had discovered the "admirable art of printing portraits and oil paintings with the same precision, same regularity and same exactitude as if they were painted with the brush," and that "paintings of this sort" after Correggio and Federico Barocci, among other artists, were on public view in the English capital.[5] Early reports of Le Blon's color printing process also stressed its utility for anatomical and natural history illustration, but Le Blon, and later Jacques-Fabien Gautier Dagoty, his former student and rival, initially sought to make their fortunes through *tableaux imprimées* (printed paintings), or substitute luxury products. In 1721, with the help of numerous investors, Le Blon established The Picture Office in London to promote and sell inexpensive "printed pictures." The company would find, it was assumed, a ready market. "There never was a more ingenious invention, nor any good furniture so cheap. Our modern painters can't come near it with their colours, and if they attempt a copy, make us pay as many Guineas as now we give shillings," exclaimed one of the many shareholders, convinced his fortune was made.[6] The Picture Office proved, however, to be a financial disaster, and Le Blon barely escaped debtor's prison.[7] After unsuccessfully attempting to apply his discoveries to the production of tapestries, Le Blon brought his invention to France in late 1735 or early 1736, and sought to profit by it there.

When Le Blon's printed portrait of Louis XV (cat. 1) was announced in the French press in 1739, the advantages of color printing for the viewing pleasure of the public were enthusiastically proclaimed. Le Blon's efforts were praised for their "perfect disguise of the burin. The whole is so like a work of the brush that I saw several people deceived by it."[8] By making the rarest paintings available in color and at a low cost, Le Blon's "ingenious invention" would make the visual pleasures of painting more widely accessible:

Its utility was proved by copies of the rarest paintings which one can now have for almost nothing, and by *portraits* of sovereigns and famous men which can, in future, be transmitted to posterity and distributed throughout the world, not with the faded air and simple black and white of *ordinary engraving*, which only immortalizes, in a certain fashion, the dead, but with their most animated characteristics. The *new engraving* can give as much life to these figures as can the brush of the painter.[9]

His portrait of the king may be wanting in some respects, the editors of the *Mercure de France* noted, but Le Blon deserved encouragement because such color prints had the advantage of "1. multiplying paintings and portraits, 2. making them available at very modest prices, [and] 3. allowing one to have, via this method, something finished enough to serve as decoration and give pleasure to the eye."[10] For 15 livres, loyal subjects who could not afford painted portraits of the sovereign could now, courtesy of Le Blon's color mezzotint process, hang a "printed painting" of the monarch in their homes.[11]

The presentation of Le Blon's French portraits reinforced their role as substitute paintings. As described in the *Mercure de France*, Le Blon's earlier portrait of Louis XV's principal advisor, Cardinal de Fleury, was pasted on canvas and attached to a stretcher as if it were indeed a painting, a "painting," moreover, that could be purchased at the minimal cost of 9 livres.[12] Like paintings, Le Blon's prints were frequently varnished, a procedure that both softened and blended the printed colors and heightened the illusion that one was viewing a painted canvas.[13] In a clever and apparently successful marketing strategy, Le Blon also offered sets of individual color separations for the portrait of Fleury at 9 livres per set (see cat. 1).[14] At the same time, Le Blon offered a printed painting after a self-portrait by the Flemish artist Anthony van Dyck.[15] He thus addressed three diverse constituencies: those with a penchant for portraits of important contemporary personages, art lovers with a partiality for paintings by and of Van Dyck, and collectors with an interest in the technical aspects of a promising new invention.

After Le Blon's death in 1741, Jacques-Fabien Gautier Dagoty not only adopted his teacher's multiple-plate process, claiming Le Blon's invention for himself, but also sued successfully for Le Blon's exclusive *privilège* (monopoly) over the technique.[16] An indefatigable entrepreneur, Gautier aggressively and repeatedly advertised his "new" invention in all available journals and suggested a variety of creative uses for his color prints to potential clients. In the December 1741 issue of the *Mercure de France,* Gautier announced the first of his modestly priced *tableaux imprimées.* His choice of imagery was calculated to appeal to a variety of tastes. Thus the prints ranged in subject and style from Salvator Rosa's *Demosthenes in Reflection* (fig. 1) to a *Landscape with Ruins* by the contemporary French painter Jacques de Lajoue, an *Old Chemist in His Laboratory* attributed to Albrecht Dürer, and a *Flemish Woman Chopping Onions* by "Girardow," the seventeenth-

century painter Gerard Dou. Also offered were a portrait of the reigning pope, a still life of peaches, and one of plums — all after pictures by Gautier himself. In an effort to stimulate demand, he provided visual evidence of his skill: an impression of a small color mezzotint of a shell was included with each copy of the December *Mercure.*[17]

To further emphasize the intended role of his prints as substitute paintings, Gautier based the dimensions of his images on *toiles de mesures* (canvases in standardized sizes). The price of each print was determined by its dimensions rather than by the subject reproduced or the fashionability of the artist. Thus Rosa's *Demosthenes*, printed in the largest size, "the size of a canvas of 15" (approximately 25½ × 20¹¹⁄₁₆ inches), cost 4 livres; Gautier's still lifes, printed "in the size of a canvas of 4" (approximately 11³⁄₁₆ × 9 inches), sold for 1 livre; and Dou's *Flemish Woman*, printed in the size of a quarter of a canvas of 4, cost a mere 10 sols.[18] Adopting the format of contemporary *toiles de mesures* for his prints was practical; such standardization meant that consumers could purchase inexpensive prefabricated frames made for paintings and use them for their *tableaux imprimées.*[19] The cost of making the prints even more deceptively like paintings, to "paste them on canvas, stretch them on frames, and varnish them" was similarly dependent on the scale of the print.[20] Thus a mounted, stretched, and varnished *Demosthenes* would cost an additional 1 livre, 10 sols, and an "adapted" *Flemish Woman*, a further 3 sols.[21] Only the framing of the pictures was left to the purchaser.

Gautier further sought to satisfy (or stimulate) demand for his substitute cabinet pictures by marketing some of his prints as pendants.[22] It was conventional in eighteenth-century houses to hang pictures of a similar size, which were often by the same artist, together as pairs.[23] Printed paintings could serve the same purpose. Gautier suggested pairing Rosa's *Demosthenes* with his color mezzotint of the same dimensions after Rosa's *Diogenes with His Friends.* For those with a preference for old masters, he produced small "pendant paintings" after Parmigianino and Giulio Romano; for those more interested in canvases by fashionable contemporaries,

1. Jacques-Fabien Gautier Dagoty, *Demosthenes in Reflection,* after Salvator Rosa, color mezzotint. Ruth Cole Kainen

Gautier printed pendant tableaux after Jean-Baptiste Siméon Chardin's *Embroiderer* (fig. 2) and *Draftsman* (fig. 3).[24]

Though there was no mistaking a black-and-white line engraving for a painting, Gautier's printed paintings, characterized by broad expanses of color and a complete absence of line, could fool even the experts. Or so he claimed. His *tableaux imprimées* were durable "true painting[s] in oil,"[25] that "have not only the coloring of each painter whose paintings have been engraved, but also have the force and softness of these same pictures. No trace of the burin appears; they conform exactly to the paintings after which they were engraved. In a word, they deceive the first glance of the connoisseur."[26] They were therefore "very pretty ornaments for cabinets, especially in country houses,"[27] and particularly appropriate to be used as overdoors, inserted into chimney mantels, or hung above pier glasses, locations for which black-and-white prints were eminently less suitable. Gautier disclosed to readers that he was working on overdoors and chimneypieces representing flowers and fruits,[28] and informed them that his two large prints after Rosa's *Diogenes* and *Demosthenes* were "suitable for the overdoors of cabinets."[29] A very large color mezzotint (measuring, impressively, just over 2 × 2½ feet) after a painting by the contemporary artist Jean-Baptiste-Joseph Pater

would be ideal for use over a mirror, as an overdoor, or as a cabinet picture.[30]

Gauging the success of Gautier's printed paintings is difficult. Studies of household inventories in the first half of the eighteenth century suggest there was a healthy market for decorative pictures and therefore perhaps also for printed paintings.[31] The grand were not alone in decorating their homes with pictures; prosperous wholesale merchants and skilled artisans owned paintings and used them as overdoors, placed them in chimney mantels, and hung them over pier glasses—precisely the uses Gautier advertised for his prints.[32] Also, Gautier announced that his prints after Rosa, for instance, were so popular that a print run of one thousand was insufficient to meet demand and that he therefore had to print a second edition. On the other hand, an anonymous critic questioned the truth of Gautier's claims: "I compliment you on the zealousness of the public to buy your works and I hope with all my heart that [your claim] is founded in truth. What may make it doubtful is the amount of work you must do to wake up the apparently sleeping public with your continual advertisements."[33] In any event, Gautier's print after Pater, announced in 1745, appears to have been his final attempt, at least his last advertised attempt, at replicating paintings. Though his sons continued to print paintings with varying degrees of commercial success, henceforth Gautier Dagoty *père* concentrated his efforts on color mezzotint anatomical and natural history illustrations.[34] These he marketed as assiduously as he had his *tableaux imprimées*, noting, for example, that in his life-size anatomical prints (cat. 3) "the human body is here finally represented after nature. One has the advantage of possessing the body as it is, with neither the horror that the presence of the subject ordinarily inspires, nor the pestilential odor that it exhales."[35] Though his edition of full-scale anatomical prints was "made for hospitals, amphitheaters, academies and public demonstration rooms," he was producing a medium-scale edition to make "his work available to everyone because of its almost universal utility."[36] At a subscription price of 90 livres, however, the "everyone" addressed by Gautier was limited indeed.

ENGRAVED DRAWINGS

Chalk manner, an innovation in color printing that was developed in the mid-eighteenth century, set itself to imitate drawings rather than paintings or representations of human anatomy. Chalk manner replicated both the colors of *crayons* (chalks) and, significantly, the texture of chalk strokes on paper. Jean-Charles François, one of the inventors of the technique, explained that chalk manner could overcome the inherent inability of the burin to reproduce the distinctive traits of chalk, a feat that even such talented engravers as Dürer and Marcantonio Raimondi had been unable to achieve:

> We know that Albrecht Dürer and Marcantonio, those famous engravers, set themselves to perfectly simulate chalk when they engraved the drawings of Raphael and other great men. But despite their repeated attempts, they could not avoid the dryness of engraving. The stroke of the chalk leaves faint traces, rendered imperfect by the grain of the paper that blunts the tip of the chalk; it is this, above all, that is difficult to imitate....You may judge for yourself, sir, of the

success of his [François'] enterprise by examining the first collection he has published, composed of six prints, or rather, six drawings, because the illusion is perfect and you will believe that they have been made with a chalk.[37]

The chalk-manner printmaker, Alexis Magny, claimed that ordinary prints simply could not duplicate the "softness, richness and smoothness" or the "spirit and finesse" of an original drawing as chalk manner could:

> With this new art, a capable draftsman can fully render the frankness of the stroke and of all the parts of an original by a great master, an object so precious and so interesting for students! Instead, in the ordinary method, it is not possible to render completely the openness of the stroke, no matter how capable one supposes the artist to be. He cannot avoid distributing a lifelessness in the expression and a coldness over the spirit of the original.[38]

As described by the printmakers, chalk manner represented a triumph of Enlightenment ingenuity over centuries of inadequate translation.

Copying drawings was fundamental to eighteenth-century artistic instruction (see fig. 3), and chalk-manner printmakers were quick to point out the advantages of their prints over ordinary line engravings or etchings for the education of artists. As François explained:

> This invention is, in fact, of great use for perpetuating the drawings of the great masters and putting into the hands of students, both in Paris and in the provinces, the best originals, rendered in a manner much more appropriate to instill in them good taste in drawings than ordinary engraving.[39]

For students of the Royal Academies of Painting and Sculpture, copying drawings was an essential preliminary phase of the academic curriculum; for pupils of the numerous *écoles gratuites* (free drawing schools established after midcentury for the education of craftsmen), copying was virtually the only training in drawing they received. Until the invention of chalk manner, they were generally limited to copying line engravings or the drawings of their provincial masters, for esteemed artists were often reluctant to lend their drawings for the purposes of instruction.[40] The advent of chalk manner meant that facsimiles of drawings by better artists could be made available to students in the academies and in the free schools. François emphasized this point in an advertisement for his first book of chalk-manner prints:

> To learn how to draw, it is necessary to copy drawings after the great masters. But these drawings are very rare, very expensive, and those who possess them are very loathe to lend them because students ruin them, wear them out, and frequently lose them. How many precious works, excellent originals, worthy of preservation for posterity have we not been deprived of owing to the lack of some happy invention that could imitate and multiply masterpieces in chalk![41]

The availability of inexpensive, accurate reproductions of drawings obviated the need for fragile originals and meant that a stock of printed drawings could be supplied to institutions without the means to acquire original sheets by the best masters.[42] Chalk-manner prints would also ensure the quality of student training. Since etchings and engravings were cold and inadequate transcriptions of drawings, copying them would promote a hardness in student work.[43] Copying chalk-manner prints, however, would encourage the desired softness and life in the drawings of young artists and artisans.

The market for these pedagogical prints was extensive— in Paris alone, the free drawing school taught fifteen hundred students per year—and since no chalk-manner printmaker had been awarded an exclusive *privilège,* the field of chalk manner was open to competition. Printmakers responded to this opportunity by producing numerous inexpensive red or black chalk-manner prints of expressive heads, hands, animals, ornament, and nude figures known as *académies.* Their

4. Thérèse-Eléonore Lingée, *Study of a Boy,* after Jean-Baptiste Greuze, chalk manner. The Metropolitan Museum of Art, New York, Gift of Mr. and Mrs. Stuart P. Feld 1983.1123.13

advertisements repeatedly emphasized the utility and low cost of chalk-manner prints. Gilles Demarteau announced books of flower studies,[44] heads after François Boucher for 15 sols,[45] and *académies* after Carle Vanloo for 20 sols (cat. 6).[46] Magny advertised expressive chalk-manner heads after Boucher for 10 sols; female *académies* after Charles-Nicolas Cochin the Younger for 1 livre, 10 sols;[47] and a *cahier* (set) of six plates of heads after Jean-Antoine Watteau "suitable for persons of the fair sex who devote themselves to drawing" for 3 livres.[48] Occasionally, unregulated competition for the chalk-manner market was criticized for having pernicious effects on quality. Thus Thérèse-Eléonore Lingée's chalk-manner heads after Jean-Baptiste Greuze (fig. 4) were promoted by the editor of *L'Année litteraire* as an antidote to the plethora of "copies that are misshapen and are even dangerous for the students who make them the object of their study."[49] More typical was an advertisement for a book of "well-composed ornaments" addressed directly to "sculptors, ironsmiths, carpenters." It concluded with a panegyric on the trickle-down benefits of chalk-manner printing: "Artists can procure prints at a very reasonable price and develop a taste for the grand and the beautiful. An avenue of communication has been opened between them and the great men who are at the head of the arts."[50] Implicit in such advertisements was a claim that chalk-manner printing contributed to the glory of France. Because chalk manner democratized access to drawings by the best masters, it contributed to the progress of the fine arts and luxury trades, and thus helped maintain French hegemony in these areas. The proliferation of mediocre chalk-manner prints, as the editor of *L'Année litteraire* worried, would undermine this effort.

Advertisements stressed that chalk-manner prints were useful, agreeable, and made "to please young artists and amateurs in equal measure."[51] If printmakers ostensibly addressed chalk-manner heads and *académies* to artists and artisans, they also targeted print collectors. The most obvious way in which printmakers of all sorts appealed to collectors was by successively numbering their prints in order to facilitate the compilation of their oeuvres. Demarteau and Bonnet numbered almost all of their prints, including expressive heads and *académies*, and frequently advertised a new print by its oeuvre number. For instance, Demarteau announced two new prints after Boucher in the *Mercure* in 1772 as "numbers 344 and 345 of this artist's oeuvre."[52] The strategy worked. The correspondence of Joachim Wasserschlebe, a Danish court official living in Copenhagen, demonstrates that this avid print collector built his collection of chalk-manner prints through a dual reliance on the *Mercure de France* for the latest print announcements and on the numbering of prints to determine which pieces he was missing.[53]

Chalk-manner printmakers also sought to benefit from the intensification of interest in drawings among amateurs of varying degrees of expertise. From the 1740s, drawings began to appear regularly in auction sales, professional matmakers emerged in response to the demand for finely mounted drawings, and artists such as Boucher began to produce finished drawings, not as part of the artistic process but for the delectation of art lovers and for the decoration of their homes.[54] Thus when Magny overtly marketed his heads after Watteau to draftswomen, he almost certainly also sought to appeal to devotees of Watteau's drawings. Expressive heads after the best French artists were similarly attractive to collectors, and printmakers such as Demarteau satisfied this market by selling chalk-manner heads after Boucher as single sheets for 15 or 20 sols, depending on their size, or "mounted like drawings" for 1 livre, 10 sols.[55] Just as a mount could turn an

expressive head into a decorative work of art, the addition of a title and some drapery could transform a female *académie*, intended for the instruction of a young artist, into a picture that a collector or a man or woman of fashion might want to buy. As an editorial comment on Bonnet's *Sleepiness of Venus* suggests, there was sometimes little distinction between female *académies* as objects of study and images of nude women intended for display or for the collector's portfolio:

> It represents a young person, who, with her head lightly resting on one of her hands, tastes the sweetness of sleep; but nothing indicates that this is Venus. One sees neither her doves nor cupid, which usually serve to designate the goddess of beauty.[56]

In this instance, the advertisement implies, only the title, with its suggestion of narrative, distinguished a female *académie* from a subject drawing.

Surveys of eighteenth-century estate inventories indicate that whereas paintings dominated the interior decor of many great houses in the first half of the century, by midcentury drawings began to compete with canvases as the decoration of choice in grander domestic interiors.[57] Chalk-manner printmakers recognized the potential of the market for drawings intended for display and fully exploited the multiple uses of their medium. In addition to the numerous chalk-manner prints produced for the use of artists and designers, Demarteau, François, Lingée, and especially Bonnet executed large compositional studies whose size, finish, and narrative subject matter enabled them to serve as substitutes for paintings in interior decoration. When François advertised his *Corps de Garde* after Vanloo in 1758 (cat. 4), he noted that "it is at once a drawing for study and a print that is a painting."[58] Demarteau's red chalk-manner print after Cochin's *Allegory of the Life of the Dauphin* was similarly described: "it is not a drawing nor a print; it is a painting of the most well-composed and most agreeable sort."[59]

The transformation of drawings and printed drawings into objects of interior decoration dictated changes in the works themselves. Like draftsmen who altered the form and content of their work in response to the requirements of display, printmakers adjusted their images to ensure their "wall power" and legibility from a distance.[60] Thus a selling point for François' portrait of Louis XV (cat. 15), priced at a mere 30 sols, was that "the head is large enough to be seen and clearly distinguished, even among paintings or large prints, in any possible place." François' announcement concludes by describing the print as a "kind of colored tableau that makes an impression."[61] The word tableau suggests a high degree of finish, a quality that was as significant as legibility for decorative works.[62] Also, just as Boucher himself modified his drawings to suit the tastes of buyers for more finished works, Bonnet "finished" Boucher's nude studies by adding accessories to make them more appealing to purchasers.[63] Demarteau similarly adjusted drawings by Boucher, altering shading and adding figures, for instance, to create more complete compositions.[64] Consumers of "finish" were routinely castigated as demi-connoisseurs by "true" connoisseurs such as Antoine-Joseph Dezallier d'Argenville and Pierre-Jean Mariette, but it was most likely this market of nonexpert consumers whom the color printmakers sought most to attract. In their advertisements, they flattered the "demi-connoisseurs" as authorities in matters of art. When François announced his *Corps de Garde*, he noted that Vanloo's drawing had been "admired by all the connoisseurs" when it was exhibited in the previous year's Salon. François thus implicitly addressed the potential purchaser as a connoisseur, enticing the consumer to buy through an ingratiating reference to his or her good taste and expertise in matters of art.[65] Such approbation of anonymous connoisseurs or amateurs was a common ploy in eighteenth-century print advertising, but it is a suggestive one. It implies that one incentive for the purchase of these works was the status it allowed the purchaser to claim. Color facsimiles permitted consumers not only to enjoy owning a fine "drawing," but also to represent themselves as both knowledgeable and fashionable.

As demand for decorative works on paper diversified to include pastels, gouaches, and colored wash drawings, printmakers responded in kind, producing pastel-, gouache-, and wash-manner prints that deceptively imitated higher priced originals. Gouache- and wash-manner printmakers such as Jean-François Janinet and Philibert-Louis Debucourt were indebted to the example of Bonnet, a printmaker both technically innovative and attuned to opportunities for profit. Building on the early efforts of François and the printmaker Joseph Varin to reproduce black chalk drawings highlighted with white, described as *aux deux crayons* (in two chalks), Bonnet adapted the multiple-plate printing process of the color mezzotinters to chalk manner, thus facilitating the replication of drawings executed in three or more colors of chalk.[66] He also discovered a stable white ink that would obviate the problems of discoloration encountered in Varin's two-color prints. Bonnet's three-chalk technique could transform ordinary heads into collector's objects. When he announced his first head in three chalks in May 1767, he did not even give it a title, calling it simply "premiere tête aux trois crayons" (cat. 9a). Although it was his technical innovation that made the print interesting, Bonnet did take care to note that his print had been approved by the most celebrated artists and described it as "this print, or rather, this drawing."[67]

When Bonnet advertised his first head printed in three chalks, he also informed readers that he would soon publish a head in "pastel manner" — his term for prints executed with more than three plates. It was his response to the fashion for pastels, which according to household inventories began to eclipse paintings in the homes of wealthy commoners and nobles by midcentury.[68] When Bonnet announced his earliest pastel-manner heads in October and November 1767, he was thus catering to a flourishing market, a market of potential consumers that Bonnet explicitly addressed as collectors when he remarked that his pastel heads "were worthy of the interest of amateurs."[69] When he advertised his most famous pastel-manner print, the *Tête de Flore (Head of Flora)* (cat. 19),

5. Louis-Marin Bonnet, *Tête de Flore (Head of Flora),* after François Boucher, pastel manner. Victoria and Albert Museum, London, Jones Bequest 540-1882

he claimed that his invention trumped the pastel medium itself because it was more durable:

> This complete imitation of pastel, with all of its light and dark shades of color, is deceptive and yields nothing to paintings in terms of its freshness nor in the vivacity of its colors. An additional advantage that amateurs will find is that this freshness cannot be altered, neither by rolling up the print, nor by transporting it in a portfolio because that which is printed cannot be effaced.[70]

Bonnet's *Tête de Flore* was thus not only an inexpensive substitute for an original pastel by an esteemed and fashionable artist but also an improvement on the very luxury item it imitated. Bonnet further offered the *Tête de Flore* "pastel" either unmatted for 6 livres or framed and ready for display at 10 or 15 livres depending on the molding. The presence of a frame and glass would heighten the deceptive, almost trompe l'oeil

quality of the work, particularly if the text at the bottom of the print was trimmed (fig. 5). When Bonnet's print was presented in this way, little could prevent a casual viewer from mistaking it for a pastel by Boucher.[71] Printed pastels, like the best chalk-manner "drawings," thus gave visual pleasure to the buyers on whose walls they were displayed; they also allowed owners to represent themselves, both to others and to themselves, as men or women of discernment and fashion.

In addition to his printed pastels, Bonnet continued to produce prints in two and three colors and to develop innovative ways of making them attractive to collectors of all sorts. Like François and Varin before him, he further heightened the illusion of the print as a drawing by using blue and tan colored papers as the support for his prints—often printing the same image once on blue and once on tan paper (cats. 8a, 8b). He also printed the same image in both pastel and two-chalk manners.[72] A print representing *Samson and the Philistines* after Van Dyck, for instance, was available in pastel manner for 6 livres or in black "chalk" heightened with white on blue paper for 3 livres.[73] Bonnet thus granted buyers a range of options and prices. At the same time, he gave collectors who were particularly engaged by the technical aspects of color printmaking, or who were completing their Bonnet oeuvres, compelling reasons to buy two prints instead of one.

One of the more fascinating chapters in the history of the eighteenth-century trade in printed color images is Bonnet's marketing of his "English" prints (cats. 30–34). Bonnet was among the first French printmakers to capitalize on the fashion for imported English luxury goods that emerged after the Seven Years' War (1756–1763), going so far as to call the shop he established in 1776 "Au Magasin Anglois."[74] In this the printmaker was emulating *marchands merciers* (fashionable French luxury merchants), who from the 1760s to the 1780s established several *magasins anglais* (English shops) to cater to the expanding market for English goods.[75] Like the *merciers* who included French imitations of English imports in their stock, Bonnet sold imitations or pirated editions of

English prints in his shop.[76] His initial foray into the market for such items was a series of spurious "imported" English chalk-manner images of women. These images were printed with English titles, signed with the abbreviated name "Louis Marin," and published with the London address of the print-maker and printseller François Vivares. To further heighten their luxury appeal, Bonnet printed the images with gold leaf borders. Because French guild regulations restricted the use of gold leaf to certain corporations, among them furniture and frame gilders and bookbinders, Bonnet's use of gold con-stituted an infringement. By employing an alias and claim-ing an English origin for his printed gold images, Bonnet not only made the prints fashionably exotic but also hoped to avoid prosecution.[77]

To announce his "English" prints, he first advertised them in the *Journal de politique et de littérature*, a publication that itself masqueraded as an import. Though the journal had a Brussels imprint, it was actually published in Paris.[78] In this "foreign" journal, Bonnet advertised his "imported" prints and identified "Marin" as a printmaker in London whose work was available in Paris *chez* Bonnet. His emphasis on the titil-lating subject matter of the prints suggests the kind of audi-ence he hoped to attract:

> Mr. Marin, printmaker in London, has invented a new kind
> of print that imitates miniatures and produces the most
> agreeable effect. At present he has published two. One repre-
> sents a young milkmaid in a pose and disarray that her
> freshness makes very piquant [cat. 30], the other, a young
> person who is taking coffee [cat. 31]….These are ovals
> enclosed in a border that is part of the print and is enriched
> with gold as are the prints themselves. They can be found in
> Paris at Bonnet's.[79]

In subsequent advertisements for his English prints, as in the quasi-official *Mercure de France*, Bonnet avoided both a description of the risqué subject matter and an identification of Louis Marin as English. Instead he chose to note that Marin's imitation miniatures enriched with gold were being sold in London by Vivares and could be purchased in Paris at Bonnet's shop for the low price of 9 livres.[80] By suggesting the prints were imported from London, Bonnet appealed to French anglophiles; by adding gold leaf he sought to meet (or create) a demand for inexpensive, imitation, small-scale luxury objects.

By marketing his gold prints as miniatures, Bonnet pre-sumably sought to profit from the market for small but costly decorative objects valued for their refined workmanship and the richness of their settings. Accordingly, in his English prints, Bonnet sought to present his clients with a luxury object suitably enhanced with precious materials. Bonnet had already addressed the market for miniatures in 1770 when he announced a small pastel-manner medallion of the royal favorite, Madame du Barry. This "miniature in the genre of pastel," he declared, was noteworthy for its high degree of finish and for the printmaker's successful negotiation of the difficulties presented by such small-scale work.[81] Bonnet's attention to the market for miniatures also points to another sector of the luxury, or rather populuxe, market to which color printmakers adapted their prints: the burgeoning market for fashion accessories. Though miniatures were fre-quently hung on the walls of cabinets, they were also a staple ornament for jewelry, snuffboxes, and even men's buttons. By producing work for all of these purposes, printmakers pro-moted their printed miniatures as substitutes for more costly small enamels or paintings on vellum or ivory.

The possibility that color prints could be used in jewelry was first recognized earlier in the century by the Swiss artist Jean-Étienne Liotard. Though he is best known today for his pastels, he began his career as an enamelist and miniaturist, and apparently sought to multiply his work through the medium of color prints. [82] He also appears to have been the first to publish three-plate color prints in Paris. In June 1735, several months before Le Blon's arrival in the French capital, Liotard advertised very small printed color portraits of cur-rent celebrities for use in rings:

6. Louis-Marin Bonnet, *Marie-Antoinette*, after Joseph Kranzinger, pastel manner. National Gallery of Art, Widener Collection 1942.9.2480

7. Jean-François Janinet, *Models for Hairstyles*, etching and wash manner. National Gallery of Art, Widener Collection 1942.9.2385

Mr. Liotard, painter and printmaker, from whom we have seen various portraits in enamel, has discovered a most ingenious way to multiply his painted works using the medium of three colors and three plates....This kind of painting can have the freshness of pastel and the force and durability of oil painting. He has just finished two portraits of Messieurs Fontenelle and Voltaire. [They are] the size of a fingernail, suitable for placement in a ring and greatly resemble [the sitters], despite their small size.[83]

Though the announcement concluded with a promise of more printed color portraits for rings, no subsequent advertisements for prints of any kind by Liotard seem to have been placed. The cause is presumably Liotard's departure from France later that year. Perhaps, however, the market for such substitute luxuries was not yet well developed, for it was not until Bonnet adapted pastel manner to the production of printed miniatures in 1770 that French color prints were marketed for use in accessories.

When color prints did reappear as substitute miniatures, they did so in a thriving market for fashion accessories, particularly for snuffboxes. The eighteenth century was the age of snuff and the *tabatière* was an essential accoutrement of any

fashionable man or woman, from a royal mistress, a court noble, or financier, to a stonecutter.[84] Demarteau, a successful color printmaker, bequeathed several gold snuffboxes to his heirs.[85] If one was wealthy enough, as Demarteau apparently was, the standard was a gold box decorated with enamels or painted miniatures on vellum under glass. For those of lesser means, miniature pastel prints such as Bonnet's portrait of the future queen Marie-Antoinette (fig. 6) were used. Bonnet explained that the print was suitable for a variety of uses: "This portrait is a pretty miniature that one can place in a box or on a bracelet. This portrait may also be placed in a square frame by retaining the printed border that encloses it."[86] Janinet, the wash-manner printmaker and a former pupil of Bonnet, catered to this market as well, producing printed miniatures of the famous modiste Rose Bertin, or of anonymous women sporting the latest hairstyles (fig. 7).[87] No black-and-white engraving could be mistaken for a painted or enameled miniature, but color prints were rather more successfully deceptive, particularly when presented under a glass or a crystal on boxes, bracelets, or rings.

An advertisement dating from the early years of the Revolution describes one final intriguing use of color prints in fashion accessories: the use of printed images on buttons. The announcement, placed in 1790 by a printmaker or printseller named Martiny, described a set of twenty medallions, printed

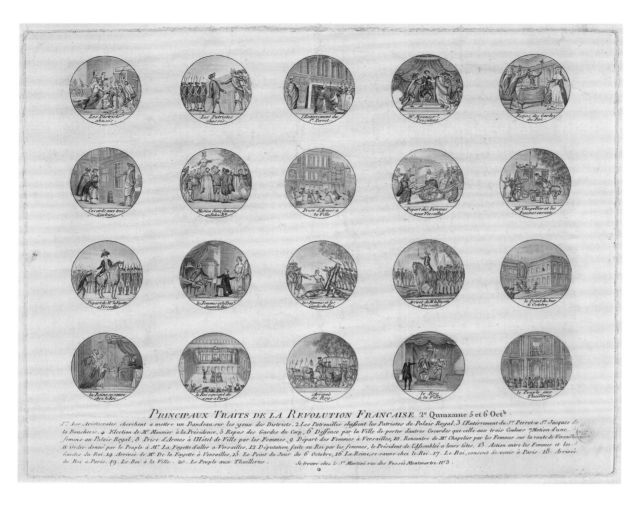

8. Anonymous (Martiny?), *Designs for Buttons Representing the Events of 5 and 6 October 1789*, etching and wash manner. Musée Carnavalet, Paris G 13194

9. Anonymous, *Revolutionary Button with Color Print* (enlarged; see fig. 8). Musée Carnavalet, Paris B 2072

in color with four plates, representing the principal events of July 1789: "The composition of these medallions is new and the author has chosen the best possible subjects so that they can serve in patriotic buttons, on fans and snuffboxes, as souvenirs, and for framing.[88] Numerous buttons representing Revolutionary scenes survive, including some which used medallions from Martiny's subsequent set of color prints relating the incidents of 5 and 6 October 1789 (figs. 8, 9). Martiny was responding to the mania for large buttons taken up by fashionable men in the late 1780s (see, for example, cat. 72).[89] These buttons were often ornamented with miniatures painted on ivory or vellum, inset, as was the Revolutionary print, into copper surrounds, and protected by glass. In her description of the excesses of male fashion in 1787, the baronne d'Oberkirch reported that some audacious "petits-maîtres" dared to display portraits of their mistresses on their buttons.[90] Janinet's color prints for buttons of lascivious gallant scenes seem perfect for just such a coxcomb (fig. 10).

10. Jean-François Janinet, *Six Designs for Buttons Representing Gallant Scenes*, etching and wash manner. Bibliothèque nationale de France, Paris Ef. 105 rés. fol., vol. 1

As proposed substitutes for miniatures on snuffboxes, bracelets, and buttons, color prints most resemble the populuxe goods defined by Fairchilds, that is, inexpensive imitations of aristocratic luxury objects. Who purchased such printed miniatures is not known. That Janinet rarely, if ever, advertised his prints for boxes and buttons, and that Bonnet did not number his prints for these purposes nor include them in the definitive catalogue of his work may suggest something about their intended consumers. [91] One can speculate that these prints were destined less for journal readers and collectors than for the middling audience of fashionable urban domestic servants, master artisans, and small shopkeepers that Fairchilds posits as the market for populuxe goods.[92] But what of the various other kinds of color prints? Chalk-manner *académies* and expressive heads were purchased, as one might expect, by such institutions as the *écoles gratuites*.[93] They were also collected by individuals such as the Danish official Wasserschlebe and the respected French drawings connoisseur Pierre-Jean Mariette.[94] A less specialized and more fashion-conscious audience for color prints is suggested by the account book of the print dealer Siméon-Charles-François Vallée. This rare surviving document of

the print trade in the late 1780s indicates that purchasers of Debucourt's color print *Le Compliment ou La Matinée du jour de l'an* (cat. 67), published in 1787, included a count, an abbé, a master printer, a bookseller, a stationer, a jeweler, an actor, a police inspector, a clerk, and a counselor of the king.[95] His clients thus included nobles, members of the clergy, and an array of wealthier members of the third estate. In his study of Vallée's accounts, Pierre Casselle concludes that the color genre prints sold in Vallée's shop were consumer products and that the market for them was driven less by considerations of their artistic merit than by the dictates of fashion.[96] This observation can be extended to the eighteenth-century market for color prints in general. Line engravings were also consumer products, but the color facsimile, by virtue of its replication of color, had a particular status. Though there was no mistaking a framed and varnished engraving for a pastel or a painting, the distinction between a framed and glazed quality color print and a unique art object was much less clear. Whether as a printed drawing after a fashionable artist or as a substitute miniature on jewelry, the color facsimile facilitated the access of greater numbers of people to fashionable items at a relatively low cost. From Gautier's *tableaux imprimées* and Bonnet's "pastels" to Janinet's "miniatures" for buttons, color prints supplied "an exact imitation acquired at little expense" of the latest fashionable objects for interior decoration and personal adornment. Color printmakers thus granted "amateurs of all sorts" the opportunity to derive pleasure from fine, finished objects and to represent themselves, both to themselves and to others, as men and women of taste and discernment. This expansion of the market to include amateurs of varying degrees of expertise was, nevertheless, a limited one. The fact that the eighteenth-century market for color prints excluded the majority of the laboring poor would not become an issue deemed worthy of debate until well into the Revolution.[97]

Ink and Inspiration

The Craft of Color Printing

Judith C. Walsh

Between 1755 and 1790 copperplate printing evolved dramatically as French printmakers strove to create ever more convincing facsimiles of chalk, pastel, or ink drawings and watercolor or gouache paintings. By ingeniously adapting traditional techniques and tools, or by devising new methods and materials as needed, these artist-printers created hundreds of full-spectrum, multiple-plate prints—some of the most complicated copperplate prints ever made. Collectively, this generation solved all the practical problems inherent in multiple-plate printing. They figured out how to transfer the artist's drawing to each of the plates in register; how to work each plate to hold a single color of ink; and how to print the plates in register to make a legible print. These artists also formulated new, quicker-drying transparent inks, and they found a plate printing paper that was soft enough to absorb each inking, yet sturdy enough to withstand the torture of multiple runs through the press.[1]

The critical idea for the prints originated with Jakob Christoffel Le Blon, who from the 1720s made full-color mezzotints after paintings by overprinting three plates—blue, yellow, and red—to create one full-spectrum image. Le Blon's insight, derived from Sir Isaac Newton's color theory, was genius even though his prints, such as the 1739 *Louis XV* (cat. 1), show only qualified success. After Le Blon's death in 1741, his ideas were publicized in France by two printmakers: From 1737 through 1749, Jacques-Fabien Gautier Dagoty made public claims of credit for the full-color printing process (which he had in fact learned during a brief sojourn in Le Blon's studio);[2] and in 1756 Antoine Gautier de Montdorge published a how-to book on the practice, *L'Art d'imprimer les tableaux: Traité d'après les écrits, les opérations et les instructions verbals de J. C. LeBlon*.[3] Montdorge's practical text describes Le Blon's solutions to the problems of drawing transfer, color separation, registration in printing, and pigments used in the ink. Although the instructions seem convoluted (Le Blon was not a printmaker himself), they do indicate how difficult the problems were and demonstrate the process subsequent printmakers modified.

The ultimate problem in multiple-plate printing is registration. In practice, registration must occur twice: first in transcribing the drawing to each plate and later in printing the several plates. Step-by-step, Montdorge describes Le Blon's method: the would-be printer should acquire the best red copperplates, free from flaws and inclusions; he should make certain that the four or five plates used in a print were cut perfectly square and trimmed to exactly the same size. The plates should be polished and textured for mezzotint by rocking.

So far, so good. Then Montdorge begins to explain the critical process of transferring the design precisely to each plate—a new consideration for printers. To accomplish this, Le Blon obtained a cardboard sheet the same thickness as one of the copperplates and two inches larger in all dimensions. Next, a hole the exact size of a plate was traced and cut into the center of this cardboard. A piece of fine cloth—Montdorge calls it a veil—was sewn onto two rings already attached to the cardboard frame. The rings were probably affixed on the left-hand side of the cardboard frame, so that the veil and cardboard could "open" like a book. The drawing to be transferred was placed below the veil and traced onto the cloth with oil paint that permeated the cloth. When the oil paint outlines dried, the transfer of the design to each plate could begin.

The veil, now holding the oil paint outline, was laid out next to the cardboard frame and the outline was brushed with a liquid white ink tempered in eau-de-vie and ox gall.[4] The alcohol-and-water-based ink beaded up on the dried oil paint outlines of the drawing. Before the ink dried, the fabric veil was laid on a copperplate held in the cardboard frame, offsetting the liquid white to the textured plate. The process was repeated for each mezzotint plate needed. When dry, the offset white was reinforced with black ink, finally resulting in a registered transfer of the design to each plate.[5]

The design on each plate was lightly engraved with a burin and the individual copperplates were burnished and scraped in the usual way of mezzotint, but as color separations—that is, each plate was worked to create the midtones and highlights for only a single color. Each color separation was proofed and corrected by engraving with the burin or with smaller rockers. When the artist was satisfied, Montdorge notes, the plates were printed in a sequence of blue, yellow, and lastly red. To further the imitation of a painting, the completed print could be mounted to canvas, put on a stretcher, and varnished.

Despite Le Blon's professed adherence to Newton's three-color theory, Montdorge reports that more than three plates were necessary to make the prints. He notes that Le Blon used a black mezzotint plate to render the dark shadings. (The use of just such a black plate had been claimed by Gautier as his own innovation.[6]) Montdorge also finds that a fifth plate was needed to impart white areas, as the registration was not precise enough to preserve the white of the paper for the hair and other fine details. The white lines were described as being entirely engraved with the burin.

Le Blon's *Louis XV*, prepared in Paris by Pierre-François Tardieu and Jean Robert and printed by Jean Mouffle,[7] appears to have been made much as Montdorge describes. The regis-

tration is soft enough to have been made with the clumsy cloth system, and the five colors Montdorge names are seen— black, blue, red, yellow, and white. All the white is indeed engraved and printed. However, a sixth color not described by Montdorge —brown—required yet another copperplate. Mouffle recalls that a second blue plate (the seventh plate) was overprinted on the king's sash and other blue areas because the first printing of blue was too faint.[8]

Careful examination under the microscope and elemental analysis were used to identify the colorants in the printing inks.[9] The results confirm Montdorge's assertion that Le Blon used an organic red, probably carmine; an organic yellow, perhaps "stil-de-grain";[10] and Prussian blue for the ink on the three main color plates. The white areas are white lead, extended with calcium and ground very fine to increase transparency. The brown color in the details of the medallion and the background is also organic and may be asphaltum, for it shows characteristic "alligatoring" of the paint film and the

1. Steps necessary in making copperplate prints, from flattening and polishing the plate to transferring the design and etching or engraving, from *Encyclopédie*, vol. 4 (Paris, 1768), pl. 1, National Gallery of Art, Library

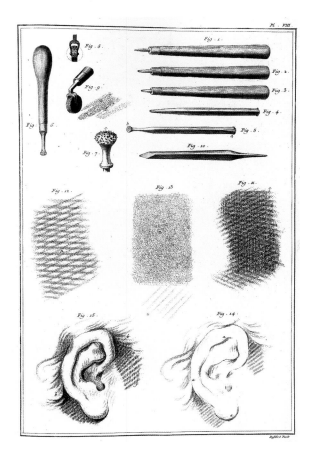

colorant was specifically mentioned by Le Blon.[11] The black appears to be "ordinary printing ink," but no evidence was found of indigo, which Montdorge recommends be added to the black.

Le Blon's rival, Gautier suggests a slightly different group of colors. As he relied on the blank sheet for his whites, Gautier proposes combinations of only four colors to re-create the effects of all the pigments used for easel painting. His pigment choices for printing are ochre and stil-de-grain yellows, vermilion red, indigo blue, and the transparent ivory black.[12] This group seems to be insufficient because vermilion is opaque; a transparent red such as carmine would also have been necessary.

The colorants had to be transparent, so that, by overlaying each other, colors could combine to make the final full-spectrum print. This requirement limited the possibilities for the printers. In the eighteenth century only a few transparent pigments were available, and these particular colorants, unfortunately, are susceptible to preservation problems. Although protected by the oil binder in the ink, indigo, carmine, and stil-de-grain are very fugitive to light and to strong solutions formerly used in restorations. The resinous colors

asphaltum brown and gamboge yellow can be damaged by solvents. Faint prints that appear to have been printed without the red or yellow plates have been described as different states of the prints or intermediate proofs. Research may yet show that such pallid impressions were created, but absent that, an alternate explanation seems quite likely—that is, the prints are simply faded or have received harsh restoration treatment at some time since the eighteenth century. The exhibited impression *Bal de la Bastille* (cat. 82) is surely an example of an altered print.

From a purely technical viewpoint, Le Blon's *Louis XV* can be criticized. The mezzotint plates were incompletely rocked, leaving an obvious crisscross texture in many places; the registration is off; the colors are muddy and pale; and the sheet is badly stained by excess oil in the printing inks. Charles-Nicholas Cochin declared the print "too blue, and that color dominates the work, wearing away all others."[13] Later French printers who built upon Le Blon's pioneering work corrected these flaws.

Denis Diderot's great *Encyclopédie, ou dictionnaire Raisonné des Sciences, des Arts et des Métiers* (1757) contains an entry entitled "Gravure" that covers the processes of copperplate printing.[14] The text was apparently taken from Abraham Bosse's 1645 booklet on copperplate printing, *Traicté des maniéres de graver en taille douce sur l'airin*. The two main methods of preparing copperplates—etching and engraving—are discussed together in this text and are illustrated as being practiced in the same studio, perhaps upon the same plate (fig. 1).[15] Diderot explains that even though etching was less controllable, it was used for three-quarters of the work on a plate. Engraving with a burin was reserved for the final treatment of the image—cleaning up the lines and harmonizing the whole.[16]

Etching and engraving were used together, as Diderot describes, to make the earliest prints in imitation of drawings, those in the chalk manner. The chalk manner is clearly described in captions by Prévost[17] and an illustration by A.-J. de Fehrt, both published as addenda to the *Encyclopédie* in 1768 (fig. 2).[18] Chalk-manner lines were made by using a roulette or *mattoir* (fig. 2, nos. 5–7) on the copperplate—tools that had

been adapted from metalworking by Jean-Charles François beginning in 1756. The many uneven teeth that protrude from the head of his version of the *mattoir* impress the copper or thin etching ground with uneven small dots.[19] The tool is run over an area several times, so that the dots merge and resolve into an imitation of a chalk line when printed (see cat. 4).

It is important to note that *mattoirs*, and probably the other hand tools De Fehrt illustrated, were designed specifically for use in either etching or engraving. Engraving tools had blunt steel handles because they were tapped with a small hammer to mark the copperplate. Etching tools were equipped with rounded wooden handles, as hand pressure was used to puncture the wax-varnish ground on the plate. Etched work with a *mattoir* (fig. 2, no. 6) or a roulette (fig. 2, nos. 8, 9) was used to make the lines and tone of fig. 2, nos. 11–13. The preliminary drawing of the ear (see fig. 2, no. 14) was also done by etching. In fig. 2, no. 15, the etching has been reinforced with an engraving *mattoir* (fig. 2, no. 5) and engraved shadows have been applied in the folds of the ear. At the base of the earlobe, in the area marked "*a*" in the illustration, the double-point engraving tool (no. 4) was used to stipple in shading. This illustration demonstrates the mingling of copperplate techniques in an image and helps explain how the printmakers achieved such subtle visual effects. In the most complicated images several such plates are overlaid, so that layers of texture and tone create these exceptional prints.

Gilles Demarteau the Elder excelled in the chalk manner. A comparison of his facsimile print and Jean-Baptiste Le Prince's original red chalk drawing *Woman in Russian Costume* (cats. 27a, 27b) shows that the printmaker rendered the chalk lines from the original with extreme subtlety. Even the

texture of the friable red chalk caught on the laid lines of the original paper (fig. 3) is indicated in the shadow of the planter (fig. 4). Demarteau must have pressed a slim toothed wheel into the copper again and again in order to create the parallel lines of red ink that look like chalk caught on the paper. Interestingly, he did not think it necessary to transcribe Le Prince's underdrawing for the standing figure: he omitted all the faint lines Le Prince used to lay out the drawing.

Drawings in two or more chalk colors were also produced. In *Head of a Woman Looking Down* (cat. 73) Demarteau printed both the blue of a trompe l'oeil collector's album page

3. Jean-Baptiste Le Prince, *Woman in Russian Costume*, c. 1770 (detail, cat. 27a)

4. Gilles Demarteau the Elder, *Woman in Russian Costume*, c. 1773 (detail, cat. 27b)

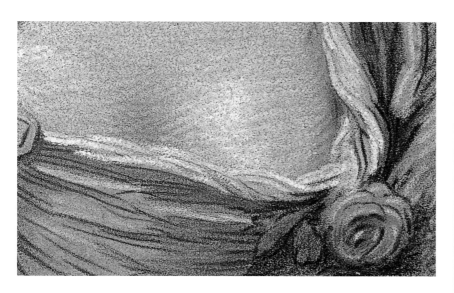

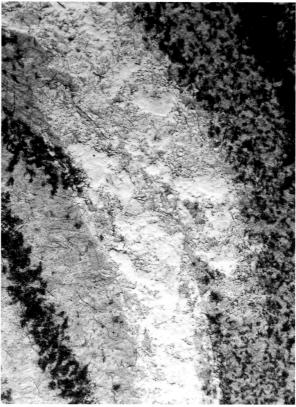

5. Louis-Marin Bonnet,
*Bust of a Young Woman
Looking Down*, 1765/1767
(detail, cat. 9a)

6. Louis-Marin Bonnet,
*Bust of a Young Woman
Looking Down*, 1765/1767
(detail, cat. 9a)

and the pale gray tone of the original sheet on a whiter sheet, reserving blank paper to represent the white chalk lines in the image. For a similar subject, Louis-Marin Bonnet, who had worked with François and then Demarteau, used a more direct method. In a print from 1765/1767, *Bust of a Young Woman Looking Down* (cat. 9a), Bonnet printed in red, black, and white on blue paper, presenting a very convincing facsimile of a François Boucher drawing. The red and black were likely printed from one plate each, but the white required two plates. The smudged white highlighting on the flesh of the sitter was printed in a small dot pattern from a deeply gouged plate, which put excess white ink on the sheet. The still wet white was evidently quickly overprinted, causing it to squash and spread slightly in a re-creation of smudged white chalk (fig. 5). The plate bearing the long, thick, white lines that describe folds in the bodice was charged with the same white ink, but as it was the last bit printed, the ink of the impasto "chalk" line dried proud of the sheet (fig. 6). Bonnet apparently calculated the depth of the etched areas, the consistency of the white ink, and the speed of overprinting required to achieve these trompe l'oeil effects.

Opaque ink was required to mimic chalk and pastel drawings; therefore, red lead, carbon black, and white lead bulked with calcium carbonate were used in chalk-manner prints. For his prints, Bonnet claimed to have invented a white ink that would not yellow or darken upon exposure to sulfur in the air.[20] The discoloration of white lead in watercolor was a serious problem for artists until 1834, when the English colormen Windsor & Newton marketed a calcined zinc pigment in watercolor known as Chinese white.[21] The discoloration of lead pigments was not a problem for oil painters, however, since the oil binder in their paints protected the individual particles of white lead from air pollutants. The oil binder used in printing inks offered similar protection. Elemental analysis of the white on Bonnet's print (cat. 9a) shows it is a combination of lead and calcium, which had already been used by Le Blon in 1739 for *Louis XV.*

Multiple-plate color prints were not described by the techniques used to make them, but by the autograph work they imitated, such as *manière de crayon* (chalk manner) and *manière de lavis* (wash manner). Indeed, any two prints of the same type, for instance, two prints replicating watercolors, could be made differently, for individual printers used whatever worked for them. *Gravure aux outils* (printmaking with tools) offered the widest range of possibilities for printmakers because any tool that would mark the copper or break through the wax-varnish etching grounds could be employed. Tools traditionally used in engraving were also used through an etching ground, and new tools were invented. The number and variety of tools available cannot be estimated, but there were certainly hundreds, for each type was made in various sizes. An 1808 inventory of Laurent Guyot's studio listed 23 roulettes and 157 *champignons* (mushroom-shaped tools for imitating washes).[22]

When techniques were mixed in any print, the copperplates were only as useful for printing as the weakest part of the plate. Contemporary writers mention reworking the plates to increase the number of pulls, and many prints show both subtle and more obvious retouches (see cats. 9a, 9b). Nevertheless, estimates for the number of prints possible from the various techniques are hard to find, as the exact number would vary by the hardness of the copper, the pressure in the press, and the depth of the plate work. No writers specifically considered the mixed technique of multiple-plate full-color prints, but William Gilpin offers his opinion that "an *engraved* plate, unless it be cut very slightly, will cast off seven or eight hundred good impressions....An *etched* plate will not give above two hundred; unless it be eaten very deep, and then it may give three hundred. After that, the plate must be retouched or the impression will be faint."[23] Gilpin also notes that mezzotint will "cast off no more than one hundred good impressions" (of which the first twenty are too dark, and the last twenty are too light).[24] Montdorge, however, contends

that continuous reworking of the mezzotint plate will give six or eight hundred.[25]

The details of the printing are not known, although solutions to a few practical problems can be inferred. The papers used in the prints seem to have enough texture and expand enough when wet to pose problems for the printer. The sheets must have been run through the press under great pressure to push the knots of fiber formed in the pulp to the back of the sheet.[26] This pressure would also permanently stretch the sheet, improving the chances for good registration.

Whether or not each color of ink had to dry between printings so as to avoid offsetting onto the next plate is of considerable interest. Contemporary references to two-colored black-and-white intaglio prints suggest that ten to twelve days elapsed between printings.[27] This amount of time seems unrealistic: multiple-plate prints routinely used five, six, or seven plates and thus many hundreds of wet prints would require drying between printings. Montdorge is no help: he notes "if it is possible" one should print all the plates without letting the colors dry. In that way the best blending of the colors could be achieved. "If there is some obstacle to quick printing, one will have to allow each color to dry and rewet the paper each time before printing."[28] Philibert-Louis Debucourt employed an efficient and possibly unique system: Chapuis and Blin printed his editions on four presses simultaneously, one for each color, pulling the yellow, red, and blue states before the final overprint with black. The printed sheets were kept evenly damp between presses by interleaving with wet papers.[29]

For multiple-plate printing, the recipe for colored ink must have been altered to dry more quickly and to resist offsetting. William Savage's exhaustive treatise *On the Preparation of Printing Inks* catalogues additives to inks that alter their working characteristics. For instance, he suggests adding litharge, a lead-based pigment, to ink to speed drying. He also directs the color printer to thin colored inks with varnish:

7. Jean-Baptiste Le Prince, *Les Pêcheurs*, 1771 (detail, cat. 21)

When a light washy tinct is required, I would strongly impress on the printer not to reduce the colour by the admixture of any white…but to thin it with varnish to the point required; to beat the subject with very little ink; and to apply a very strong pressure, by which means any tinct may be produced…still retaining all its spirit.[30]

Lead salt driers or dilution with resinous varnish would have rendered the boiled and burned oil used in the inks ready for overprinting much sooner.[31] Savage also reminds ink-makers that soaps help the ink to print "clean," that is to come off the plate completely. Presumably, the soaps would also make inks less susceptible to offsetting on subsequent copperplates.

The honor for the invention of aquatint is disputed, but Le Prince's variation of it, his so-called *gravures au lavis* (wash prints), dates from about 1768.[32] *Les Pêcheurs* (cat. 21), a print after a sepia wash drawing, was made in 1771. In 1791 a description of the method appeared in the *Encyclopédie*, and Jules Hédou reprinted that text in his biography and catalogue of the artist in 1879.[33]

Le Prince's method is ingenious and efficient. It requires only one plate, obviating the problems of multiple plates.

Instead, he relied on multiple etching bites to achieve the same range of tones in the print that are achieved in drawing by diluting the ink. His one copperplate would have been prepared for printing as all were—flattened, cleaned, and polished—then covered with a hard ground made of varnish alone. On this ground, he brushed an ink composed of lamp black suspended in olive oil and turpentine, as if he were making a wash drawing. The turpentine softened the underlying varnish, allowing the olive oil to seep in and prevent the varnish from reforming below the brushstrokes. The softened varnish was blotted off and the revealed copper cleaned and degreased. The cleaned copper was then tamped with a sticky sugar-soap mixture. The aquatint grain was applied by tapping a silk bag of finely ground varnish powder above the plate. The excess could be removed by holding the plate upright and tapping it on an edge. Of course, the dry powder adhered to the sticky sugar-soap on the plate, but not on the dry hard varnish. The plate was warmed to melt the varnish into an aquatint ground, and the plate was then ready for etching.

The etching was tricky. Le Prince described two etching solutions, one weaker than the other. To be able to create the variety of tones needed, he made a test aquatint etch on a long thin piece of copper—he called it a "tuning fork" for the print. Each section of the strip was etched slightly longer to make a stepped scale of tones—light to dark—that corresponded to regular intervals of time in the etching bath. Le Prince suggested two minute intervals, in six steps for each test strip.

The areas to be etched were compared against this tonal scale, then systematically blocked out with varnish as they were finished. The areas that were to be the lightest, such as the sky and the faintest details, were the first blocked from the acid, the next-lightest areas followed, and the next, as the plate was given repeated exposures to the etching fluid. When cleaned and printed, the plate could render the tones of ink as sensitively as seen in a detail of *Les Pêcheurs* (fig. 7).

Late in the era, aquatint was combined with hand tools to replicate specific techniques in watercolor drawing.[34] Gilles-Antoine Demarteau created *"Regarde, ma bien-aimée"* (cat. 45) using transparent inks for the aquatint washes and opaque brown for the ink outlines. The quill pen lines seen in the

original drawing were probably transcribed using a tool made from two flexible sewing needles set in a handle. One needle was set a little shorter than the other, so that when the tool was drawn through the soft etching ground, the needles eased apart, as did the two points in a cut quill, re-creating the turns in a pen line.

French printmakers knew of another acid-biting method that would create areas of tone on a copperplate. They could shake grains of sugar or sea salt into a warm varnish on a plate. When the varnish cooled and hardened, the sugar or salt grains would be dissolved, leaving small craters in the varnish that when exposed to etching fluid and printed would make areas of tone in the image.[35] Such salted varnishes might look very much like the remains of a scraped mezzotint or stippled passage when printed. In fact, anything that would puncture the ground could be used to create pattern in the plate, as the least opening in the varnish ground exposed the copper to corrosion by the etching fluid.

Tonal methods were critical for imitating the washes of color seen in prints made after watercolors and gouaches. For most of the period, however, printmakers seem to have relied upon engraving with hand tools for re-creating the even tones of watercolor washes. This is a departure from the method described in the *Encyclopédie*, in which most of the work was

8. Charles-Melchior Descourtis, *Noce de village*, 1785 (detail, cat. 55a)

9. Transcribing an image to a copperplate, from *Encyclopédie*, vol. 4 (Paris, 1768), pl. 4, no. 1, National Gallery of Art, Library

done by etching. However, the use of hand tools, while laborious, offered printmakers complete control over the work. Areas could be worked slowly and reworked in minute sections; neither was possible in etching or aquatint.[36]

A set of proof sheets of the *Noce de village* by Charles-Melchior Descourtis demonstrates how he, and by implication other French printmakers, made full-color prints in imitation of watercolor or gouache paintings (cats. 55a–j). His method shows a few critical improvements over the method pioneered by Le Blon. Descourtis would have obtained five flattened and polished copperplates of exactly the same size. Into these he drilled holes at the center of each of the four sides to act as registration points.[37] The plates were probably drilled at the same time, in a stack, so that the holes would line up. The artist prepared to transfer the drawing to all the plates by first etching an outline of the drawing on one plate, known as the *planche-mère* (mother plate). A still-wet, black ink print of the etched outline was apparently counterproofed onto each of the remaining copperplates. As the sheets were put through the press for the first time, imprinting them with the black outline, the registration holes made four dimples in the margins outside the printed area. The dimples could be realigned with the holes in each subsequent plate, thereby creating perfect alignment of the transferred design. The offset black lines on each plate were lightly traced with a needle and etched, creating a basic image for each color. Descourtis may have applied a white watercolor ground to the plates in order to increase the visibility of the faint counterproofing.[38]

The etched line underdrawing for the print (fig. 8) used shorthand notations similar to those Diderot illustrated in his discussion of engraving (fig. 9). Dotted lines mark the boundaries of shading for the forms in engraving, but in this print they are used to locate the highlights in the separations, for instance, in the folds of the mother's dress.

Although it was not much used in France, mezzotint rocking with a *berceau* is clearly seen in the sky of the red, blue, and black plate proofs of *Noce de village* (cats. 55c, e, and i). However, the work is less than even one complete "turn."[39] Despite the clear identification of this tool with mezzotint, here the *berceau* appears to be used in the same spirit as any

other engraving hand tool for prints. The plates were burnished to create the lights and then carefully worked with many different hand tools directly on the copper in order to create the myriad textures and tones needed for each part of the color separations.

Color separation is very difficult: each shade and shadow has to be isolated and broken down into its component parts. The different amounts of blue and yellow needed for each branch of a tree, for instance, have to be decided. The yellow parts and the blue parts have to be located on a sketch of the image and each plate worked to hold various amounts of the ink from the faintest to the thickest applications to create modulated color. Today, separations are made using filters and photography. That these printmakers reasoned out the details of each print, in small areas and large, all by hand and eye, is truly remarkable.

Noce de village was printed in an order—yellow, red, blue, carmine, and finally black—different from the one Montdorge suggests. The image seems to become more confused as each color is added, until the final black tonal plate focuses the colored image, lending it an impression of good registration that the penultimate printing does not show (fig. 10). Apparently the colors were laid on a little more broadly than necessary, in expectation that the black tones would cover the excess, and all the finest details—such as facial features—were only delineated in black (fig. 11). This method made clear images possible, even in the most delicate details, without perfect registration (fig. 12).

The order of printing the inks is important in an image. If the black plate is printed last, it covers all the slight differences in registration that are bound to arise in multiple-plate images. The colors were generally printed from least obvious to most obvious in any image.[40] The exception was carmine, which was expensive[41] and was generally printed just before the last, black, tonal plate. In some prints, the order of printing was revised to achieve certain effects. For example, in Bonnet's *L'Amant écouté* (cat. 53) and *L'Éventail cassé* (cat. 54)

the plates were printed in this order: blue, black, red. Where the opaque orange-red is printed directly on the paper, it looks orange-red; where it covers the black, it looks brown, thus economically introducing another color to the prints.

From 1774 to 1777, Bonnet made a series of gilded pastel-manner prints (cats. 30–34). He carefully transcribed pastel and chalk drawings to his etching plates and printed them in full color; on the same sheet of paper, however, he also created fancy gold frames around the figures. The printed frames were drawn to replicate contemporary styles and, incredibly, Bonnet also incorporated actual frame-making techniques in the printing. *The Woman ta King Coffee* (cat. 31) is a very fine pastel-manner print in several colors, all of which were mixed with lead white to render them opaque and pastel-like. The gold framing surrounding the print was constructed in a meticulous re-creation of contemporary frame-making practices. A deeply worked plate was printed in thick white lead to

create a textured "gesso ground" for the inner liner of the frame. The white lead underprinting creates what appear to be carved lines in the border of the image, lines around the oval liner that radiate from the center of the image. The other areas to be gilded were also underprinted with white lead. The white lead was then printed with an oil-based mordant, on which gold leaf was laid by hand.[42]

Details in the frame that were to remain free of leaf, although they were within the general area to be gilded, were simply not printed with the mordant, as gold will not stick to paper or dry printing ink. After the gold leaf was laid, the print was run through the press twice more to apply the blue and black shadings over the gold leaf that define the ornaments found in the corners and top of the frame.[43]

But, this tour-de-force was apparently not enough for Bonnet. In another print, *The Milk Woman* (cat. 30), he again used lead white to opacify the printing inks, but here he incorporated gold in the image by laying gold leaf over the printed green milk jug.[44] The frame for this print was even more complicated than the frame for *The Woman ta King Coffee*. Both

10. Charles-Melchior Descourtis, *Noce de village*, 1785 (detail, cat. 55h), overprinting of all four color plates

11. Charles-Melchior Descourtis, *Noce de village*, 1785 (detail, cat. 55i), black

12. Charles-Melchior Descourtis, *Noce de village*, 1785 (detail, cat. 55j), completed image

were constructed over an ersatz gesso layer, but at the corners of *The Milk Woman* frame, the three-dimensional gesso was overprinted with red lead to approximate the bole layer in gilding. The red lead ink had small white crystals—perhaps sand—admixed, giving the corners and sides of the frame a pebbled texture under the gold leaf. This same method was employed by contemporary frame-makers to get the sanded gilding that was then in vogue in Paris.[45] After gilding by hand, the frame elements were again overprinted in black and blue shadows.

Some of the "sand" crystals in the red lead printing ink have been lost, and in the cavities they left behind, an energetic pointillistic pattern of white and red inks is visible. Whether Bonnet calculated or induced the loss of the sand grains is not known, but given everything else he did in copperplates, he probably intended this effect as well.

When Le Blon set out to mimic paintings, he began a process that revolutionized color printmaking in France. Printers in Paris quickly began to duplicate chalk drawings and pastels, then turned to watercolors and gouache paintings. Scenes of the boudoir or seductive frivolities from everyday life gave artists and painter-printmakers topics that would intrigue their patrons and decorate elaborate town houses. As such, these prints can be grouped with decorative arts in the Louis XV style. During this period of tremendous creativity for all artisans, high technical merit and a significant degree of craftsmanship were stressed.

Colored prints were created with the same feeling. Although much of the technical means was hidden, the degree of craftsmanship used in creating the colored prints was unsurpassed. The thrill of creation as artists and artisans vied to produce new effects in copperplate printing is easily imagined—time after time, the printers raised the threshold of expectations by presenting increasingly complicated prints to the public. Such a sensational period of invention in Western printmaking did not recur until nearly two hundred years later, when professional printers offered their skills to fine artists in the collaborative printmaking studios of the mid-twentieth century.

A Collector's Perspective

Ivan E. Phillips

My collecting of eighteenth-century French color prints began by chance in the late 1960s in Paris. At that time, I was a young lawyer and had started a small collection of prints by Edouard Manet. In the mid-1950s, my parents had begun to acquire French impressionist and early twentieth-century French paintings and drawings. Through a friend of mine at Yale, Ted Coe—the son of the great impressionist collector Ralph Coe—I met John Rewald, the preeminent historian of French impressionism, who became a close friend of, and advisor to, my family. John suggested that I visit the R. G. Michel Gallery on quai Saint-Michel in Paris, which is presently run by Françoise Michel-Arguillère, the granddaughter of the original owner.

A visit to the Michel Gallery was, and still is, like stepping into a print by Honoré Daumier. Whole folios of prints are brought out and presented to the clients, who sit on rickety

1. Gilles Demarteau the Elder, *Three Young Women by a Brook*, 1772, after François Boucher, chalk manner. Lisa Phillips Collection

wooden chairs. During one of these visits in about 1966, my former wife, Lisa, came across a print by Gilles Demarteau the Elder reproducing a sanguine drawing by François Boucher, which we purchased (fig. 1).[1] At the time, we had moved to a new home and had bought some eighteenth-century French furniture and works of art. The print was perfect for the setting; an original Boucher drawing was then beyond our reach.

In September 1970, I acquired three more chalk-manner prints, all by Demarteau.[2] A year later, I purchased a set of full-color wash-manner prints of the four seasons by Gilles-Antoine Demarteau after Jean-Baptiste Hüet (cats. 49b, 50b, 51, 52b). By this time, I had become fascinated with the scope and technical ability of the great French eighteenth-century color printmakers—Bonnet, Demarteau the Elder, his nephew Gilles-Antoine, Debucourt, Descourtis, and Janinet, in particular. I began to seek out their works on my visits to dealers in London, Paris, and New York, and managed to acquire a few each year for the next several years.

One of the happiest coincidences of my collecting career came in April 1973. Just a month or so earlier, I had acquired the print *Woman in Russian Costume* (cat. 27b) by Demarteau the Elder and had taken it to be framed at Lowy and Co. in New York. After picking up the framed print, I stopped off to see Regina Slatkin, the dealer and Boucher expert. There on the gallery wall was the original drawing by Jean-Baptiste Le Prince (cat. 27a)! Of course I had to buy it, and splitting the purchase with my older brother Neil, I did. Reuniting the two works gave both of us a great deal of satisfaction: We could truly appreciate, through studying the print and the drawing side by side, how faithfully Demarteau was able to reproduce every detail of Le Prince's sketch.

The next year we were able to buy the two Boucher drawings *Les Œufs cassés* and *Le Maraudeur* from the sale of the collection of Mrs. Alan L. Corey (cats. 16a, 17a).[3] I had purchased one of the prints, *Les Œufs cassés*, from Michel a couple of years earlier (cat. 16b); I later acquired two impressions of the pendant, one of which I gave to the National Gallery of Art (cat. 17b). Then two of Hüet's watercolors for the set of the four seasons came our way from Galerie Cailleux in Paris in 1981 (cats. 49a, 52a).[4] But another twenty years passed before

I was able to acquire the watercolor *Summer* (cat. 50a) from Emanuel von Baeyer in London. Neil unfortunately had died in 1997. Somewhere out there lurks the missing *Autumn* and someday, unless it has been lost to the ravages of time, I hope to be able to complete the set.

In my collecting over the years I have developed a number of criteria that have helped me in deciding what works to acquire. The subject matter and a print's aesthetic appeal have always been of prime importance to me. If I do not respond to the image, I will not buy the print, no matter how much it might be admired by others. Academic and anatomical studies (cats. 2, 6, 29) are of little interest to me, for example. Other subjects I choose not to collect are what I call "the travelogue print," such as the views of the principal buildings of Paris (cat. 69) and landscapes of other parts of France and Europe (cats. 42, 43); representations of the French Revolution and other historical subjects (cats. 82, 84); and portraits of the "movers and shakers" of late eighteenth-century Paris (cats. 75–77, 87), except Marie-Antoinette (cat. 39), though I suppose she may be called the biggest "mover and shaker" of them all.

If the image appeals to me, I then go on to consider the artist who made it. I have concentrated for the most part on the few great creators of color prints—Demarteau, Bonnet, Janinet, Descourtis, and Debucourt. A great name, however, is not always a guarantee of the best quality. Not only did the best-known color printmakers produce a startling number of bad prints,[5] but they also often published the works of their assistants under their own names. The problem is well described by Marcel Roux, who, after discussing Bonnet's great *Tête de Flore* (cat. 19), went on to explain:

> Unfortunately, works of this quality are the exception in the voluminous work of Bonnet, where one must say the bad and the worse dominate. Besides being an engraver, he was an engraving entrepreneur. A whole team worked in his studio and flooded the international market with commercial prints, often of gallant subjects. These works, which are marked "Bonnet direxit," are very tiresome and only have a distant relationship with art.[6]

2. Studio of Louis-Marin Bonnet, *Head of a Young Woman*, 1777, after Pierre-Thomas Le Clerc, chalk manner with applied gold leaf. The Ivan Phillips Family Collection

Within my own collection, one need only compare one of Bonnet's so-called "English" prints, such as *The Milk Woman* (cat. 30), with one of the studio-produced prints—*Head of a Young Woman* after Pierre-Thomas Le Clerc (fig. 2), for example—to recognize the truth of Roux's assessment.

For some artists the prints they produced early in their careers are considerably more desirable than their later works. Such is the case with Janinet, whose last great works are the large boudoir prints of the late 1780s (cats. 59–61, 74), when he was still in his thirties. His prints of Revolutionary subjects are rather weak in execution and artistically insignificant in comparison. Debucourt's eighteenth-century prints rarely disappoint, but those executed in the early nineteenth century

3. Louis-Marin Bonnet, *L'Amant écouté*, 1783, after Jean-Frédéric Schall, stipple and wash manner. The Ivan Phillips Family Collection

and thereafter show a marked decline in quality. Sometimes the works of the secondary masters—Joseph de Longueil, Laurent Guyot (cats. 70, 71), and Louis Le Coeur (cats. 64, 82), for example—are as fine as their better-known contemporaries, and I have acquired a few examples that I found particularly pleasing.

Ideally, I try to find clear and bright impressions, with fresh colors, crisp contours, and no sign of wear in the plates. Color prints were produced in large editions and over a period of many years. The engravers had catalogues of their works, which could be ordered on demand. The Bonnet and Demarteau catalogues each list over seven hundred works, while that of Debucourt numbers almost six hundred. With the passage of time, the plates wore down through the printing process and the impressions deteriorated in quality. Late impressions are therefore of much less interest than early ones, and proofs before the title are the most sought after. The absence of a title, however, is not a guarantee that the print in question is an early proof. Many of the prints were dedicated to members of the nobility or to the wealthy owners of the original drawing. Following the Revolution these dedications were removed from the plates, since it was no longer socially acceptable to buy (or sell!) a work dedicated to a duke or marquis who had lost his head to the guillotine.

Each time a color print was produced, the plates had to be re-inked with the result that the colors often varied from impression to impression. I have in my collection two impressions of a print by Bonnet entitled *L'Amant écouté*, one of which is in this exhibition (cat. 53). The color of the chair in the impression with the letters (exhibited) is silvery gray, while in the proof before letters (fig. 3) it is brown. A couple of other examples of these kinds of printing differences are included in the show (cats. 37a, 37b, 58a, 58b). Were such variations made consciously by the artist, or were they due to the vagaries in the inking of the plates? The answer is not always clear.

Condition is yet another critical factor in considering a print for purchase. The colors must be fresh and the paper should be in good shape. Many of these prints were made and bought for decoration, and were thus framed and hung with pride on their owners' walls. Hence, they were often exposed for long periods of time to light and broad fluctuations in temperature and humidity. Overexposure to light could darken white paper, fade colored papers, and bleach out some light-sensitive inks such as carmine. Excessive humidity could cause foxing or rippling of the sheet. Harsh restoration treatment could also lead to different kinds of damage in the form of overcleaning and bleaching. As I have learned from Judith Walsh, senior paper conservator at the National Gallery of Art, some of the solvents used in conservation might leach out certain colors, such as gamboge yellow, which once gone can never be recovered (see page 25).

As I have said, many of the color prints were intended from the beginning to be matted, framed, and hung on the walls of their owners' homes. Today I choose to hang them in the same manner, but I take every precaution to keep them safe. It is imperative to use acid-free, museum quality mats and ultraviolet-filtering glazing to protect the delicate papers and inks. Several of my prints hang in corridors without windows. In rooms that do have windows, I keep the curtains drawn and the blinds closed during the day so that no direct sunlight will fall on the art.

As is the case in any collecting area, authenticity is a matter of prime importance for French eighteenth-century color prints. Because of their popularity in the late nineteenth century and early twentieth century, many were counterfeited very deceptively and copies were sold as originals to unsuspecting collectors. The fakes range from twentieth-century colored versions of eighteenth-century black-and-white prints, which one can still buy from the stalls that line the banks of the Seine in Paris, to extremely sophisticated reproductions of the most popular Janinet and Bonnet prints.[7] Fortunately, the counterfeiters did not usually match the dimensions of their fakes to the sizes of the originals. Thus, one critical way of distinguishing between the imitations and the actual prints is to measure the images and the platemarks and to compare them with the dimensions published in standard catalogues raisonnés. The educated collector, however, should train his eye to weed out real prints from imitations. I have therefore spent many enjoyable hours in the great print rooms of the United States and Europe studying the originals, learning what the ink colors should look like and how the paper should look and feel. Nothing can replace this kind of direct experience of the art.

Ideally, when I am considering the purchase of a particular print, I like to look at other impressions of the same print. Even with good notes, though, my memory of the exact colors and the precise quality of the lines can be faulty. I have discovered therefore that the very best way to gauge the quality of a print on the market is to compare it side by side with other good impressions. Such examinations have saved me from buying works that looked good on their own. When they were placed next to other impressions, however, the flaws and weaknesses became immediately evident. In a perfect world, I would always use this method when I buy my prints, but it is unfortunately a luxury that is not always available.

Once I decided that I would make French color prints a focus of my collecting, I spent quite a lot of time familiarizing myself with the standard references. A major problem for the North American collector is that the bulk of the literature is written in French and to a lesser extent in German, with very little available in English. The excellent catalogue of the 1984 exhibition *Regency to Empire, French Printmaking 1715–1814*, curated by Victor Carlson and John Ittmann, is a

notable exception.[8] Even if language poses no problem for a collector, the main catalogues raisonnés and reference books are long out of print and are not easily available. As my own collection of French color prints grew, I made a point of "collecting" a small library to go with it. Otherwise the necessary books are generally available only in museum or university libraries or in specialized research facilities such as the Frick Art Reference Library in New York City.

The one indispensable resource for all aficionados of French eighteenth-century prints is the collection catalogue of the Bibliothèque nationale in Paris, the *Inventaire du fonds français, Graveurs du XVIIIe siècle*, published between 1930 and 1977. The inventory (a frequently cited source referred to throughout this volume simply as *IFF*) consists of fourteen volumes organized in alphabetical order. Unfortunately, however, it ends with an artist named "Lequien," and there are no present plans to publish any more volumes. Nor are there published catalogues of other important collections of French prints, such as the one in the Kupferstichkabinett in Veste-Coburg, Germany, and the Collection Edmond de Rothschild in the Musée du Louvre in Paris. For the Rothschild collection, the only "catalogue" is a rather tattered and dog-eared typescript list that is kept in the collection's study room.

I have been fortunate in my collecting to have had the help of many knowledgeable scholars, curators, and dealers who have been willing to give me their advice and moral support. It is not a large group; we would not need Yankee stadium to hold a convention. Nevertheless, I cannot name everyone who has encouraged and advised me, but I must at least mention Andrew Robison and Margaret Morgan Grasselli of the National Gallery of Art, who have generously shared their enthusiasm and expertise with me over the years and have become good friends in the process.

I have also been aided by several honest and reliable dealers. Building a personal relationship with the best dealers in the field has been an important and personally rewarding aspect of collecting French prints. I keep in regular touch with them, and upon occasion one of them will call me about a recent acquisition that might be suitable for my collection. The most thrilling such call came only recently from Michèle Prouté. The members of the Prouté family had been trying to think of a personal way to participate in this exhibition, and had finally decided to part with one of the color prints from the family's own private collection. Mme Prouté was therefore calling to offer me the opportunity to buy the magnificent and exceptionally rare impression of the first state, before letters, of the Janinet *Toilette de Vénus* (cat. 47a), which I had long coveted. The chance to acquire this spectacular impression, especially from such good and generous friends, and thus fill an important gap in my collection was not to be missed.

The last element that guides the fortunes of a collector is luck, mostly good, but occasionally bad. I have had both: the former when I came across something unexpectedly, such as

4. Jean-François Janinet, *Zephire and Flore*, 1776, after Antoine Coypel, wash manner with applied gold leaf. The New York Public Library, Astor, Lenox and Tilden Foundations, Print Collection, Miriam and Ira D. Wallach Division of Art, Prints and Photographs

the Le Prince drawing from Regina Slatkin; the latter when through indecision and delay, I lost something to a more astute and decisive collector. I rue the day, for example, that I failed to take an hour to go see a brilliant pair of Janinet gold-bordered works at Paul McCarron's in New York. The prints are now in the collection of the New York Public Library (fig. 4).

In all, assembling my collection has been a wonderful and rewarding experience, enhanced over the last ten years by my wife Winnie's good eye and advice. Together we have fun searching for these rare gems. When I first met her, I asked her if she liked going to museums and galleries. She replied in the affirmative. Little did she know what she was in for!

There was once a great and thriving demand for these color prints. Just as a collector today who cannot afford a painted *Marilyn* by Andy Warhol buys instead a silkscreen version, so too in eighteenth-century Paris someone who could not afford an original drawing by Boucher, Fragonard, Hüet, or Le Prince could acquire a print. In the late nineteenth century, after several decades of neglect, these finely crafted color prints came back into favor and the market for them revived dramatically. By the time of the Debucourt exhibition in 1920, the authors of the catalogue noted that great examples were then almost unobtainable and only then at enormous prices.[9] Subsequently, the market deteriorated and one can today sometimes find prints for the same prices—and often less—that they had reached three-quarters of a century ago. It is not hard to understand why these beautiful works fell out of collecting favor after their heyday in the years leading up to World War II: they undoubtedly came to be regarded as devoid of serious content, not worthy to be spoken of in the same context as prints by Dürer, Rembrandt, or even Munch and Picasso. As frivolous as much of their subject matter may seem, French eighteenth-century prints and the printmakers who made them nevertheless played a crucial role in the evolution of the art of color printing. These prints are remarkable not only for their technical complexity but also for their superb craftsmanship. These works deserve to be recognized again as one of the glories of artistic creation in eighteenth-century France.

Catalogue

MEDIA descriptions, for the most part, follow the French system of using terms that describe the works being imitated by the prints: for example, chalk manner (*manière de crayon*) and wash manner (*manière de lavis*). Despite our best efforts, we were unable to decipher the precise means by which these very complicated prints were made. Although we knew that each plate of the multiple-plate prints could have been worked in several copperplate techniques, as the plates were overlaid in printing, the characteristic patterns associated with specific methods were obscured. In the finished prints, we could not confidently identify the technique used to make any specific mark. However, "aquatint" and "mezzotint" are used to describe prints that were clearly or entirely executed in those printmaking techniques. For definitions of individual printmaking techniques and terms, see the glossary.

DIMENSIONS are given in millimeters, height before width.

WATERMARKS found in the exhibited sheets, except cat. 1, are reproduced in the appendix *Paper Used in the Prints*.

1

Jakob Christoffel Le Blon
1667–1741

Louis XV

1739
after Nicholas Blakey
color mezzotint and engraving, printed in blue, carmine, yellow, brown, black, and white inks
sheet: 600 × 443 (trimmed within platemark)
IFF 13:4
watermark: double-headed eagle

NATIONAL GALLERY OF ART,
ROSENWALD COLLECTION 1954.12.177

"Painting can represent all visible Objects, with three Colours, Yellow, Red, and Blue; for all other Colours can be compos'd of these Three, which I call Primitive." Surprising as it may seem, this important theory about the basic components of all pigments was not formulated until the mid-1720s by the rather obscure German painter and engraver Jakob Christoffel Le Blon. Le Blon then turned his theory to practical purpose by inventing primitive versions of three- and four-color multiple-plate printing processes that formed the basis for the halftone color reproduction techniques still used today.[1] Even before his treatise was published in London in 1725, Le Blon had already been making full-color reproductions of pictures using only blue, red, and yellow inks. He made these "printed paintings," as he called them, by separating the colors that made up his painted models into the three basic "primitive"—or primary—colors: Dividing up the parts of the composition according to the colors in which they would be printed and using the mezzotint printmaking technique that had thus far been used only for black-and-white prints, Le Blon worked each part onto a separate

1–4. Jakob Christoffel Le Blon after Hyacinthe Rigaud,
Cardinal de Fleury, 1738, color mezzotint progress proofs.
Bibliothèque de l'Arsenal, Paris

copperplate, three in all, one for each color. He inked the plates and printed them in succession—blue first, then yellow on top of that, and finally red on top of the other two. He carefully superimposed each layer of ink on the one before to re-create as nearly as possible the image and palette of the original painting (see pages 23–25). Thus did Le Blon lay the technical foundation for the great innovations made in color printing in eighteenth-century France.

Le Blon's writings and the royal privilege he was granted by Louis XV in 1737 all refer to this three-color printing process. In his prints, however, Le Blon often used four inks—the three primary colors and black—because images printed only with the primaries usually lacked definition and clarity. He discovered that printing a black plate before the other three resulted in a sharper, more unified image. But he was so wedded to his three-color theory that he never admitted, at least in writing, to using more than three plates in the execution of his prints. Even in the sets of progress proofs of other portraits that were printed up for sale to amateurs, Le Blon included only the impressions taken from the blue, yellow, and red plates separately and from the blue and yellow plates together (figs. 1–4).[2] For the National Gallery's impression of *Louis XV*, however, Le Blon actually used six inks: he added not only black and brown, but also white, which though usually described as being applied by hand, was certainly printed in this example. For some impressions, he even added a second, lighter shade of blue.[3]

Aged seventy-two when the print of *Louis XV* was announced in the *Mercure* in September 1739, Le Blon left the actual execution of the print to assistants—probably Jean Robert (active

1739–1766/1782) and Pierre-François Tardieu (1711–1771), and the printer Jean Mouffle (dates unknown). The number of impressions made from the full-color portrait is not known, but fewer than ten impressions have been identified today.[4] Many of these prints were varnished to make them look more like actual paintings. Some were even laid down on canvas in order to give texture to the paper surface, as was probably once the case with the exhibited sheet. Many of these prints were then framed and hung like paintings. Evidently few impressions were able to survive such treatment.

The model for Le Blon's print was a painting by a little-known Irishman, Nicholas Blakey (active 1739–1775), which in turn was painted after a sculpture by Jean-Baptiste Lemoyne the Younger (1704–1778). The whereabouts of the painting are not known.

1. See J. C. Le Blon, *Coloritto or the Harmony of Colouring in Painting* (London, [1725]), 28, reprinted in Paris in 1756 under the title *L'Art d'imprimer les tableaux*. In this brief tract, Le Blon seeks to differentiate between the properties of "material" colors, such as paint pigments, and immaterial or intangible colors, such as light, which are the subject of Sir Isaac Newton's famous book, *Opticks*, published in London in 1704. Specifically, Le Blon attempts to explain how the entire spectrum of light rays, when mixed together, can produce white, yet the same colors of paint pigments mixed together produce black. The difference, he posits, lies in the opacity of the "material" colors and in the immateriality or translucency of light.

2. Le Blon's decision not to mention the fourth plate led to angry disagreements between his assistants, who tried to carry on his work, and Jacques-Fabien Gautier Dagoty (cats. 2, 3), who had worked briefly in Le Blon's shop and claimed to be the inventor of the four-color printing process.

3. Le Blon's assistant Jean Robert, in response to Gautier's claims that he had invented the four-color printing technique, stated unequivocally that Le Blon had regularly used four plates for his prints—as Gautier well knew. Further, Le Blon himself had told Robert that it was advisable for the beauty of the execution to use as many as five and six plates, depending on the paintings one undertook to copy; see *Mercure* (June 1749), 150–154, reprinted in part in *L'Anatomie de la couleur: L'Invention de l'estampe en couleurs* [exh. cat., Bibliothèque nationale de France and Musée Olympique] (Paris and Lausanne, 1996), 146, appendix 7.

4. In addition to the impression exhibited here, only six others are currently known: two in the Bibliothèque nationale, Paris, and one each in a Parisian private collection, the Kupferstichkabinett, Berlin, the British Museum, London, and the Art Institute of Chicago. One sold at Boerner's, Leipzig, 13–15 May 1929, no. 51, may well be one of those already mentioned.

2

Jacques-Fabien Gautier Dagoty
1716–1785

L'Ange anatomique (The Anatomical Angel)
or Dissection of a Woman's Back
1746
color mezzotint, printed in blue, red, yellow, and black inks
plate: 612 × 460
IFF 10:45

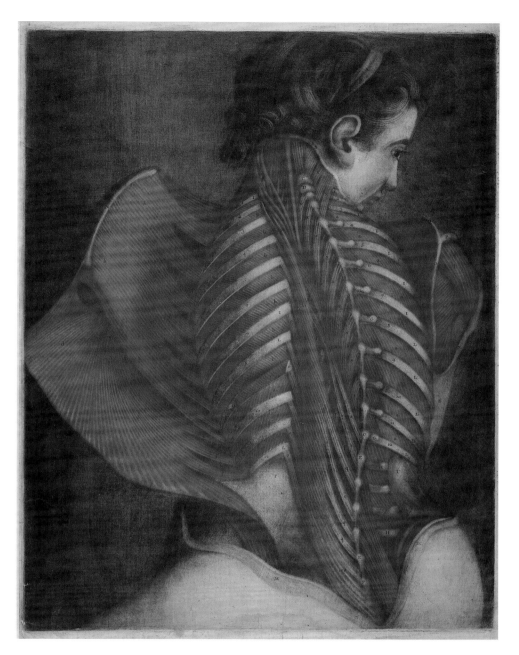

Le Blon (cat. 1) was the first to perceive the importance of full-color printing for medical illustration. As early as 1721 he had published a curiously beautiful print of a man's testicles, and two decades later he published another showing the intestines and abdomen of a boy.[1] One of Le Blon's disciples, Jan L'Admiral (1699–1773), made a specialty of anatomical prints, producing a number to illustrate medical treatises published in Leyden between 1736 and 1738.[2] The artist most identified with the genre, however, was Jacques-Fabien Gautier, who had worked in Le Blon's atelier for a mere six weeks in the spring of 1738 (and shortly thereafter added Dagoty to his surname). He apparently had time enough to familiarize himself with Le Blon's color printing methods and theories, for after Le Blon's death in 1741, he managed to obtain a thirty-year royal *privilège* for the color printing process that Le Blon had invented. For many years Gautier pressed the claim, to loud objections from Le Blon's students and heirs, that he himself had actually invented four-color printing.

Gautier's first great anatomical project was the illustration of a book on the muscles of the human body, *Myologie complète en couleur et grandeur naturelle*. Gautier observed the dissections performed by the surgeon M. Duverney, made paintings of them, and based engravings on the paintings. Work on the twenty plates for the book (all full color and full sized) began in 1745 and was completed in 1748. The most famous plate, the dissection of a woman's back (number XIV), is generally known as the *Ange anatomique* because of the winglike shape of the large mass of muscle opening out to the left. Incongruously, however, the figure is presented as a living being: although the back is laid open to expose the muscle and bone from the nape of the neck to the base of the spine, the woman calmly poses as if she were a model for an ordinary life-drawing class.

1. See Paris and Lausanne 1996, nos. 51, 62.
2. Paris and Lausanne 1996, nos. 63–81.

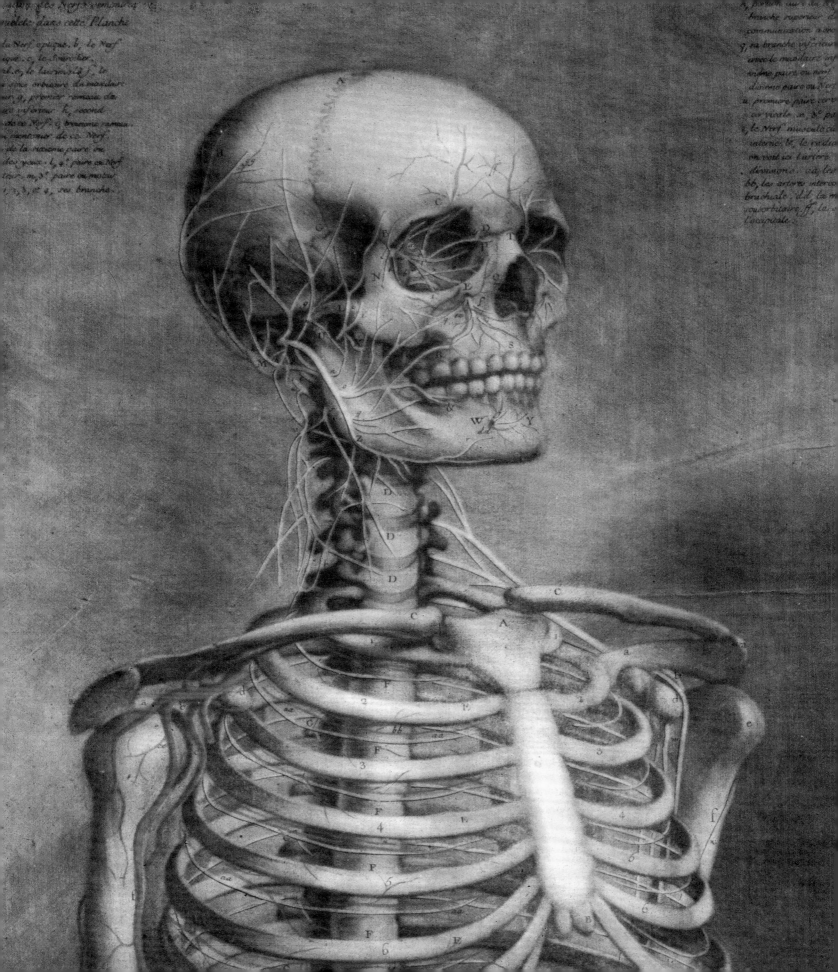

3

Jacques-Fabien Gautier Dagoty
1716–1785

Skeleton

c. 1754
color mezzotint, printed in black, yellow, red, and blue inks
plate: 1,869 × 460 (on three joined sheets)[1]
IFF 10:152–154

NATIONAL GALLERY OF ART, ROSENWALD PRINT
PURCHASE FUND AND AILSA MELLON BRUCE
FUND 2002.40.1

Even more spectacular than Gautier Dagoty's book on muscles (cat. 2) was his book on the internal organs of the human body, *Anatomie générale des viscères, et de la névrologie, angéologie et ostéologie du corps humains…*, published by Gautier himself and the printing house Delaguette in Paris in 1754. It was illustrated with a total of eighteen plates, twelve of which were joined in groups of three to make up four natural-sized renderings of the human figure: a partially dissected standing woman (plates I–III); a standing man, fully flayed, from the front and the back (plates IV–VI and X–XII); and an entire skeleton (plates XVI–XVIII), including some of the veins and nerves, as well as a separate detail of the spinal column, the brain, and the associated network of nerves.

For his previous anatomical illustrations, including the first three plates of the *Anatomie générale*, Gautier had depended on a surgeon to do the dissection and demonstration. Starting with the fourth plate in this book, however, Gautier was responsible for performing the dissection, making drawings of it, engraving and printing the plates, and even writing the explanatory texts. For this reason, specialists regarded this book, which Gautier presented as a medical text, with a certain amount of derision. Although the plates are undeniably arresting and seem at first glance to portray the internal structure of the human body in extraordinary detail, they are actually seriously flawed, lacking the "exactitude and anatomical truth in the figures" that are essential for an instructional book.[2]

1. The image is composed of three separate prints that were cut and pasted to make one complete, life-size human skeleton.
2. J. C. W. Moehsen, *Verzeichnis einer Sammlung von Bildnissen groesstentheils beruehmter Aertze* (Berlin, 1771); cited in Paris and Lausanne 1996, 124, no. 108.

4

Jean-Charles François
1717–1769

Corps de Garde (Guard Corps)

1758

after Carle Vanloo

etching, soft-ground etching, and chalk manner, printed in brown ink

plate: 459 × 678

watermarks: dovecote; T DUPVY FIN / AUVERGNE 1742

Hérold 1931, 67 iii/iv; IFF 9:89

The first printmaker to succeed in replicating the actual appearance of chalk lines in his prints was Jean-Charles François, whose modest goal was to find a way to make cheap, drawing-like prints that could be used as models by art students. Over a period of eighteen years, beginning in 1740, François came up with progressively improved methods to achieve his aim. The proudest proof of his eventual success in the late 1750s is the *Corps de Garde* after a drawing by Carle Vanloo (1705–1765). It is the largest and most impressive print François ever made.

At first François tried to adapt traditional engraving and etching tools and processes to his purposes, but was dissatisfied with the results. In 1756, he published a set of trophy prints with Gilles Demarteau the Elder (cat. 5), who had trained in metalwork decoration. During their collaboration, François was introduced to some special tools—most importantly, toothed roulettes—that led to a critical breakthrough (see

page 25, fig. 2). He discovered that when a copperplate was worked directly with a roulette or when a roulette was rolled carefully across a prepared etching plate, the prongs on the roulette wheel created a pattern of dots that could be varied in width according to the size of the wheel. When inked and printed, the resulting dot patterns simulated the effect of grainy chalk lines quite well. François soon found that the even spacing of the teeth on Demarteau's original roulettes was too regular to impart the proper visual effect, and he turned to Alexis Magny (1711–1795), a maker of fine hand tools, to design and manufacture tools with irregularly spaced teeth of varying sizes set at odd angles to the shaft. With these new roulettes and other similarly modified metalworking tools, François finally realized in mid-1757 his dream of making prints that accurately, deceptively, and quite cheaply replicated the appearance of actual chalk drawings.

Even with this success, François continued to experiment, and by early 1758 he had perfected yet another new technique—one that used a soft acid-resistant varnish (*vernis-mou* or soft ground) on the etching plate in place of the traditional hard ground. In this method, François covered the copperplate with the soft ground and sprinkled a gritty material such as sand or ground copper filings on top. He then placed a drawing on a thin sheet of paper (face up) directly on the prepared plate and firmly traced the drawing with a blunt, rounded tool. Wherever he pressed, the sticky ground stuck to the back of the paper and was lifted off the copperplate except where the gritty material (which lay between the paper and the ground) prevented the ground from being lifted off the plate. When

the plate was bitten, the printed lines had the breadth and graininess of chalk lines and, because the design was traced directly onto the plate, were somewhat less mechanical in appearance than those created by roulettes and other chalk-manner engraving tools. François chose to keep the details of this soft-ground etching technique secret and only one other printmaker of his generation, Ploos van Amstel in Holland (1726–1798), is known to have used it. The process was later "invented" again in England, where it enjoyed considerable success.

Thanks to the good offices of the marquis de Marigny, brother of Madame de Pompadour, François was awarded a small royal pension in October 1757 for his invention of the chalk-manner technique. In January 1758, he was given permission to make prints after works in the royal collection. Very shortly thereafter, François executed the *Corps de Garde*, a powerful combination of chalk-manner and soft-ground etching, and dedicated it, appropriately enough, to the marquis. In the advertisement published in the *Mercure de France* of April 1758, François was by no means modest in his claims for the print: "The boldness and precision of the drawing, the softness and breadth of the chalk are faithfully copied in it [the print]. It is at once a drawing for study and a print that is a painting."[1] He also identified himself proudly on the print itself as the "author of the art of engraving in the chalk manner, Pensioner of the King and Engraver of Drawings of His Majesty's Cabinet." Ironically, Gilles Demarteau, François' rival claimant as inventor of the chalk-manner technique, bought François' original copperplate for

Se Monsieur Le Marquis de Marigny Conseiller du Roy en ses Conseils, Comandeur des Ordres de Sa Majesté, Directeur et Ordonnateur General de ses Batiments, jardins, Arts, Academies et Manufactures Royales.

Carle Vanloo

Corps de Garde in 1773. He completely reworked it and republished it as no. 467 of his own oeuvre with a new inscription, "retouched by Demarteau."

Vanloo exhibited an oil sketch of the *Corps de Garde* at the Salon of 1757.[2] He then presumably copied this sketch in a chalk drawing that served as a model for François' chalk-manner print. The drawing remained in Vanloo's possession until his death, when it was sold as part of his estate.[3] Its location was unknown for more than two centuries; it resurfaced on the London and New York market in 2002.[4]

1. *Mercure de France* (April 1758), 163.
2. This work (oil on canvas, 44.5 × 52 cm) was recently on the art market with Alex Wengraf, Ltd., in London. It first reappeared in a sale at Christie's, Monaco, 4 December 1992, lot 52 (reproduced in color).
3. See *Carle Vanloo 1705–1765* [exh. cat., Musée Chéret] (Nice, 1977), 154, no. 489. The drawing was mentioned in the inventory of Vanloo's effects after his death in 1765 (no. 39) and was included in the estate sale held in Paris on 12 September 1765, lot 13.
4. *An Exhibition of Master Drawings* [exh. cat., Jean-Luc Baroni, Ltd.] (New York and London, 2002), no. 22.

5

Gilles Demarteau the Elder
1722–1776

A Farmyard
1759
after François Boucher
chalk manner, printed in red ink
plate: 333 × 431; 1st framing line: 265 × 375
watermark: dovecote
Leymarie 11; Jean-Richard 597

Gilles Demarteau, called "the elder" to distinguish him from his younger brother Joseph, was a master metal engraver who transferred his skill in chasing designs on metal objects to copperplate engraving in the mid-1750s. In 1756 he collaborated on a set of ornament prints with Jean-Charles François, who turned Demarteau's metalworking tools and techniques to the new purpose of chalk-manner engraving (see cat. 4). Formerly François' friend, Demarteau quickly became one of his chief rivals and over the course of the next twenty years published literally hundreds of chalk-manner prints. A large percentage of these were made after drawings by François Boucher (1703–1770), but a significant number of prints were executed after the drawings of a wide variety of other artists ranging from Antoine Watteau (cat. 28) to François-André Vincent (cat. 73).

One of Demarteau's earliest chalk-manner prints, *A Farmyard* after Boucher was published in October 1759 at a price of 1 livre, 5 sols. Even in his first efforts he shows considerable mastery of this new printmaking technique—the direct result, no doubt, of his many years of experience in metal engraving. Even more, he demonstrates remarkable fidelity in his translation of Boucher's drawing style onto the copperplate. The earliest impressions of this print were apparently published in black ink, following the medium of the original drawing,[1] but Demarteau soon switched to red ink. Such a departure may seem surprising for a printmaker who was intent on making facsimile prints of drawings. However, as an entrepreneur interested in turning a profit, Demarteau was apparently guided by aesthetic and market concerns as well. Not only did he select images that he thought would have a general appeal, but he also sometimes manipulated them to be even more attractive and saleable.

Almost all of Demarteau's prints bear numbers that were inscribed into the copperplate at the time of publication. These numbers record the approximate order in which the prints were executed and later served as the basis for a catalogue—actually more of a price list—compiled in 1788 by Demarteau's nephew and collaborator, Gilles-Antoine (see cat. 38).[2] Louis de Leymarie used these same numbers in establishing the order for his 1896 catalogue of Demarteau's oeuvre.

1. The drawing, which is in reverse to the print, was executed in black chalk with touches of white on gray-green paper and measures 265 × 380, almost exactly the same as the print. The drawing was last recorded in a sale at H. Gilhofer & H. Ranschburg, Lucerne, 28 June 1934, lot 50, reproduced.
2. See Leymarie, page 5.

Boucher in. Del.   Demarteau Scul.

DEDIÉ A MONSIEUR BLONDEL D'AZAINCOURT, LIEUTENANT COLONEL D'INFANTERIE, CHEVALIER DE L'ORDRE ROYAL ET MILITAIRE DE St LOUIS.

N.º VI.   A Paris, chez Demarteau, Ruë de la Pelletrie, à la Cloche, près le Palais, avec Privilege du Roi.   Par son très humble et très obéissant
                                                                                                                                                    Serviteur Demarteau l'ainé.

6

Gilles Demarteau the Elder
1722–1776

Seated Nude Man, Seen from Behind,
Pulling a Rope
c. 1760
after Carle Vanloo
chalk manner, printed in red-brown ink
plate: 397 × 532
watermark: sun
Leymarie 30; *IFF* 6:30

Jean-Charles François' primary reason for inventing a printmaking technique that could imitate the appearance of chalk lines was to produce "engraved drawings" that could be copied by art students as part of their early training. At the time of the publication of his third booklet on the principles of drawing in 1753 (executed in an experimental engraving technique that was not yet the full chalk manner), an announcement in the October issue of *Mercure* specifically states that the price had been set at a particularly modest level in order "to give young people who are learning to draw more facility in obtaining them [these prints]." The announcement goes on to applaud François' attempts as having "great utility in perpetuating the drawings of the great Masters and in putting into the hands of pupils, both in Paris and in the provinces, the best originals, rendered in a manner much more suitable for forming in them a taste for good drawing than would be possible from ordinary engraving."[1]

One of the first to exploit François' idea of producing prints for instructional purposes, Demarteau focused his attention for a time on large academic nudes. His first print of this type (Leymarie 15), probably produced early in 1760, copied a drawing by Boucher and was apparently priced at 12 sols;[2] the second, the print pictured here after Carle Vanloo, sold for 1 livre, which was perhaps not quite the bargain that François had hoped for. Drawings of the nude figure were traditionally quite large, however, and producing prints after them on the same scale was expensive—the price of the copperplates alone was high.

Academic nudes were standard fare for both students and masters, and prints after the best of these drawings would presumably have had a ready market. Demarteau, even at this early stage in his career as a chalk-manner printmaker, proved himself to be particularly skilled in adapting his technique to the special requirements of the genre while also capturing the specific character of the style of the artist he was copying. After publishing this print after Vanloo,

he rapidly produced eight more (Leymarie 32, 36–42), followed shortly by three others (Leymarie 51, 52, 60). He then made one after a drawing by Louis Gabriel Blanchet (1705–1772; Leymarie 66).[3] But by 1762, he had almost entirely abandoned the reproduction of male academic nudes, and over the course of the next fourteen years he made only a handful of such prints. Perhaps Demarteau had found the genre too limited (or limiting) and not as profitable as he had hoped.

1. The announcement is cited by Edmond Pognon and Yves Bruand in *IFF* 9: pages 305–306.
2. Reproduced in Jean-Richard 598. The prices quoted for the various prints of male nudes come from the price list established by Gilles-Antoine Demarteau in 1788. See Leymarie, page 5.
3. Nine of the prints and the three drawings after which the others were made are reproduced in Nice 1977, nos. 551, 561 (drawings); 581 (counterproof of the original drawing); 583, 587, 591, 596–598, 600, 608, 609 (chalk-manner prints).

7

Louis-Marin Bonnet
1736–1793

Head of a Young Woman Wearing a Cap
before 1764
after Jean-Baptiste Greuze
chalk manner, printed in red ink
plate: 465 × 346; framing line: 427 × 319
watermark: chaplet with Maltese cross
Hérold 40a

NATIONAL GALLERY OF ART, GIFT OF
IVAN E. AND WINIFRED PHILLIPS 1997.17.1

Bonnet first trained as a printmaker in the studio of Louis-Claude Le Grand (1723–1807), his uncle by marriage. He began working with Jean-Charles François (cat. 4) in 1756, and therefore learned the chalk-manner technique even as it was being developed. About 1759, he spent a brief period in the shop of Gilles Demarteau (cats. 5, 6), who took advantage of the opportunity to learn from him as many of François' secrets as possible. Bonnet became Demarteau's greatest rival, and likewise produced a large number of chalk-manner prints over the course of his career.

Contemporary artists such as François Boucher, Carle Vanloo, and Jean-Baptiste-Marie Pierre (1714–1789) clearly recognized the economic and reputational merits of having their drawings reproduced. Both Bonnet and Demarteau early in their careers made many prints after the works of those painters. Other artists may have been more skeptical or may not have proven to be congenial business partners for the printmakers. The large red chalk head studies that were a specialty of Jean-Baptiste Greuze (1725–1805) were perfectly suited to reproduction in the chalk-manner technique, and Bonnet was clearly very adept at translating them in that manner, as the exhibited print shows. Yet Bonnet made only four chalk-manner prints after Greuze's red chalk drawings (Hérold 39a, 40a, 113, 176), and Demarteau made none.[1] Bonnet's first print after Greuze (Hérold 39a), the pendant to this one, was actually dedicated to Greuze's wife, who had posed for the original drawing. Thus, a collaboration that seems to have begun warmly clearly did not prosper. Perhaps Greuze, an astute businessman, wanted to maintain tight control over the publication process, just as he did with black-and-white engravings after his paintings.[2]

The location of the drawing by Greuze that served as the model for this print is not currently known.

1. A few other chalk-manner prints after Greuze are known. One by Thérèse-Eléonore Lingée is reproduced on page 14.
2. See Antony Griffiths, "Greuze et ses graveurs," *Nouvelles de l'estampe* 52/53 (July–October 1980), 9–11.

8a

Louis-Marin Bonnet

1736–1793

Marie-Rosalie Vanloo

c. 1764

after Carle Vanloo

chalk manner, printed in black and white inks
on gray-brown paper

plate: 400 × 302; image: 355 × 289

Hérold 55a ii/v

8b

Louis-Marin Bonnet

1736–1793

Marie-Rosalie Vanloo

c. 1764

after Carle Vanloo

chalk manner, printed in black and white inks on blue
paper

plate: 402 × 302; image: 358 × 289

Hérold 55a iii/v

DEDIÉE A MONSIEUR CARLE VANLOO

Bonnet was not content simply to turn out print after print in the standard chalk-manner technique. Instead, this inspired and determined innovator expanded the possibilities of the medium in a variety of directions. One of his first innovations was the formulation in about 1763 of a white printer's ink that could effectively imitate the appearance of white chalk and white gouache, but would not turn yellow or black over time. This new ink revolutionized chalk-manner engraving and greatly expanded the types of drawings that could be reproduced in prints. Not only could studies made in black and white chalks or in red and white chalks be replicated, but drawings made *aux trois crayons* (three chalks, specifically red, black, and white; see cat. 9a) could also be imitated, yielding eye-catching prints. Bonnet eventually developed a pastel-manner technique that resulted in some of the most complex and beautiful prints of the eighteenth century (cat. 19). Since Bonnet never shared the secret of his white ink with anyone, he was the only chalk-manner printmaker to use it. He quickly capitalized on his monopoly, making a specialty of multicolored prints.

Like Demarteau, Bonnet did not always publish prints that exactly copied his model drawings. Both men turned out impressions in different inks and on different papers that became in effect new and often improved versions of the original drawing—imitative prints with a spark of originality. Printing black-and-white impressions on blue paper was a favorite variant, for the blue of the paper not only added an extra dimension of color, but also enhanced the brightness of the whites and their contrast with the blacks.

The child in these two prints has always been identified as "Anna" Vanloo (see Hérold 55a), but Carle Vanloo's only daughter, born in 1740, was actually named Marie-Rosalie. The original drawing by Vanloo—or possibly a copy after either the original drawing or after the print by Bonnet (which is in the same direction)—is in the collection of the Metropolitan Museum of Art, New York.[1] Since the drawing is on brown paper, the impression printed on gray-brown is closer to it in appearance.

Bonnet is known to have lived at the address indicated on the second state of the print (cat. 8a)—"Pont St Michel, aux Armes de France, vis à vis la rue du Hurpoix"—in 1764. The print was therefore published just before Bonnet's departure for Russia in October 1764, where he hoped to find favor with the court and to teach the chalk-manner printmaking technique at the Russian Academy of Fine Arts. Having met with little success there, he returned to Paris toward the end of 1766.

1. Inv. 1974.366, black and white chalks on brown paper, 359 × 283. See Jacob Bean and Lawrence Turčić, *15th–18th Century French Drawings in The Metropolitan Museum of Art* (New York, 1986), no. 294.

Dessiné par Carlo Vanloo   Gravé par Louis Bonnet

DEDIÉE A MONSIEUR CARLE VANLOO

A Paris, chez la V.de F. Chereau   Par son très humble, et très-
rue S. Jacques aux 2. Piliers d'or.   obéissant serviteur, Louis Bonnet.

9a

Louis-Marin Bonnet
1736–1793

Bust of a Young Woman Looking Down
1765/1767
after François Boucher
chalk manner, printed in red, black, and white inks
on blue paper
plate: 310 × 232; 2d framing line: 237 × 167
Hérold 9 i/iv; Jean-Richard 339

NATIONAL GALLERY OF ART, COLLECTION OF
MR. AND MRS. PAUL MELLON 1995.47.72

9b

Louis-Marin Bonnet
1736–1793

Bust of a Young Woman Looking Down
1773 or later
after François Boucher
chalk manner, printed in red and black inks
plate: 309 × 232; 2d framing line: 235 × 166
watermark: chaplet (partial)
Hérold 9 iv/iv; Jean-Richard 339

NATIONAL GALLERY OF ART, GIFT OF
IVAN E. AND WINIFRED PHILLIPS IN
MEMORY OF NEIL PHILLIPS 2003.12.1

*Premiere Estampe aux trois Crayons d'après le dessein de M.ʳ Boucher
premier Peintre du Roy. Gravé par Louis Bonnet le seul qui possede le
secret d'Imprimer les blancs tiré du Cabinet de M.ʳ de la Garégade,
Thresaurier Général de la Marine.*

*a Paris chés la Veuve Chereau rue S.ᵗ Jacques aux 2 Pilliers d'Or
et chés Bonnet rue Galliante la porte Cochere entre un Chandellier et un Lecteur vis-à-vis la rue du Fouar.*

As Bonnet proudly states in the caption of the
first state of this print (cat. 9a), it was the first
print ever executed in the *trois crayons* manner,
that is, in red, black, and white inks. Its publication was announced in the *Avant-Coureur* of 18
May 1767 at a price of 1 livre, 16 sols, though the
print was surely completed well before that date.
Bonnet had taken some copperplates and prints
with him when he departed for Russia at the end
of 1764, and during his stay there he offered to

teach, for a large fee, promising young artists to
make chalk-manner prints in two and three colors.[1] Having already produced a few images
printed in black and white inks from two plates
by 1764 (see cats. 8a, 8b), Bonnet could easily add
a third plate to the mix. To enhance the effect of
the whites and to add even more color to the
image he could also vary the hue of the paper,
as he did here.

Bonnet appears to have been quite a prag-
matic printmaker: by often reworking and
adapting his images and adding and subtracting
plates in order to maximize the number of
impressions produced, he could extend the commercial value for quite a long time. Surprising as
it may at first seem, the red and black two-color
version (cat. 9b) is made from two of the same
plates that Bonnet had used to make his first
print in the *trois crayons* manner. Both plates

have been considerably reworked with many additional lines and some strengthening of already existing lines. This last state was published several years after the first—certainly no earlier than 1773, when Bonnet moved to the rue Saint-Jacques, the address indicated on it. By that time, the image had already passed through two other incarnations before arriving at this final version. Indeed, within just five months of announcing the publication of the three-chalk version of the *Bust of a Young Woman Looking Down*, Bonnet had added two more plates, one for blue ink and one for yellow ink, in order to transform the image into his first pastel-manner print. He had also erased the original inscription, which remained partially visible even in the last state; added several framing lines and panels printed in color to simulate a mount; inscribed "N° 9" at upper right; and added a new inscription below the outermost framing line. This completely revised second state was announced on 12 October 1767 at a price of 2 livres, 8 sols.[2]

Thereafter at an unknown date, Bonnet published a second *trois crayons* version, using gray paper, but still featuring the framing lines and inscriptions found in the second state. (An impression of this state is in the Collection Edmond de Rothschild at the Louvre.[3]) Finally, in or after 1773, Bonnet transformed the image into the two-color state exhibited here.

1. See Hérold, pages 10–12.
2. An impression of this state is reproduced in color in *Rokoko und Revolution, Französische Druckgraphik des späten 18. Jahrhunderts* [exh. cat., Wallraf-Richartz-Museum] (Cologne, 1987), 15, no. 42.
3. Inv. no. 19111 L.R. Reproduced in Jean-Richard 339.

10

Jean-Claude-Richard, abbé de Saint-Non
1727–1791

Eros and Psyche
1766
after François Boucher
etching and aquatint, printed in brown ink
image: 248 × 318 (oval, irregularly trimmed outside the image)
watermark: T DUPVY FIN / AUVERGNE 1742
Baltimore 1984, no. 60

NATIONAL GALLERY OF ART, GIFT OF
REGINA SLATKIN 1984.57.3

Just as important as the invention of a chalk-manner engraving in the mid-1750s was the invention a decade later of a new technique, aquatint, that could replicate the appearance of ink washes.[1] Various experimental methods of achieving tone through a "wash-manner" technique (*manière de lavis*) on a copperplate were tried by a number of printmakers, including Jean-Charles François (cat. 4), who had already invented the chalk-manner technique; François-Philippe Charpentier (cat. 11); and the Swedish printmaker Per Gustaf Flöding (1731–1791). The development of a true aquatint method, which is essentially the same as the one used today, is generally credited to an amateur printmaker, the abbé de Saint-Non, and his professional advisor, Jean-Baptiste Delafosse (1721–1775). The abbé produced his first aquatints in 1765, three years before aquatints were published by Jean-Baptiste Le Prince (cat. 20), who also claimed to be the inventor.

For most etchings, an unbroken hard ground is used to prepare the copperplate. The preparation for an aquatint, however, consists of a porous ground, usually created by sprinkling powdered resin or asphaltum liberally and evenly over the plate and then heating the plate from below to liquefy the powder and fuse it to the copper. When dipped into an acid bath, the irregularities in the ground allow the acid to bite into the plate in an allover pattern that, when inked, prints as tone. Depending on the fineness of the resin powder and the number of times the plate is prepared and bitten, the aquatint can yield quite solid, even tones that imitate very closely the appearance of ink washes. Because aquatint is purely a tonal medium and does not simulate pen lines effectively, it is usually used in combination with traditional etched lines to replicate drawings made in pen and wash.

Eros and Psyche was one of five aquatints produced in 1766 by Saint-Non, after drawings by François Boucher. All but one of those prints are exceptionally rare.[2] The impression of *Eros and Psyche* in the Metropolitan Museum of Art, New York, was actually thought to be unique as late as 1984,[3] but two other impressions have since come to light: the one exhibited here and another acquired in 1995 by the Archer M. Huntington Art Gallery, The University of Texas at Austin.[4]

The original drawing by Boucher, virtually identical in size to the print but in reverse, is in the collection of the Art Institute of Chicago.[5]

1. Aquatint was first used by Jan van de Velde IV in the 1650s. See Paris and Lausanne 1996, 44–45.
2. Four of the prints are recorded in Louis Guimbaud, *Saint-Non et Fragonard, d'après des documents inédits* (Paris, 1928), nos. 37–40. *La Leçon* (no. 40) is the one print of this group that is not rare. Guimbaud makes no mention of *Eros and Psyche*, which was apparently unknown to him.
3. See Baltimore 1984, no. 60.
4. Inv. 1995.21. Reproduced in *Prints of the Ancien Régime* [exh. cat., Archer M. Huntington Art Gallery, University of Texas] (Austin, 1966), 32, no. 37.
5. Inv. 1960.357, pen and brown wash over black and red chalk on ivory paper, 240 × 315. Reproduced in *François Boucher in North American Collections: 100 Drawings* [exh. cat., National Gallery of Art] (Washington, 1973), no. 55.

LA CULBUTE
A Paris chés Basa...

11

François-Philippe Charpentier
1734–1817

La Culbute (The Tumble)

1766
after Jean-Honoré Fragonard
etching and aquatint, printed in brown ink
plate: 300 × 417
watermark: D TAMIZIER / AUVERGNE 1742 / FIN
IFF 4:37

NATIONAL GALLERY OF ART,
WIDENER COLLECTION 1942.9.2312

Charpentier was an engraver who also had a gift for mechanics and engineering. His work on developing a technique for making wash-manner prints eventually earned him a lodging at the Louvre and a royal pension, but the invention of the true aquatint process is now generally credited to the abbé de Saint-Non (cat. 10) in about 1765. News of Saint-Non's technique spread quickly, for just a year later in 1766 Charpentier used it to translate with remarkable fidelity the vigor and panache of a brown wash drawing by Jean-Honoré Fragonard (1732–1806): *La Culbute,* which was announced in the *Avant-Coureur* of 15 September 1766. In this print, Charpentier not only conveyed the sweep of Fragonard's brushwork and the vitality of his pen line, but also captured the humor and lighthearted eroticism of the subject. *La Culbute,* Charpentier's masterpiece, has been called one of the "prettiest" facsimiles of a drawing made in the eighteenth century.[1]

Fragonard's original drawing, formerly in the Goncourt collection, was last exhibited in Japan in 1980, on loan from an unidentified private collection.[2] The drawing is in reverse to the print.

1. Marcel Roux, *IFF* 4:207.
2. See *Fragonard* [exh. cat., The National Museum of Western Art and Kyoto Municipal Museum] (Tokyo and Kyoto, 1980), no. 123.

12

Louis-Marin Bonnet

1736–1793

Young Woman Seated on a Bed

1767

after François Boucher

chalk manner, printed in black and white inks
on blue paper

5th framing line: 409 × 292; image: 355 × 238

Hérold 13 iii/iii; Jean-Richard 341

NATIONAL GALLERY OF ART, GIFT OF
IVAN E. AND WINIFRED PHILLIPS IN
MEMORY OF NEIL PHILLIPS 1998.63.2

The first state of this print, taken from a single
plate inked only in red, must have been made
before 1764, for the dedicatee, Monsieur le
Chevalier de Bausset, became a marquis before
his departure (with Bonnet) for Russia in October of that year. (An impression of this first state
is in the Rothschild collection at the Musée du
Louvre.[1]) The addition of the white plate, which
defines the second state, seems to date from the
period after Bonnet's return to Paris at the end
of 1766. At this stage, even though the original
drawing was executed in red and white chalks,[2]
Bonnet chose to print the image in black and
white inks on blue or gray paper. Impressions of
the third state, in which an added piece of drapery covers the woman's thighs, were printed
either in red chalk alone (from one plate) or in
black and white inks on colored paper (from two
plates), as here.

1. Inv. 19066 L.R. Reproduced in Jean-Richard 341, page 113.
2. The drawing was formerly in the collection of Paul
   Mathey (sale, Paris, 18 May 1901, no. 10). The dimensions
   of Bonnet's print are very close to those of Boucher's
   drawing (350 × 240).

13

Gilles Demarteau the Elder
1722–1776

Head of a Woman Looking Up
1767
after François Boucher
chalk manner, printed in black and orange-red inks
3d framing line: 209 × 160; image: 195 × 149
Leymarie 149; Jean-Richard 720

NATIONAL GALLERY OF ART, GIFT OF
PHILIP AND JUDITH BENEDICT 1997.88.7

In the 25 May 1767 issue of the *Avant-Coureur,*
Demarteau announced the publication of five
prints in "several colors," by which he actually
meant that they were printed in just two, red
and black, from two separate plates. This one
was the second in the group. Just one week
before, Bonnet had announced his first print
aux trois crayons (cat. 9a), which was printed in
red, black, and white inks from three plates on
blue paper. Since Demarteau was never able to
print with white, he could not make true facsimiles of *trois crayons* drawings (see cats. 35, 38),
nor could he rival Bonnet's production of multicolor prints from several plates. With rare excep-
tions he therefore limited himself to publishing
one- and two-color prints for the duration of
his career.

Demarteau seems to have made multicolored prints in spurts, producing nine in 1767
(Leymarie 148–156, including this one), two in
1768 (Leymarie 187, 188), three in 1770 (Leymarie
217–219), and two in 1771 (Leymarie 249, 250).
Thereafter, his production was irregular.

The model for this print was a study (location
unknown), in reverse, for the head of Aurora at
upper right in one of Boucher's most famous
paintings, *The Rising Sun* of 1753 (Wallace
Collection, London).[1]

1. Reproduced in Alexandre Ananoff and Daniel Wildenstein, *François Boucher* (Geneva, 1976), 2: no. 422. Jean-
Richard, under no. 720 and Ananoff and Wildenstein
1976, 2:114, no. 422/5, suggest connections with other
Boucher figures, but the head of Aurora in *The Rising Sun*
seems to match most closely the pose and expression of
the head in Demarteau's print.

14

Gilles Demarteau the Elder
1722–1776

Young Woman with Her Head Covered
1767
after François Boucher
chalk manner, printed in red and black inks
2d framing line: 331 × 251
watermark: dovecote (partial)
Leymarie 156; Jean-Richard 724

NATIONAL GALLERY OF ART, GIFT OF
IVAN E. AND WINIFRED PHILLIPS IN
MEMORY OF NEIL PHILLIPS 2002.90.1

Identified in the caption as Demarteau's ninth
multicolored print, this *Young Woman* was
made within a very short time of *Head of a
Woman Looking Up* (cat. 13). The technique used
to create the effect of stumped chalk is the same
in both prints: Areas of the plate are worked very
lightly with chalk-manner tools, but in a way
that creates a tonal effect rather than the appearance of chalk strokes.

Boucher's drawing (location unknown) was
surely based on a rather sketchy study by Antoine
Watteau (1684–1721) of a woman wearing a black
mantle, now in the Amsterdams Historisch
Museum (fig. 1).[1] The poses are identical (though
the figure in the print after the Boucher is in
reverse), and the costume is similar, even to the
scarf or ribbon draped around the model's neck.
The very sketchiness of Watteau's drawing
seems to have inspired Boucher to make a more
highly finished version. He set out not to imitate
Watteau's style, however, but to transform the
figure into one that was completely his own. That
Boucher had turned to Watteau for inspiration
is not surprising, for in the 1720s he made more

than one hundred etchings after Watteau's
drawings, including one after a more finished
version of the same mantled woman in the
Amsterdam drawing.[2]

1. Inv. A. 10985, red and black chalks with stumping on
   beige paper, 154 × 132.
2. Reproduced in Pierre Rosenberg and Louis-Antoine Prat,
   *Antoine Watteau 1684–1721, Catalogue raisonné des des-
   sins* (Milan, 1996), 2:964, fig. 568a.

1. Antoine Watteau, *Bust of a Woman with
Her Head Covered by a Mantle*, c. 1717, red
and black chalks. Amsterdams Historisch
Museum

15

Jean-Charles François
1717–1769

Louis Quinze, Roy de France (Louis XV)
1767
plate: 343 × 231
chalk manner, stipple, and soft-ground etching,
printed in red ink
watermark: T DUPVY MOYEN / AUVERGNE 1742
Hérold 1931, 53

NATIONAL GALLERY OF ART, GIFT OF
A. THOMPSON ELLWANGER III AND
GREGORY E. MESCHA IN HONOR OF
MARGARET MORGAN GRASSELLI 2003.50.1

In a letter dated 12 July 1767, François offered the
marquis de Marigny six impressions of his new
portrait of the king, writing that it had been "a
very long time since I have made something that
is worthy of being presented to you."[1] Indeed,
during the nine years since he had completed the
Corps de Garde (cat. 4), he had spent almost all
of his time on a long, ambitious, and not entirely
successful project: illustrating Alexandre Savér-
ien's *Histoire des philosophes modernes* (Paris,
1760–1767 in quarto; 1761–1767 in duodecimo), at
first with chalk-manner portrait prints, frontis-
pieces, and title pages, but later with simple etchings, printed in red in some editions and in black
in others.[2]

François made three chalk-manner prints of
members of the royal family: the portrait of
Louis XV; one of the queen, Marie Leczinska;
and one of the dauphin, Louis, who had died in
December 1765.[3] All are presented in an oval
format set within a rectangle that was broadly
worked in a pattern of diagonal stripes. In all
three portraits, the faces are handled with con-

siderable care, beautifully modeled with modulated and quite dense stippling and roulette
work. The clothing and hair, by contrast, are
treated more broadly and with a certain flair that
lifts these portraits above the ordinary.

This print is also discussed by Kristel
Smentek on page 16.

1. Quoted in Hérold 1931, page 27.
2. See Hérold 1931, 111–217.
3. Reproduced in Hérold 1931, figs. 53, 57.

16a

François Boucher
1703–1770

Les Œufs cassés (Broken Eggs)
c. 1755
red chalk with touches of black chalk
249 × 172

THE PHILLIPS FAMILY COLLECTION

16b

Gilles Demarteau the Elder
1722–1776

Les Œufs cassés (Broken Eggs)
c. 1769
after François Boucher
chalk manner, printed in orange-red ink
plate: 285 × 207; image: 250 × 177
watermark: AVUERNE 1742
Leymarie 128; Jean-Richard 702 ii/ii

THE IVAN PHILLIPS FAMILY COLLECTION

17a

François Boucher
1703–1770

Le Maraudeur (The Thief)
c. 1755
red chalk with touches of black chalk
248 × 167

THE PHILLIPS FAMILY COLLECTION

17b

Gilles Demarteau the Elder
1722–1776

Le Maraudeur (The Thief)
c. 1769
after François Boucher
chalk manner, printed in red ink
plate: 285 × 207; image: 256 × 173
watermark: unknown fragment
Leymarie 129; Jean-Richard 703 i/ii (proof before letters)

NATIONAL GALLERY OF ART, GIFT OF
IVAN E. AND WINIFRED PHILLIPS 1996.132.1

Having pendant drawings by Boucher together with the two prints after them by Demarteau provides an important opportunity to compare the originals to the reproductions.[1] The printed strokes may be a little harder, a little flatter, and a little less nuanced than the chalk strokes, but the prints nevertheless capture much of the appearance and spirit of the models. Indeed, Demarteau did not painstakingly copy every one of Boucher's strokes as they appear in the original drawing. Instead he sought to create a print that

LES OEUFS CASSÉS.

Se vend chez Demarteau l'aine, rue de la Pelterie, à la cloche.

N° 128

looks like an exact replica without actually being one. To enhance the resemblance, he executed his prints on the same scale as the originals and appears to have mixed the printer's inks to give a good approximation of the sanguine chalk.[2] The most notable difference in the two prints after Boucher is the reversal of the image, a result of the printing process that could be avoided if the printmaker chose to reverse the image before copying it onto the copperplate. This "mirroring" of the image seems not to have been an important concern, for the large majority of chalk-manner prints are in reverse to their models. Indeed, on the rare occasion when a print is in the same direction as a drawing, the drawing should be regarded with a certain amount of suspicion: many chalk-manner prints were copied by amateurs and art students and some of

the best copy drawings can be mistaken as models *for* the prints rather than copies made *after* them.

Chalk-manner masters like Demarteau and Bonnet executed their facsimiles with such skill that their prints can be mistaken for actual drawings themselves, especially when framed under glass (see page 17). In addition, the printmakers were so attuned to the individual touches of the draftsmen they copied that the author of a particular drawing may often be identified from the print just as easily as from the drawing on which it was modeled. These two prints, for example, are clearly after works by Boucher and look significantly different from prints after Vanloo (cats. 4, 8a, 8b), Greuze (cat. 7), or Le Prince (cat. 27b).

The proof impression of *Le Maraudeur*—printed before the title and credits were added—is quite an accurate rendering of Boucher's drawing in every respect, with no major additions or subtractions. However, after faithfully replicating the model drawing, the printmaker sometimes made changes to the print, often for reasons that remain unknown. In *Les Œufs cassés*, for example, Demarteau at first copied the drawing quite carefully using exactly the same touch and technique as he had in *Le Maraudeur*. At some point thereafter, however, he (or an assistant) returned to the print and added quite a number of strokes that do not appear in Boucher's drawing. At first the additions appear to be rather limited, but close study of the print and the drawing side by side reveals considerable new work throughout the entire composition. The most obvious additions are in the sky, which is nearly blank in the drawing but in the print is completely filled with hatching and cross-hatching. These new strokes were made with a

roulette that produced broader, more coarsely grained lines than the ones first used to copy the drawing. Close scrutiny reveals that the same roulette was used to add other hatchings and touches throughout the print. Why these additions were made is not clear: they do not materially improve the appearance of the image and depart significantly from the Boucher original. Perhaps they were made to conceal early signs of wear in the plate, or perhaps Demarteau, possibly even with Boucher's knowledge, felt that the printed image should be strengthened and enriched with further work.

1. See also cats. 27a, 27b for a drawing by Le Prince and the corresponding print, and cats. 49, 50, 52 for three watercolors by Jean-Baptiste Hüet and the prints after them.
2. The print after the Le Prince drawing (cat. 27b) is especially remarkable in this respect.

18

Louis-Marin Bonnet
1736–1793

The Awakening of Venus

1769

after François Boucher

pastel manner, printed in black, red, blue, white, and yellow inks on blue paper

sheet: 312 × 393 (trimmed within platemark); image: 281 × 382

Hérold 20 i/v (proof before letters); *IFF* 3:14

NATIONAL GALLERY OF ART,
KATHARINE SHEPARD FUND 1998.63.1

As Bonnet himself noted, his first six so-called pastel-manner prints were actually black and white prints with a few other colors added.[1] Here he added red, blue, and yellow inks and chose to print the image on a blue paper. The end result is very striking, especially in the way the two blues work together, but the dominant colors are clearly the black, red, and white. Indeed, the drawing that probably served as the inspiration for this print was not itself a pastel, but rather Boucher's three-chalk *Venus with a Dove,* in reverse, which includes the bedding but lacks the rest of the setting found in the print (National Gallery of Canada, Ottawa).[2] Regina Slatkin proposed that another drawing may have been made by Bonnet to serve as his own model (formerly in the collection of Marius Paulme).[3] That version is also in reverse but is more finished in execution and closer to the print in certain details of Venus' pose.

The print was announced in the *Avant-Coureur* in January 1769 at a price of 6 livres. By 22 October 1770, when a second announcement was published, only two plates were being used to produce a print executed in just red and black inks. Many of Bonnet's multicolor prints suffered a similar fate (see, for example, cats. 9a, 9b). The price was correspondingly reduced to 1 livre, 4 sols.[4]

1. See *L'Avant-Coureur* (3 July 1769), the first announcement of the publication of *Tête de Flore* (cat. 19). The text of the announcement is quoted in its entirety in Hérold 192, page 125.
2. Inv. 6897, 276 × 380. Reproduced in Washington 1973, no. 75.
3. Regina Shoolman Slatkin, "Some Boucher Drawings and Related Prints," *Master Drawings* 10, no. 3 (1972), 264–269, pl. 31.
4. See Hérold 20.

19

Louis-Marin Bonnet
1736–1793

Tête de Flore (Head of Flora)

1769

after François Boucher

pastel manner, printed in red, green, yellow,
blue-green, light blue, bright blue, black, tan,
brown, white, and pink inks

2d framing line: 409 × 327; sheet: 418 × 336
(trimmed within platemark)

watermark: dovecote

Hérold 192 i/ii

NATIONAL GALLERY OF ART,
ROSENWALD COLLECTION 1946.21.48

The single most ambitious color print attempted
by Bonnet or any of his rivals was the *Tête de
Flore*. Printed from eight separate plates, it captured with amazing richness the effect of a full-
color pastel. Bonnet was justifiably proud of this
exceptional print, going so far as to assemble a
unique set of eight progress proofs and to write
a plate-by-plate description of how it was made
(figs. 1–8). His testimony is so invaluable to
understanding the complexity of the technique
and the skill with which he worked out the
printing of this extraordinary facsimile, that
it deserves to be translated here in toto.[1]

*Pastel in Engraving, Invented and Executed
by Louis Bonnet 1769*

1st. Proof from the first plate printed in
green and blue-green to form the reflections,
in blue to express the color of blood perceived
under the skin, and likewise to prepare the
background of the painting and a part of the
flowers.

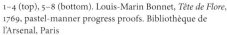
1–4 (top), 5–8 (bottom). Louis-Marin Bonnet, *Tête de Flore*,
1769, pastel-manner progress proofs. Bibliothèque de
l'Arsenal, Paris

2nd. Proof composed from the impression of the first and second plate. The second plate is printed in white and a little lake and carmine, destined to produce a pale flesh tone; the grain of its impression is very broad, because, since this plate will pass six times through the press it will be crushed and united to the necessary degree.

3rd. Proof composed of the impression of the first two plates together with the third. This third plate is printed in dark blue to finish the background of the painting, a part of the flowers, the pupil and the crystalline white of the eye. The work appears coarse, but it will be softened by the compression of the other plates.

4th. Proof composed of the impression of the first three plates together with the fourth. This fourth plate is printed in a delicate lake color and is destined to give the red tones and to break up the first colors. The green and the yellow serve to paint the bouquets.

5th. Proof of the fifth plate printed in a bistre color destined to draw the contours, to express the shadows, and to blend the first tints. The bistre and the earth colors employed in painting could not be used to print these plates since they are dull and opaque. All the work of the author was lost. Finally, after infinite research, he discovered that petrified wood reduced into a powder worked for him.

6th. Proof of the sixth plate printed in carmine to give the last tones of red.

7th. Proof of the seventh plate printed in very dark brown, this plate determines the contours and gives the last touch to the shadows. It is engraved in such a manner as to produce hard tones that will be softened by the last plate.

8th. Proof of the eighth and last plate. This plate printed in white gives light to the painting, softens the hardness of the blacks, and destroys the acridity of the reds. The whites used up to this time had the defect of becoming yellow or black; but the author had discovered several years earlier a white that is not at all subject to this drawback and that served to give the last value to his work.

Perhaps the most surprising revelation in Bonnet's description is his use of two and three colors, inked *à la poupée* (applying more than one color to a plate at a time) on three of the plates (nos. 1, 2, and 4). Also remarkable is his coarse working of the second and third plates in anticipation of the effects that many passes through the press would have on the inks. Clearly, this print was the result of much experimentation—even to the invention of a new ink using powdered petrified wood!—and much trial and error. Bonnet does not indicate how long he worked on perfecting the image, but many months, if not years, were probably devoted to solving all the technical problems.

The print was based on a pastel portrait of Boucher's younger daughter, Marie-Émilie (born 1740), which was last recorded in a Parisian private collection in 1976.[2] The pastel was executed in 1757, the year before Marie-Émilie married one of Boucher's pupils, the painter Pierre-Antoine Baudouin (1723–1769).

The publication of the print was announced in 1769 in the *Avant-Coureur* on 3 July and again on 2 October, when the price was quoted as 6 livres. The print could also be purchased already framed at a price of 10 or 15 livres, depending on the type of molding chosen. By the time another announcement ran in the *Avant-Coureur* on 25 October 1773, the print had become a three-plate chalk-manner engraving printed only in black, red, and blue. Other impressions with more than three plates but less than eight also exist, however, including an impression in the National Gallery of Art (1942.9.2145), printed without white and light pink and with only one blue. Perhaps to maximize the return on the considerable effort he had put into the making of the original print, Bonnet continually altered and adapted the image as the individual plates wore down and could no longer be used.

1. The full French text is transcribed in Hérold 192; and in Baltimore 1984, 194, 196, under no. 63.
2. See Ananoff and Wildenstein 1976, 1:97, fig. 135.

20

Jean-Baptiste Le Prince
1734–1781

La Danse russe (The Russian Dance)
1769
etching and aquatint, printed in brown ink
plate: 384 × 306; image: 301 × 238
watermarks: dovecote; I A SAUVADE FIN / AUVERGNE 1742
Hédou 137; *IFF* 14:130

NATIONAL GALLERY OF ART,
WIDENER COLLECTION 1942.9.1639

21

Jean-Baptiste Le Prince
1734–1781

Les Pêcheurs (The Fishermen)
1771
etching and aquatint, printed in brown ink
image: 322 × 232 (trimmed within platemark)
Hédou 163; *IFF* 14:169

NATIONAL GALLERY OF ART,
AILSA MELLON BRUCE FUND 1990.134.5

La Danse Russe

Trained as a painter and draftsman in the studio of François Boucher, Jean-Baptiste Le Prince was also an innovative printmaker who perfected his own very refined version of the aquatint etching process in 1768. His method, in which he used mastic instead of resin, was described in detail in the eighteenth century.[1] For a discussion of his technique, see page 29. Unlike Saint-Non (cat. 10) and Charpentier (cat. 11), whose prints display a comparatively limited tonal range, Le Prince followed a painstaking process of bit-ing, stopping out, and rebiting his plates multiple times in order to re-create the visual effect of richly varied wash drawings. He was thus able to achieve not only a full range of tones, but also printed "washes" that are so finely grained that to the naked eye they seem to be completely smooth and have none of the characteristic flecking so evident in the aquatints by Saint-Non and Charpentier. Many of Le Prince's aquatints were printed in black, but most, like *La Danse russe* and *Les Pêcheurs*, were printed in shades of brown to imitate the appearance of bistre ink drawings. All of them were printed on bright white papers to sharpen the contrast with the inks and enhance the pictorial richness of the images.

1. Binding of *L'Oeuvre de Le Prince*, 1770s. National Gallery of Art, Widener Collection 1942.9.1639

les Pêcheurs

2/2

Le Prince's first *gravures au lavis* (wash prints), as he called them, were published in 1768; the last appeared in 1774, only six years later. During that relatively short period, however, Le Prince produced seventy-nine aquatints. In late 1769 or early 1770, Le Prince assembled outstanding impressions of 124 prints he had made up to that time—including *La Danse russe* and 33 other aquatints printed in brown ink—and gave them, with his personal manuscript dedication, to Pierre Poissonier, a prominent doctor and collector. That volume, still in its handsomely decorated eighteenth-century red morocco binding with Poissonier's arms stamped in gold (fig. 1), passed through several important collections before coming to the National Gallery as part of the Widener gift in 1942.[2]

All but a handful of Le Prince's aquatints were made after his own drawings. The locations of the models for both *La Danse russe* and *Les Pêcheurs* are not known.

1. See the 1791 edition of Diderot's *Encyclopédie méthodique*, "Procédé de la Gravure au lavis," under the Beaux-Arts section, 2:622. This long description is quoted in its entirety in Hédou, pages 179–188.
2. See Cohen and Ricci, col. 627.

22

Gilles Demarteau the Elder
1722–1776

Young Woman Reading "Héloise and Abélard"
1770
after François Boucher
chalk manner, printed in black, red, and blue inks
1st framing line: 198 × 151; 3d framing line: 219 × 166
Leymarie 218; Jean-Richard 783

The addition of a blue plate to the red and black makes this print one of Demarteau's most elaborate chalk-manner works, yet it is light-years behind Bonnet's achievements in pastel manner, especially the *Tête de Flore* from the preceding year (cat. 19). Nevertheless, this beautifully rendered little piece makes one wish that Demarteau had made more forays into multicolor, multiple-plate chalk-manner prints.

Another impression of the same print, with the third plate printed in green ink instead of blue, is in the Musée du Louvre.[1]

As the title *Eloyse et Abailar* on the spine of her book indicates, the young woman is reading a version of the medieval romance between the brilliant philosopher Peter Abélard (1079–1142) and his equally gifted pupil Héloise (1101–1164). Seduction, passion, a secret marriage, violent castration, and forced separation make their story both dramatic and tragic; their eventual entrance into holy orders—he by choice, she at his command—and the letters they wrote to each other raise their love to a purely intellectual and spiritual plane. The story was therefore both racy and edifying, making attractive reading for a young woman in the eighteenth century.

1. Inv. 19374 L.R. See Jean-Richard 783.

23

Atelier of Gilles Demarteau the Elder
1722–1776

Head of a Man Wearing a Plumed Turban
1772
after Carle Vanloo
chalk manner, printed in red and black inks
5th framing line: 234 × 167; image: 186 × 133
Leymarie 374; *IFF* 6:374

NATIONAL GALLERY OF ART,
AILSA MELLON BRUCE FUND 1986.66.1

This striking print belongs to a group of five (the others are Leymarie 372, 373, 375, 391) that reproduce the heads of nine figures from Vanloo's painting of 1737, *The Grand Turk Giving a Concert to His Mistress* (Wallace Collection, London).[1] Four of the prints, including this one, date from 1772; the fifth was published early in the following year. None of the model drawings for these prints are known. However, the evidence of the prints, which correspond exactly to the painted images, suggests that the drawings were very likely made after Vanloo's painting rather than in preparation for it.

All five prints in the group are marked "Demarteau direxit" (Demarteau directed), which indicates that Demarteau was in charge of the project but did not himself execute the prints. The identity of the actual printmaker is not known, though he (or she) was clearly very talented.

1. Reproduced in John Ingamells, *The Wallace Collection, Catalogue of Pictures, III, French before 1815* (London, 1989), 255.

Vanloo fecit   *Demarteau direx .*

A Paris chés Demarteau Graveur du Roi, rue de la Pelterie a la Cloche).   Nº. 374

24

Gilles Demarteau the Elder
1722–1776
and
Jean-Baptiste Hüet
1745–1811

*Hunting Trophies and Vignettes with Dogs
Chasing a Boar and a Stag*

1773
after Jean-Baptiste Hüet
etching and chalk manner, printed in red ink
plate: 267 × 197
watermark: grapes
Leymarie 380; *IFF* 6:380

NATIONAL GALLERY OF ART, PROMISED GIFT
OF THE ELLWANGER/MESCHA COLLECTION

25

Gilles Demarteau the Elder
1722–1776
and
Jean-Baptiste Hüet
1745–1811

Singerie with Four Vignettes of Dogs Hunting

1773
after Jean-Baptiste Hüet
etching and chalk manner, printed in brown-red ink
plate: 202 × 304
watermark: IHS in a circle (partial)
Leymarie 381; *IFF* 6:381

NATIONAL GALLERY OF ART, PROMISED GIFT
OF THE ELLWANGER/MESCHA COLLECTION

26

Gilles Demarteau the Elder
1722–1776
and
Jean-Baptiste Hüet
1745–1811

*Two Pastoral Vignettes, Two Hunting Vignettes,
and a Trophy*

1774
after Jean-Baptiste Hüet
etching and chalk manner, printed in red ink
plate: 204 × 304 (trimmed at platemark at left and right)
watermark: IHS with cross in a circle
Leymarie 397; *IFF* 6:397

NATIONAL GALLERY OF ART, PROMISED GIFT
OF THE ELLWANGER/MESCHA COLLECTION

From 1770 onward, the Demarteau workshop
published more than 150 prints after drawings by
Jean-Baptiste Hüet, making him second only to
Boucher as the atelier's favorite designer. Hüet
himself knew how to etch, having probably
learned the craft from his teacher Jean-Baptiste
Le Prince (cat. 20) in the mid-1760s. Although
Hüet made a few prints in the early 1770s and
produced a few more before 1789, most of his
own printmaking activities took place during
and after the French Revolution.

Hüet seems to have participated in the
actual making of these three prints after his own
designs. Each of the motifs is set down with a
lively, freely etched line that is different from
Demarteau's usual execution, but is very similar
to the type of stroke found in Hüet's own prints.[1]

Also, Hüet etched his own signature and the date into each plate, specifically using the "f." or "fecit" that indicates he had "made" the print. Using "del" or "delineavit" would have indicated that he had designed it, that is, made the model drawing. That Demarteau is also inscribed as the engraver, with the term "sculpsit," suggests that he completed Hüet's line etchings using chalk manner and perhaps some aquatint. This type of collaborative effort seems to have been quite unusual—none of the other artists whose designs were engraved by Demarteau seem to have participated in the actual printmaking process—but it yielded some prints of remarkable charm.

The exact purpose of these particular prints, priced at 12 sols apiece, is not known, though one can surmise that they served as models for decorators and designers for works in other media, such as textiles, porcelains, *boiseries* (wood carvings), embroideries, paintings, and metalwork. Designs such as these undoubtedly led to Hüet's engagement in 1783 as the chief designer of cotton fabrics for the Oberkampf textile factory in Jouy-en-Josas.[2]

1. Compare, for example, Hüet's print *Pastorale*, illustrated in Baltimore 1984, 73, dated 1778.
2. For illustrations of some of the fabrics designed by Hüet, see Laure Hug, "Jean-Baptiste Huët and the Decorative Arts," *Antiques* (August 2002), 54–61; and Anita Jones, *Patterns in a Revolution, French Printed Textiles, 1759–1821* [exh. cat., Taft Museum] (Cincinnati, 1990).

27a

Jean-Baptiste Le Prince
1734–1781

Woman in Russian Costume
c. 1770
brownish-red chalk
259 × 226

27b

Gilles Demarteau the Elder
1722–1776

Woman in Russian Costume
c. 1773
after Jean-Baptiste Le Prince
chalk manner, printed in brownish-red ink
plate: 267 × 225
watermark: T DUPVY MOYEN
Leymarie 389; *IFF* 6:389

Le Prince spent five years in Russia, from 1758 to 1763, recording in innumerable drawings the customs and costumes of the people he encountered there, mainly peasants and country folk. Upon his return to France, he exploited this exotic subject matter in his art and enjoyed a certain amount of success with his so-called *russeries* (Russian subjects). To help him in this work, he acquired a large collection of foreign costumes, some full-size, but many made for doll-size mannequins.[1] He could therefore have made the drawing exhibited here at any time after his return to Paris, perhaps even to serve as a model for Demarteau.

27b

Le Prince inv. del.

A Paris chés Demarteau Graveur du Roi, rue de la Pelterie à la Cloche.

Demarteau sc.

N.° 389

Starting in about 1770, Demarteau made chalk-manner prints after almost three dozen drawings by Le Prince, who had been making aquatints after his own pen-and-wash drawings since 1768 (cat. 20). Perhaps he realized himself or Demarteau persuaded him that there would also be a ready market for prints after his chalk drawings.

As the juxtaposition of Le Prince's drawing and Demarteau's print after it shows, Demarteau translated his model with exceptional fidelity, both in the actual copying of the lines and in the choice of an ink that matches very closely the brownish tones of Le Prince's chalk. Le Prince's strokes have a bit more freshness and variety and a greater sense of the immediacy that comes from the direct application of chalk on paper, but Demarteau's facsimile is remarkably effective and shows how very sensitive he was to the style of the draftsman and the nuances of his touch. The print was priced at 12 sols.

At the time of his death, Le Prince owned a very large collection of prints, including more than 5,000 of his own impressions together with 163 of his original copperplates, as well as works by a wide variety of artists, mainly Netherlandish and French. The catalogue of the estate sale mentions hundreds of chalk-manner prints by Demarteau, including two lots (lots 72, 99) with a total of 122 impressions after Le Prince's drawings.[2] These works were presumably the remainder of his share of the prints that would have come to him in fulfillment of whatever deal he had made with Demarteau to reproduce his drawings.

1. In Le Prince's estate sale, held in his studio on 28 November 1781 and thereafter, lots 111 and 112 contained a large number of costumes, mainly Russian, but also Circassian, Chinese, and "savage." The auction catalogue is reprinted in toto in Hédou, pages 297–313.
2. See Hédou, pages 306–310.

28

Gilles Demarteau the Elder
1722–1776

Head of a Young Woman
1773
after Antoine Watteau
chalk manner, printed in red and black inks
4th line: 241 × 165; inner line: 217 × 149
Leymarie 419; *IFF* 6:419

Antoine Watteau is generally regarded as the
great master of chalk drawing, especially of the
trois crayons technique in which red, black, and
white chalks were used together to colorful effect.
That some of his drawings were used as models
for chalk-manner prints, then, is not at all
surprising.

Demarteau borrowed this young woman
with the dashing hat from a sheet by Watteau
with four sketches of the same model (fig. 1).[1]
Not being as attuned to Watteau's style as he was
to Boucher's, Demarteau did not capture with
quite the same success Watteau's touch or the
idiosyncrasies of his draftsmanship. In addition,
since Demarteau had never penetrated the secret
of printing with white, he could only use—with
mixed results—red and black inks on white
paper to convey the effect of Watteau's three
chalks. Demarteau also took considerable liber-
ties with his model, not only adding all the
strokes behind the figure and completing the
shoulders, which Watteau had simply suggested,
but also lengthening the bust-length figure
almost to the waist and inventing most of her
gown. The print sold for 15 sols.

To serve as a pendant, Demarteau made a
print after another study of a young woman
from the same Watteau sheet, similarly changing
and adapting the image in the process (Leymarie
420).

1. Black, red, and white chalks on beige paper, 258 × 235.

1. Antoine Watteau, *Four Studies of a
Woman's Head*, 1716–1717, red, black, and
white chalks. Private collection

29

Jean-François Janinet
1752–1814

Two Male Nudes

c. 1774
after Charles-Nicolas Cochin the Younger
chalk manner, printed in bright red ink
plate: 388 × 473
watermark: T DUPVY FIN / AUVERGNE 1742
unpublished

NATIONAL GALLERY OF ART, PROMISED GIFT
OF THE ELLWANGER/MESCHA COLLECTION

Chalk-manner prints continued to fulfill their
first purpose—providing cheap, easily available
models for struggling young artists (see cat.
4)—for as long as they were made. Quality, however, varied enormously depending on the abili-
ties of the artist who made the original drawing
and the skill of the printmaker who transcribed
it into print form. This rendering of two male
figures by Janinet after Charles-Nicolas Cochin
(1715–1790) is a strikingly beautiful example that
shows the high artistic level this genre could
reach. Surprisingly, this particular work seems
to be unpublished, for it does not appear in any
list of Janinet's works.[1]

Janinet lived at the address given on the
print, "Rue de Lirondelle," in 1774, when he was
only twenty-two years old. He had trained in
Bonnet's workshop in 1771 and 1772, and had
quickly established himself as his teacher's best
disciple. Janinet went on to distinguish himself
as one of the greatest color printmakers of the
eighteenth century, yet at this early stage of his
career he devoted as much care and energy in

transcribing a simple study of nudes into a chalk-
manner print as he would later take in perfecting
his most complex full-color compositions.

1. See for example Michèle Hébert and Yves Sjöberg, *IFF*
12:1–94, which includes 244 prints and purports to be a
complete catalogue of Janinet's oeuvre as a printmaker;
see also Portalis and Béraldi, 2:476–487, which includes
only 143 prints. Neither catalogue includes a single print
by Janinet after C. N. Cochin.

30

Louis-Marin Bonnet

1736–1793

The Milk Woman

1774

pastel manner, printed in red, blue, yellow, and black inks with two colors of applied gold leaf

outer framing line: 285 × 235; sheet: 321 × 249 (trimmed within platemark)

Hérold 294

31

Louis-Marin Bonnet

1736–1793

The Woman ta King Coffee

1774

pastel manner, printed in blue, red, carmine, purple, yellow, and black inks with applied gold leaf

outer framing line: 285 × 235; sheet: 324 × 251 (trimmed within platemark)

Hérold 295

32

Louis-Marin Bonnet

1736–1793

Provoking Fidelity

1775

after M.A. Parelle

pastel manner, printed in blue, carmine, yellow, brown, green, and black inks with two colors of applied gold leaf

outer framing line: 283 × 234; sheet: 321 × 248 (trimmed within platemark)

Hérold 296

33

Louis-Marin Bonnet

1736–1793

The Pretty Noesgay Garle

1775

after Jean-Baptiste Greuze

pastel manner, printed in blue, red, carmine, yellow, green, and black inks with applied gold leaf

outer framing line: 285 × 235; sheet: 321 × 250 (trimmed within platemark)

Hérold 297

34

Louis-Marin Bonnet

1736–1793

The Pleasures of Education

1777

pastel manner, printed in red, carmine, blue, purple, black, and yellow inks with applied gold leaf

outer framing line: 292 × 238; sheet: 323 × 246 (trimmed within platemark)

Hérold 299

In 1774, Bonnet began to produce a unique series of prints that featured frames printed with gold leaf. Because the use of gold leaf was closely regulated and only certain artisans, such as bookbinders and furniture makers, were permitted to work with it, Bonnet invented an elaborate fiction: he pretended that his prints were actually made by an English printmaker named "L. Marin" and published by a London printseller named Vivares. The first name was derived from Bonnet's own given names; the second was the name of an actual family of printsellers who did indeed have a shop on Great Newport Street in London, as Bonnet's captions state. Although Bonnet may have known the family personally, he more likely saw the name on an English print and appropriated it to make his ruse all the more believable. The deception was completed by titles printed in English, but oddly misspelled.

The first of these so-called *estampes anglaises* (English prints) were *The Milk Woman* and *The Woman ta King Coffee*, both of which were specifically mentioned in an announcement published in the *Journal de politique et de littérature* on 25 December 1774. In the announcement the fictional Marin was given credit for inventing this entirely new type of print, which imitated the appearance of framed miniatures. Bonnet himself is actually listed as the Paris dealer for these works, which sold for 9 livres each. All depict attractive young women seen in half-length and engaged in simple everyday activities. These central motifs were executed in pastel manner printed in several colors, a particularly complex technique for which Bonnet was already well known (see cats. 18, 19). The frames consist of an initial layer printed in red or white, which served as the bole for the gold leaf. The gold was

The Milk Woman.

To be sold at F. Vivares in great Newport Street London.

The Woman ta King Coffee

Provoking fidelity.

The Pretty Nosegay Garle.

then laid in by hand when the "bole" was still moist. Once the gold was adhered, designs in black and sometimes blue were then printed on top of it to simulate the appearance of an actual decorated and gilded frame (for a more in-depth discussion of this process, see page 32). In some of these prints, Bonnet extended the use of gold even into the central scenes, using it, for example, as a separate color in the milk can in *The Milk Woman*. With their obvious commercial appeal, these prints must have enjoyed an instant success in spite of their high price.

Bonnet reveled in the cleverness of his deception and even named his new shop, to which he moved in 1776, "Au Magasin Anglois" (At the English Shop). He continued to produce

gold prints into 1777, but the truth about the identity of L. Marin and the fact that these "English prints" were actually French in origin must finally have come out. Official steps were presumably taken to prevent the use of gold leaf in any future prints and none were published thereafter.

Whereas Bonnet himself provided the models for at least two of the prints (cats. 30, 31), he looked to other artists for others in the series: Greuze (cats. 33 and probably 34)[1] and M.A. Parelle (cat. 32). Only one of the works copied by Bonnet is currently known: the painting *Provoking Fidelity* by Parelle.[2] For the most part, the colors in Bonnet's print follow Parelle's palette quite closely, except that the bright orange dressing gown in the painting was rendered in black in the print.

1. No source is credited on *The Pleasures of Education,* though Greuze has been suggested (Hérold 299).
2. Signed and dated 1766, M. A. Parelle's oil painting on panel (in the same direction as the print) was sold in New York at Christie's on 2 November 2000, lot 140, reproduced in color.

L. Marin invenit 1777.

The Pleasures of Education.

To be sold at F. Vivares in great Newport Street London.

35

Gilles Demarteau the Elder
1722–1776

Young Woman with a Dog
1775
after Jean-Baptiste Hüet
chalk manner and tool work, printed in black and blue inks
1st framing line: 255 × 178
Leymarie 517; *IFF* 6:517

Never having learned the secret of printing with white ink, Demarteau had to rely on the white of the paper for his highlights. He turned to the solution that had been used in chiaroscuro woodcuts since the early sixteenth century and in the woodcut-and-etching prints made by Nicolas Le Sueur earlier in the eighteenth century (page 6, fig. 9): printing a background tone that makes the sheet look like colored paper, but working the plate in order to leave strategic areas of the page blank. Demarteau, however, created tone with chalk-manner tools. He then printed the lines of the composition over the "prepared" paper in black or red ink so that the reserved areas of the paper read as white highlights. A third plate could also be used to create the effect of a *trois crayons* drawing on colored paper (see cat. 38). Thus a print such as *Young Woman with a Dog* can give the appearance of having been printed in black and white on blue paper, even though Demarteau printed the blues and the blacks and simply left blank paper for the whites. The visual effect is quite different from Bonnet's *trois crayons* manner (see cat. 9a, for example), but it is still an effective solution to a challenging technical problem. Even so, Demarteau seems to have shied away from multicolored printmaking, for he published relatively few during his lifetime. Bonnet, on the other hand, thrived on them and made dozens over the course of his career.

36

Jean-François Janinet
1752–1814

Restes du palais du pape Jules (Remains of the Palace of Pope Julius)

1775
after Hubert Robert
wash manner, printed in red-orange, blue, yellow, and black inks
image: 291 × 245
watermark: FIN / D TAMIZIER / AUVERGNE 1742
IFF 12:170; Portalis and Béraldi 2:84

THE IVAN PHILLIPS FAMILY COLLECTION

Within a short time of leaving Bonnet's studio in 1772, Janinet created yet another revolution in French printmaking of the eighteenth century: He conceived a new way of making full-color prints from multiple plates that produced for the first time smoothly toned and richly colored facsimiles of paintings, watercolors, and gouaches. For this "wash manner" technique, Janinet did not invent any new processes but took advantage of the various tonal printmaking techniques that were already available—including aquatint, tool work, and mezzotint. He then combined them with the multiple-plate color-separation printing techniques that he had learned in Bonnet's studio (and which had originated with color mezzotints, cats. 1–3). An extraordinary set of ten progress proofs of the wash-manner print *Noce de village* by Janinet's pupil Charles-Melchior Descourtis gives a very clear indication of how Janinet's process worked (see cats. 55a-j). The first of Janinet's color prints made in this manner was *L'Operateur* after a drawing by Peter-Paul Benazech (c. 1744–1783), published in 1772.

In the caption of the print, the twenty-year-old artist claimed the technique as his own: "This plate engraved in imitation of colored wash by F. Janinet, the only one who has discovered this technique."[1]

The model for *Restes du palais du pape Jules* was a painting of about 1759 by Hubert Robert (1733–1808), which is now in the Musée des Arts-Décoratifs, Paris.[2] Janinet's print, dated 1775 in the plate, was announced in the *Mercure* in March 1776. Robert's paintings and watercolors proved to be congenial models for Janinet, who translated them into color prints with excep-

tional fidelity and charm. This print is the first of four after Robert made by Janinet between 1775 and 1778; all are featured in this exhibition (cats. 37, 40, 41).

1. See Hébert and Sjöberg, *IFF* 12:1.
2. Inv. PE 51, oil on canvas, 69 × 58 cm. Reproduced in *J.H. Fragonard e H. Robert a Roma* [exh. cat., Villa Medici] (Rome, 1990), 70, fig. 20a.

37a

Jean-François Janinet
1752–1814

*Colonade et jardins du palais Medicis
(Colonnade and Gardens of the Palazzo
Medici)*

c. 1776
after Hubert Robert
wash manner, printed in blue, red, yellow, and black inks
plate: 292 × 245
watermark: dovecote
IFF 12:172; Portalis and Béraldi 2:83 (proof before letters)

37b

Jean-François Janinet
1752–1814

*Colonade et jardins du palais Medicis
(Colonnade and Gardens of the Palazzo
Medici)*

c. 1776
after Hubert Robert
wash manner, printed in red, blue, yellow, and black inks
on pale green paper
plate: 291 × 244 (trimmed to platemark at top and bottom)
watermark: AUVERGNE 1742
IFF 12:172; Portalis and Béraldi 2:83

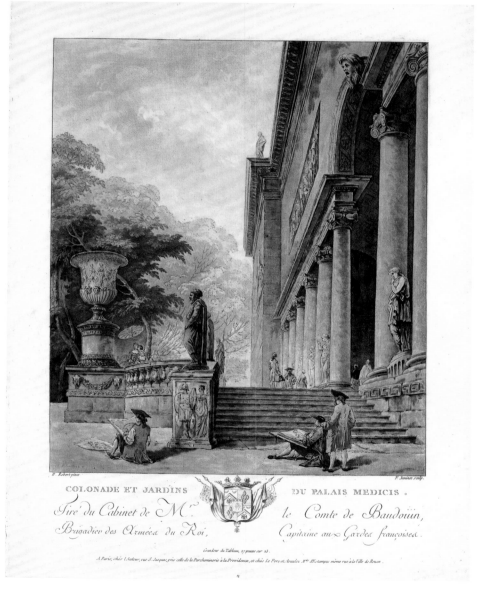

H. Robert pinx.   *F. Janinet sculp.*

COLONADE ET JARDINS   DU PALAIS MEDICIS .

Tiré du Cabinet de M^r.   *le Comte de Baudoüin,*

Brigadier des Armées du Roi,   *Capitaine au Gardes françoises.*

Grandeur du Tableau, 27 pouce sur 23 .

A Paris, chés l'Auteur, rue S. Jacque, près colle de la Parcheminerie à la Providence, et chés Le Pere et Avaules A^d M^{ds}. d'Estampe même rue à la Ville de Rouen .

Janinet's second print after Hubert Robert depicts the Palazzo Medici in Rome. Different inkings give these two impressions distinctly different characters: one has a darker, more threatening sky and more brown in the stones of the buildings; the other has a lighter feel overall, with more gray throughout and perhaps the suggestion of a little more sunlight throughout the scene. In such complex prints made from four different plates such subtle differences in inking occur regularly, both in impressions from different states of the same print and in impressions of the same state. Sometimes the differences are caused by slight variations in the batches of inks or even in the paper colors, as here, but on some occasions the artist apparently chose to alter more radically one or more of the ink colors in order to change the visual effect of the print as a whole (see, for example, cats. 58a, 58b).

Robert included similar views of the façade of the Medici villa in several of his paintings,[1] but the location of the particular painting or watercolor that served as the model for Janinet's print is not currently known.

1. See, for example, Rome 1990, figs. 141a, 152, and 152b.

38

Gilles Demarteau the Elder
1722–1776

Young Woman with a Rose

c. 1776

after François Boucher

chalk manner and tool work, printed in green, red, and black inks

plate: 314 × 224

Leymarie 563; *IFF* 6:563 (as Demarteau the Elder)

Gilles Demarteau, who died in July 1776, was succeeded as *chef d'atelier* by his nephew Gilles-Antoine, then twenty-six years old. The numbering of the prints continued uninterrupted, with number 560 (a head of an old man after Edme Bouchardon, 1698–1762) generally considered to be the last print in the oeuvre of the elder Demarteau; those numbered 561 to 729 are all credited to the nephew. Several of the earliest in that range, however, may possibly have been completed or at least begun by the uncle, but only published after his death. In the announcement of the publication of *Young Woman with a Rose* in the *Mercure de France* of March 1777, the print (priced at 1 livre, 10 sols) is described as "no. 563 of the oeuvre of the late M. Demarteau, who left his stock of all his plates to M. Demarteau his nephew." If the younger Demarteau had wanted to claim authorship of this particular print for himself, surely he would have phrased the announcement differently.

The technique used for *Young Woman with a Rose* is exactly the same as the one the elder Demarteau had used in 1775 for the *Woman with a Dog* (cat. 35): white highlights were not printed but were created instead by reserves of white paper. In this print, too, the black and red lines that shape the figure and the green background that gives the effect of a colored paper are all printed, but the whites are not. Thus did Demarteau cleverly give the appearance of a *trois crayons* study drawn on colored paper with particularly handsome results. In many ways this print is just as effective as Bonnet's closely similar first print in the three-chalk technique (cat. 9a), though naturally Demarteau's "whites" are considerably more subtle in their effect than Bonnet's bright white inks.

A drawing in the same direction as Demarteau's print, executed in *trois crayons* with touches of pastel on pinkish paper, was formerly in a Swiss private collection.[1] This work could be Boucher's original drawing that served as Demarteau's model, but it is very possibly a copy after Demarteau's print.

1. Reproduced in Alexandre Ananoff, *L'Oeuvre dessiné de François Boucher (1703–1770)* (Paris, 1966), no. 324, fig. 63.

39

Jean-François Janinet
1752–1814

Marie-Antte. d'Autriche, Reine de France
et de Navarre (Marie-Antoinette)

1777

after Jean-Baptiste-André Gautier Dagoty

wash manner, printed in blue, pink, yellow, and black inks,
cut into an oval and set into a printed frame in orange-red,
tan, and blue inks

portrait: 253 × 206 (oval); frame: 409 × 318

IFF 10:56; Portalis and Béraldi 2:132

THE IVAN PHILLIPS FAMILY COLLECTION

The model for Janinet's print is a full-length
portrait of Marie-Antoinette (1755–1793) by Jean-
Baptiste-André Gautier Dagoty (1740?–1786?), a
member of the printmaking family (see cats. 2, 3)
and painter to the queen.[1] It was first engraved
in color mezzotint by his brother Fabien Gautier
Dagoty (1747–1782), but the result was not satis-
factory.[2] Janinet was called in to make another
print, which was far more successful both technically and artistically.

The elaborate frame surrounding the portrait was intended to be decorated with gold leaf
in the same manner Bonnet had used in his so-
called English prints (see cats. 30–34), and
indeed Janinet must have learned the technique
from his former master.[3] Relatively few impressions with the gilded frame survive, for shortly
after Janinet first published the portrait in 1777,
the use of gold leaf in prints ceased.[4]

The frame and the portrait are actually
printed on two separate pieces of paper. In some
impressions, the center of the frame is cut out
and the print is attached to the back of it so that
the portrait is seen through the opening. In

those impressions, the portrait print is usually
uncut, and the title and inscriptions below the
image remain intact but are covered by the
printed frame. In others, like this one, the portrait print is trimmed to the edge of the image
and then glued onto the sheet bearing the
printed frame. Some impressions without the
frame are also known.[5]

1. Château de Versailles, inv. M V 8062, oil on canvas, 160 ×
128 cm. Reproduced in Claire Constans, *Musée national
des châteaux de Versailles et de Trianon, les peintures*
(Paris, 1995), 358, no. 2040.
2. Gautier Dagoty's print is reproduced in Paris and Lausanne 1996, 141, no. 134.

3. Two impressive prints with gold borders, *Zephire and
Flore* and *Vertumne and Pomone* after paintings by
Antoine Coypel, are thought to have been the work of
Janinet, in spite of an inscription naming "F. Bzzi" (Francesco Bartolozzi) as the author. See Hérold, page 25. Like
Bonnet, Janinet apparently pretended that these prints
originated in England by using the name of an artist
working there, crediting a London printer as the pub-
lisher, and giving the prints English titles. Stellar examples of these two prints were recently acquired by the New
York Public Library; one is reproduced on page 39.
4. One impression with gold in the frame is in the Museum
of Fine Arts, Boston (reproduced in Baltimore 1984,
no. 66). Another is in the collection of Mr. and Mrs.
David P. Tunick (reproduced in *The Age of Elegance,
Eighteenth Century French Prints from the Collection of
Mr. and Mrs. David P. Tunick* [exh. cat., Nassau County
Museum of Art] (Roslyn Harbor, New York, 1997), 29.
5. The Bibliothèque nationale, Paris, has an impression
without the frame (reproduced in Paris and Lausanne
1996, 142, no. 135).

Sachettorum Villæ rudera imitabatur.

40

Jean-François Janinet
1752–1814

Villa Sacchetti

1778

after Hubert Robert

wash manner, printed in blue, orange-red, yellow,
and black inks

sheet: 346 × 466 (trimmed within platemark)

watermark: double-headed eagle

IFF 12:173; Portalis and Béraldi 2:86

THE IVAN PHILLIPS FAMILY COLLECTION

41

Jean-François Janinet
1752–1814

Villa Madama

1778

after Hubert Robert

wash manner, printed in blue, orange-red, yellow,
and black inks

sheet: 344 × 465 (trimmed within platemark)

watermark: double-headed eagle

IFF 12:174; Portalis and Béraldi 2:85

THE IVAN PHILLIPS FAMILY COLLECTION

The watercolor models for these two prints are
both in the Albertina, Vienna.[1] Other than
reversing the images, as he usually did, Janinet
translated them into print with remarkable
accuracy and spirit. Not only did he match the
size of the watercolors with his copperplates—these are among the largest prints he
made—but he also captured the monumental
grandeur of the compositions and the translucency of the watercolor washes.

The Villa Madama, built in the sixteenth
century on designs by Raphael, is situated on the
right bank of the Tiber River on Monte Mario, in

Villa cui nomen *Madama*, Temporis injuriâ pene diruta

the northwest section of Rome. The fishpond, located below and to the east side of the north garden terrace, has changed little since Robert drew it in the middle of the eighteenth century.[2] The villa was a favorite motif of Robert's; he first visited it in 1759 and was inspired in the following years to execute some grand views that exploited the massive stone forms of the architecture. He especially enjoyed the play of arches offered by the deep grotto-like niches of the pond and the high arcade of the villa's garden façade.[3] The same general view is found in

another watercolor and painting in the Hermitage, Saint Petersburg.[4]

Not far away from the Villa Madama, at the foot of Monte Mario, is the Villa Sacchetti, or more properly the Casino del Pigneto Sacchetti, which was built between 1625 and 1630 on designs by Pietro da Cortona. Its appeal for the artist, who was known as "Robert des Ruines" (Robert of the Ruins) was undoubtedly its tumbledown condition, for by the time he made his watercolor in 1760, the villa was little more than a crumbling shell. It was essentially destroyed by the end of the century.[5]

1. Invs. 12431, 12432. Reproduced in Rome 1990, no. 52, pl. XVII (in color), and Hubert Burda, *Die Ruine in den Bildern Hubert Roberts* (Munich, 1967), 142, fig. 45.
2. Compare photographs in Isa Belli Barsali, *Ville di Roma* (Milan, 1970), 147, 148.
3. See Rome 1990, nos. 52, 53; and Jean de Cayeux, *Les Hubert Robert de la Collection Veyrenc au Musée de Valence* (Valence, 1985), no. 30.
4. Both are reproduced in Cayeux 1985, figs. 39, 41.
5. A print by Alessandro Specchi (1668–1729) after one of Cortona's original designs shows the villa as it was originally intended to look. See Burda 1967, fig. 44.

42

Jean-François Janinet
1752–1814

*Chûte de Staubbach dans la vallée de
Lauterbrunnen (Falls at Staubbach in the
Valley of Lauterbrunnen)*

c. 1780

after Caspar Wolf

wash manner, printed in blue, red, yellow, and black inks

outer framing line: 232 × 321; sheet: 299 × 450 (trimmed
within platemark)

IFF 12:175c; Portalis and Béraldi 2:92

NATIONAL GALLERY OF ART,
ROSENWALD COLLECTION 1945.5.81

43

Charles-Melchior Descourtis
1753–1820

Falls at Schaffhausen

c. 1784

after Friedrich Rosenberg and Johann Heinrich Troll

wash manner, printed in blue, red, yellow, and black inks

outer framing line: 236 × 324; plate: 322 × 448

watermark: AMP

IFF 7:7

NATIONAL GALLERY OF ART, GIFT OF
IVAN E. AND WINIFRED PHILLIPS IN
MEMORY OF NEIL PHILLIPS 2002.14.2

CHÛTE DU STAUBBACH DANS LA VALLÉE DU LAUTERBRUNNEN

Dédié à S. A. Royale F Henri Louis Prince de Prusse

These two prints were made for *Vues remarquables des montagnes de la Suisse dessinées et colorées d'après Nature, avec leur déscription*, a handsome Swiss travelogue conceived and directed by Rodolphe Hentzy (1732–1803) and published in Amsterdam by J. Yntema in 1785. The publication consisted of forty-two color prints by Janinet and his pupil Descourtis, with two additional plates by Antoine Carrée (active 1781/1790) and Pierre-Michel Alix (1762–1817). These prints were executed primarily after watercolors and paintings by Swiss artists Caspar Wolf (1735–1798) and Friedrich Rosenberg (1758–1833), with a few after works by Johann Wolfgang Kleemann (1731–1782; identified on the prints as Clément), Heinrich Füssli (1755–1829), and Johann Heinrich Troll (1756–1824). The production of the prints was supervised by the French painter Claude-Joseph Vernet (1714–1789) and the descriptive texts were written by Albrecht von Haller (1708–1777) and Jacob Samuel Wyttenbach (1748–1838). A first collection of twenty-four of the color prints, all by Janinet after Wolf, was published in three parts by Wagner in Bern

43

LEOPOLDO II. AUSTRIACO
Imperatori Semper Augusto Regi Apostolico
Hanc Rheni Cataractam in Pago Scaphusiano
Humillime Offerebat
Chalcographia Hentziana R. Hentzy, Liber Civis Bernensis.

Troll. del. Rosenberg pinx. Descourtis sculp.

between 1780 and 1782 under a slightly different title.[1] It included, as plate 5, the view of the falls at Staubbach (cat. 42), which was then republished as plate 11 in the 1785 Amsterdam volume.[2] Descourtis probably did not complete the view of Schaffhausen before 1784. Thus it was likely one of the last views to be executed (as plate 39) for the 1785 publication.

The quality of these Swiss views varies considerably, depending not only on the artist who rendered the painting or drawing that served as a model for the printmakers, but also on the interest of the actual scene itself. Views of the towns, for example, tend to be somewhat less exciting than scenes of mountains and waterfalls. The print by Descourtis is a particularly fine example from the series, showing off the skills of the newly fledged printmaker in excellent fashion and letting it be known that he was already a worthy rival for his master, Janinet.

1. *Vues remarquables des montagnes de la Suisse avec leur déscription* (Bern, 1780–1782). Hébert and Sjöberg, *IFF* 12: under no. 175, confuse this publication with one of 1776 (also published in Bern by Wagner), which included ten hand-colored outline engravings by several Swiss artists after designs by Wolf: *Merkwürdige Prospekte aus den Schweizer-Gebürge und derselben Beschreibung.*
2. Useful bibliographic information about the various books of Swiss views published between 1776 and 1785, including lists of the plates, is included in Willi Raeber, *Caspar Wolf, 1735–1783, Sein Leben und sein Werk* (Zurich, 1979), 341–344.

44

Gilles-Antoine Demarteau
1750–1802

"Comme il va rire!" ("How he will laugh!")
1783
after Jean-Jacques-François Le Barbier
wash manner, printed in red, carmine, blue, yellow, brown, and black inks
plate: 295 × 362; image: 235 × 310
watermark: FIN DE / D TAMIZ ER / AUVERGNE
Leymarie 622; *IFF* 6:35

THE IVAN PHILLIPS FAMILY COLLECTION

45

Gilles-Antoine Demarteau
1750–1802

"Regarde, ma bien-aimée" ("Look, my beloved")
1783
after Jean-Jacques-François Le Barbier
wash manner, printed in blue, brown, yellow, green, red, and black inks
plate: 298 × 365; image: 240 × 319
watermark: FIN DE / D TAMIZYER / AUVERGNE / 1742
Leymarie 623: *IFF* 6:36

THE IVAN PHILLIPS FAMILY COLLECTION

Whereas Gilles Demarteau the Elder dedicated himself almost exclusively to chalk-manner prints, his nephew Gilles-Antoine added full-color wash-manner prints to the atelier's repertoire. Using as many as six separate plates and a combination of etching, aquatint, and some roulette work, Gilles-Antoine and his assistants produced prints that were considerably more complex and ambitious than any of those produced by his uncle. This redirection was necessary for Demarteau and his workshop to be able to compete in the changing marketplace. Jean-François Janinet was beginning to make a name for himself at the time of the elder Demarteau's death (cats. 36, 37), and Louis-Marin Bonnet, who had long since added pastel-manner printing to his repertoire (cat. 19), was also moving toward full-color printing (cats. 53, 54).

These pendant prints show just how brilliant the younger Demarteau's multicolor prints could be, with a bright, fresh palette and nicely blended tones. Their importance for him is indicated by their price, 8 livres each, which far exceeded the price of any individual prints produced by the Demarteau workshop up to that time.

The prints illustrate episodes from two stories by the contemporary Swiss writer and artist Salomon Gessner (1730–1788). The first represents a scene from "Chloé," *chant* 15 from Gessner's *Idylles.* The young Chloé, secretly enamored of the sleeping Lycas, drapes him with flowers. "How he will laugh!" she says. "How he will be astonished to see his head and his flute entwined with garlands." The second comes from *Le Premier navigateur* (The First Navigator). An unnamed young man crosses the sea in a rudimentary boat to find the innocent young woman, Mélide, who had been revealed to him in a dream. Here he tells her, "Look, my beloved. Here is the trunk that carried me across the waves of the sea and guided me into your arms."

Jean-Jacques-François Le Barbier (1736–1826) was so deeply inspired by Gessner's stories and poems that he decided to publish, with the author's blessing, a three-volume edition of his collected works illustrated with many black-and-

white prints.[1] Begun in 1779, the project took fourteen years to complete. The two color prints published by Demarteau in 1783 were not made in connection with those volumes, for they differ significantly in size and format from the prints in the books. They were contemporary with Le Barbier's work on that project, however, and were presumably inspired by it. Indeed, the captions on Demarteau's two prints are etched in the same style as the book illustrations and are framed within the same kind of cartouches. *"Comme il va rire!"* even shows the same episode (see fig. 1) chosen to illustrate the story of "Chloé" in the *Oeuvres,* with the same basic story elements organized in a different way.[2]

The location of the original watercolors by Le Barbier is not currently known.

1. Nicolas Ponce after Jean-Jacques-François Le Barbier, *"Comme il va être étonné,"* 1786, etching and engraving. National Gallery of Art, Katharine Shepard Fund 2002.74.1

1. *Oeuvres de Salomon Gessner (traduits en français par Huber, Meister et Brut de Loirelle),* 3 vols. (Paris, 1786–1793). A copy of this book was recently acquired by the National Gallery of Art, 2002.74.1.
2. The book illustration was engraved by Nicolas Ponce (1746–1831) and appears in *Oeuvres de Gessner* 1786–1793, 1: opposite page 59.

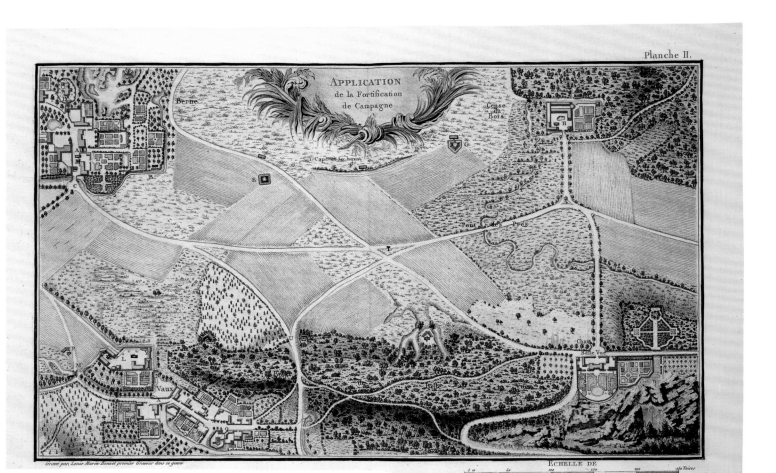

46

Louis-Marin Bonnet
1736–1793

Map of the Countryside around Berne and
Map of the Environs of Rouville

from Charles-Louis-François de Fossé, *Idées d'un militaire
pour la disposition des troupes…* (A Soldier's Ideas for the
Disposition of Troops) (Paris, A. Jombert, printed by Didot
the Elder, 1783), in-quarto

etching, chalk manner, and stipple, printed in orange, blue,
green, red, yellow, mauve, and black inks

page: 301 × 234; fold-out plates: 215 × 351

Hérold 878; *IFF* 3:117–127

In 1781, Bonnet was presented with an opportunity to use his color printmaking skills for an
entirely new purpose, the illustration of a manual on the production of color-coded military
maps. Charles-Louis de Fossé (1734–1812) was
an infantry officer and amateur artist who
wanted to use color to lay out potential battle-
grounds in easily legible form. Bonnet's ability
to produce prints in several colors made Fossé's
ambitious project possible: he executed Fossé's
own watercolors in chalk manner and stipple on
multiple plates. Surprisingly, given the subject
matter, the book's eleven plates turned out to be
among the most utterly charming color illustrations produced in the eighteenth century (reproduced here are plates II and VII). Each plate is

precisely executed with bright colors, and the
simple forms follow Fossé's own instructions
in the text as to how specific landscape features
such as bushes, water, vineyards, cultivated
fields, and woods should be represented. Delightful little landscape vignettes in the lower right
corners add to the special appeal of these prints.

To facilitate production, the color plates were
printed separately from the text pages on a finer
paper that was more suited to printmaking. Each
print was trimmed to or within the platemark,
except for a long (6–7 inch) tab of paper left at
the bottom right-hand corner. Paste was applied
to the back of the tab area and the print was

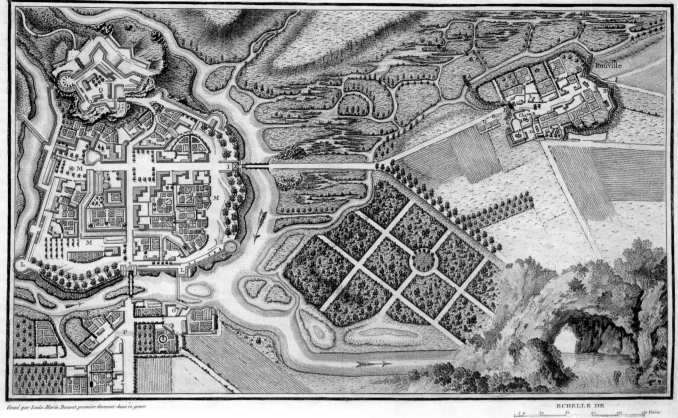

attached by hand onto a page that had already been printed with a numbered key corresponding to the numbers included in the print. The print was then folded in half, the left side of the page covering the right. In the National Gallery's copy of the book, some of the prints were pasted onto the page with the tab placed quite close to the bottom edge. In those cases, the prints cover the text and have to be unfolded and lifted forward from the top to reveal it. On other pages, however, the print is attached by the tab to the very top of the page and is folded not only in half, but also down at the tab to fit between the pages of the book. When the book is open and the print is unfolded, the print actually sits above the page and can be viewed simultaneously with the text. Why this ingenious solution to a difficult logistical problem was used for only some of the prints is unclear.

This handsome volume is very rare: the amount of handwork involved in putting each copy together almost certainly restricted the number of books made. Louis XVI's own copy is preserved in the Bibliothèque nationale, Paris.[1]

1. *IFF* 3:117–127.

47a

Jean-François Janinet
1752–1814

La Toilette de Vénus

1783

after François Boucher

wash manner, printed in blue, red, carmine, yellow,
brown, and black inks

plate: 495 × 389; outer framing line: 375 × 294

IFF 12:39 i/iv; Portalis and Béraldi 2:3 i/iii
(proof before letters)

THE IVAN PHILLIPS FAMILY COLLECTION

47b

Jean-François Janinet
1752–1814

La Toilette de Vénus

1783

after François Boucher

wash manner, printed in green-blue, red, carmine,
yellow, and black inks

plate: 493 × 386; outer framing line: 373 × 292

watermark: FIN DE / D TAMIZIER / AUVERGNE / 1781

IFF 12:39 iii/iv; Portalis and Béraldi 2:3 ii/iii

NATIONAL GALLERY OF ART,
WIDENER COLLECTION 1942.9.2382

For serious collectors of prints, the earliest proof states without titles and other inscriptions are often more desirable than impressions of the published states. The lack of "letters" or captions on those prints not only serves as a kind of guarantee that the plates were still as fresh as could be when they were printed, but also suggests that the artist himself was either pulling the impressions or at least directly supervising the printing.[1]

Just how much richer a proof can be, as compared to an impression of the published state, is amply demonstrated by these two examples of one of Janinet's most important prints, *La Toilette de Vénus* after a painting by François Boucher (The Metropolitan Museum of Art, New York).[2] The exceptionally rare first state (cat. 47a), a proof before all letters, is remarkably fresh and crisp in every detail, with strong, harmonious colors, glowing highlights, and beautifully modeled forms. Especially fine are such delicately worked areas as the diaphanous satin-striped veil and the grays and roses that shade Venus' flesh. The impression of the third, published state (cat. 47b), complete with the title and dedication, is also very handsome, with many admirable features. Although the palette is considerably lighter overall, with a somewhat powdery green now dominant, the composition as a whole is still relatively strong and clear. Unusually bright and well-preserved yellows are especially effective in the rendering of the brocade drapery and the gilded carvings on Venus' bed.

LA TOILETTE DE VENUS
Dédiée à Madame la Comtesse de Coaslin
Née Mailly.

A Paris, chez Chereau, Rue des Mathurins, près celle de Sorbonne.

rococo style was well out of fashion by the time Janinet produced his print in 1783 (Boucher had died in 1770), but Janinet had no trouble adapting himself to Boucher's manner. The print was announced in the *Affiches, annonces, et avis divers* of 23 March 1784 at a price of 12 livres, which was the highest charged for any of Janinet's individual prints except the framed version of the portrait of Marie-Antoinette (see cat. 39).[3]

The decision to make a print of such an outmoded picture probably came from the print's publisher, the Chéreau family, a member of which had acquired the painting at auction in 1782.[4] The Chéreau publishing firm had issued large numbers of prints after Boucher's paintings and drawings over the years and therefore would quite naturally produce an expensive color print after a Boucher painting from the family's own collection—even though the picture was out of step with the times and harked back to the love affairs and court politics of the previous reign.

1. As Ivan Phillips notes (page 37), captions and dedications were sometimes burnished off the copperplates or masked during printing—often in response to a changing political or social climate. Thus late impressions can sometimes appear to be early proofs. Such false "proofs" can often be recognized by weaknesses in the print itself or by the detection of faint traces of the erased inscription in the blank title area.

2. Inv. 20.155.9, oil on canvas, 108.5 × 85 cm. The painting, which is in reverse to the print, was reproduced in color in *François Boucher* [exh. cat., The Metropolitan Museum of Art] (New York, 1986), 256.

3. As Alastair Laing pointed in New York 1986, 257, the dedication of *La Toilette du Vénus* to Mme de Coislin (spelled "Coaslin" on the print) is highly ironic, for she had actually been for a short period in the 1750s one of Madame de Pompadour's chief rivals. What an artist or publisher could gain by dedicating a work after one of the Pompadour's paintings to one of her enemies is hard to imagine. Presumably someone found a good reason—whether political, economic, or personal.

4. See the discussion in Baltimore 1984, 260, under no. 91.

The blonder tones of this impression were surely due in large part to the wearing down of the copperplates by the repeated pressure of the press. Such wear is quite obvious, for instance, in the sky at upper center, where the original clouds have almost completely disappeared. Janinet certainly reworked some parts of the plates—most notably some of the shadows and highlights in the curtains at left and right. He also seems to have used adjustments in the ink colors to keep the composition unified and thus to maximize the number of saleable prints he could produce. In a final, fourth state, he made an even more radical change: he completely eliminated the putto dressing Venus' hair, presumably because of some irreparable damage to one of the plates.

Commissioned by Madame de Pompadour, favorite of Louis XV, Boucher's original painting was completed in 1751 and hung in her bathroom in the Château de Bellevue. The picture's high

48

Jean-François Janinet
1752–1814

Combat of the Horatii and the Curiatii
1783
after Jean-Jacques-François Le Barbier
wash manner, printed in blue, red, and black inks
plate: 390 × 494; framing line: 329 × 442
watermark: A M P
IFF 12:85; Portalis and Béraldi 2:68 (proof before letters)

The story of the Horatii and the Curiatii is told by Livy in his *History of Rome* (chapters 22–31). During the reign of Tullus Hostilius, the legendary king of Rome who is said to have ruled from 672 to 640 B.C., Rome went to war against neighboring Alba. Instead of having an all-out battle between their two armies, however, they agreed on hand-to-hand combat between two sets of triplets, the Horatii for the Romans and the Curiatii for the Albans. Whoever won would win the war for his side.

Janinet's print shows the moment when Horatius, the lone survivor of the Roman triplets, is about to slay the last of the three Curiatii as the two armies look on. Seated in the clouds above, Peace extends an olive branch to each side, signifying the end of the conflict. The embracing figures at left are probably Tullus Hostilius and Mettius Fufetius, leader of the Albans.

Produced in the same year as *La Toilette de Vénus* after Boucher (cat. 47), *The Combat of the Horatii and the Curiatii* could hardly be more different in execution and appearance. These prints clearly reflect the divergent characters of the works that served as Janinet's models, a high rococo painting of 1751 by Boucher versus a contemporary watercolor by Le Barbier. The latter exemplifies the broad shift in style and subject matter that was taking place in French art as a neoclassical style took hold and inspirational subjects from ancient history gained popularity.

Even though the number S.*XXXIV* is inscribed at upper right in the published state of this print, no other classical history subjects in similar format by Janinet are known. The print is almost identical in dimensions to a quartet of biblical illustrations by him from the same year, 1783: *The Creation, Adam and Eve, The Death of Abel* (numbered S. 11) and *The Death of Cain*, also after Le Barbier.[1] Otherwise, however, *The Combat of the Horatii* appears to stand alone in Janinet's oeuvre.

1. Hébert and Sjöberg, *IFF* 12:85, note the similarity and suggest that all five prints were part of a project that must have been abandoned. The four biblical prints were catalogued by Portalis and Béraldi, 64–67. Only two of those, *Adam and Eve* and *The Death of Abel*, are in the Bibliothèque nationale, Paris (*IFF* 12:83, 84).

49a

49b

49a

Jean-Baptiste Hüet

1745–1811

Nymphs Lighting a Torch (Spring)

1785

pen and gray ink with gray wash and watercolor

243 × 325

signed and dated in pen and brown ink at lower right:
J. B. hüet 1785..

THE PHILLIPS FAMILY COLLECTION

49b

Gilles-Antoine Demarteau

1750–1802

Le Printemps (Spring)

1785

after Jean-Baptiste Hüet

wash manner, printed in blue, orange-red, and black inks

outer framing line: 252 × 335; plate: 292 × 364

watermark: dovecote

Leymarie 632; *IFF* 6:45

THE IVAN PHILLIPS FAMILY COLLECTION

50a

Jean-Baptiste Hüet

1745–1811

Bathers (Summer)

1784

pen and gray ink with gray wash and watercolor

239 × 324

signed and dated in pen and brown ink at lower left:
J. B. hüet .1784..

THE IVAN PHILLIPS FAMILY COLLECTION

50b

Gilles-Antoine Demarteau

1750–1802

L'Été (Summer)

1785

after Jean-Baptiste Hüet

wash manner, printed in blue, orange-red, and black inks

outer framing line: 247 × 336; plate: 290 × 370

Leymarie 633; *IFF* 6:46

THE IVAN PHILLIPS FAMILY COLLECTION

51

Gilles-Antoine Demarteau

1750–1802

L'Automne (Autumn)

1785

after Jean-Baptiste Hüet

wash manner, printed in blue, orange-red, and black inks

outer framing line: 248 × 334; sheet: 289 × 365
(trimmed to platemark)

Leymarie 634; *IFF* 6:47

THE IVAN PHILLIPS FAMILY COLLECTION

52a

Jean-Baptiste Hüet

1745–1811

Boar Hunt (Winter)

1784

pen and gray ink with gray wash and watercolor

242 × 323

signed and dated in pen and brown ink at lower left:
J. B. hüet 1784..

THE PHILLIPS FAMILY COLLECTION

52b

Gilles-Antoine Demarteau

1750–1802

L'Hiver (Winter)

1785

after Jean-Baptiste Hüet

wash manner, printed in blue, orange-red, and black inks

outer framing line: 251 × 331; sheet: 293 × 363
(trimmed to platemark)

watermark: dovecote

Leymarie 635; IFF 6:48

THE IVAN PHILLIPS FAMILY COLLECTION

The most ambitious project undertaken by Gilles-Antoine Demarteau and Jean-Baptiste Hüet was this series of full-color prints representing the four seasons. The set sold for 24 livres, an inordinately high price that was exceeded in Demarteau's price list on a per item basis only by the 8 livres charged for each of the two Gessner-inspired color prints after Le Barbier (cats. 44, 45).[1] Perhaps the success of those two exceptionally fine prints encouraged Demarteau to seek to establish himself more securely at the high end of the color-print market.

The dates inscribed on these three drawings and four prints place them all within a limited period in 1784 and 1785. Indeed, Demarteau was probably working on the prints even before Hüet had completed all four drawings. The print *Autumn* (cat. 51), for instance, is dated 1784

51

52a

52b

within the image even though the publication date is given in the caption as 1785.

Separately, the two sets of works form very handsome groups that are remarkably coherent within themselves: The drawings share Hüet's light pen stroke and pretty watercolor washes, mainly blues, yellow-greens, and gray-browns. The prints present quite a different palette of colors, dominated by pinks, blues, and browns. The visual effect produced by the two groups is therefore quite different, with the delicate harmonies of the watercolors transformed in the prints to brighter, more contrasted hues and a

somewhat more intense light. However, the prints quite possibly were once much closer to the watercolors in appearance, with color schemes conveying the same rich variety rendered in the two prints after Le Barbier (cats. 44, 45). Perhaps some of the fugitive yellows that would have subtly shaded the pinks and blues into flesh tones and greens have been lost over the years, or perhaps the yellow plates were simply not used in these particular impressions. That this set has been together for many years,

possibly even since the eighteenth century, seems highly likely given the overall uniformity of the colors in all four prints.

Two of the drawings, *Spring* and *Winter*, had remained together in France and were purchased from the Galerie Cailleux by Ivan and Neil Phillips in 1981. The third drawing, *Summer*, came to light in late 2001 with the London dealer Emanuel von Baeyer and was purchased by Ivan Phillips in the spring of 2002. The location of the fourth drawing, *Autumn*, is not known.

1. See Leymarie 622, 623, 632–635.

53

Louis-Marin Bonnet

1736–1793

L'Amant écouté (The Lover Heard)

c. 1785

after Jean-Frédéric Schall

stipple and wash manner, printed in orange-red, blue, yellow, and black inks

image: 264 × 218 (trimmed within platemark)

Hérold 836 ii/ii; *IFF* 3:111

THE IVAN PHILLIPS FAMILY COLLECTION

54

Louis-Marin Bonnet

1736–1793

L'Éventail cassé (The Broken Fan)

c. 1785

after Jean-Frédéric Schall

stipple and wash manner, printed in orange-red, blue, yellow, pink, and black inks

plate: 338 × 257; framing line: 269 × 216

watermark: AUVERGNE 1742

Hérold 835 i/ii; *IFF* 3:110 (proof before letters)

THE IVAN PHILLIPS FAMILY COLLECTION

Contemporaneously with the gold prints (cats. 30–34) and continuing thereafter, Bonnet produced a number of prints in "stipple," a technique that was known in France as *la manière anglaise* (the English manner) because it had been developed in England by Francesco Bartolozzi (1727–1815) and William Wynne Ryland (1732–1783). Stipple, a dotted technique that is either etched or engraved on the copperplate, is generally used to create areas of tone. Like the gold prints, many of Bonnet's stipple prints were given English titles and inscribed with the address of an English print shop. *L'Amant écouté* and *L'Éventail cassé*, however, were both unabashedly French and catered to the French market for elegant—and sometimes not so elegant—scenes of dalliance and courtship. Each one was priced at 6 livres.

Hérold, in his catalogue raisonné on Bonnet's prints, suggests that these two prints may actually have been the work of Charles-Melchior Descourtis. However, in 1785, when these prints

passed through the sale rooms in 1986, it was sold as by Hüet, but six years later, when it was auctioned again, it was attributed to Schall.[4] The 1992 sales catalogue offers a plausible explanation for this confusion: Schall made the original paintings; Hüet copied them in drawings; and the drawings served as Bonnet's models when he made the prints.[5] Thus the facial types of the figures in Bonnet's prints look more like Hüet's, but the compositions are more characteristic of Schall's.

Laure Hug has recently pointed out that the two figures in *L'Amant écouté*, in the same pose but in reverse, were used in a textile pattern printed in Nantes about 1790.[6]

1. See Hérold 835. The Schall paintings, described as being on copper measuring 10 × 8 *pouces* (inches), were lot 6 in Bonnet's estate sale (Paris, 7 November 1793).
2. André Girodie, *Un Peintre de fêtes galantes, Jean-Frédéric Schall (Strasbourg 1752–Paris 1825)* (Strasbourg, 1927), 18.
3. Gustave Mühlbacher sale, Galerie Georges Petit, Paris, 15–18 May 1899, lots 33, 34.
4. See Sotheby's, Monte Carlo, 22 February 1986, lot 305, and Sotheby's, New York, 22 May 1992, lot 74.
5. This explanation is credited to Girodie in the 1992 auction catalogue, but I was unable to locate the reference in Girodie's book on Schall.
6. Laure Hug, "Jean Baptiste Hüet and the Decorative Arts," *Antiques* (August 2002), 60–61, pl. XII, where she maintains the attribution of the painting to Hüet.

were most likely made, Descourtis was fully occupied with *Noce de village* (cat. 55), assiduously and successfully working in the wash manner he had learned from Janinet. That Descourtis would suddenly switch to stipple, a technique that does not otherwise appear in his oeuvre, seems highly unlikely.

The author of the original paintings is not identified on Bonnet's prints. Hérold, however, points out that in Bonnet's estate sale in 1793, two small paintings with the same titles were

listed as by Jean-Frédéric Schall (1752–1825), who was still very much alive at the time.[1] In his monograph on Schall, Girodie, in his turn, notes that *L'Éventail cassé* was signed by Schall and dated 1785,[2] which happens to be the likely date for the two prints. In 1899, however, the paintings passed through the sale rooms as the work of Jean-Baptiste Hüet,[3] and the attribution has remained confused since. When *L'Amant écouté*

55

Charles-Melchior Descourtis
1753–1820

Noce de village (Village Wedding)
1785
after Nicolas-Antoine Taunay
set of ten color proofs in etching and wash manner,
printed from five plates
each, outer framing line: 311 × 234; inner margin: 305 × 229
watermark: IHS in a circle (cat. 55a); FIN / T DUPVY /
AUVERGNE 1742 (cats. 55d, 55f, 55h)
IFF 7:8

NATIONAL GALLERY OF ART,
ROSENWALD COLLECTION 1958.8.77–86

55a. Plate 1 (1st state, recto)
etching, printed in black
ink

Like Jakob Christoffel Le Blon (see cat. 1) and
Louis-Marin Bonnet (see cat. 19) before him,
Descourtis showed off the brilliance and complexity of his printmaking skills by publishing
sets of progress proofs of one of his best prints.
Although he did not invent the process at which
he excelled, as the others had, he had learned it
directly from the inventor, his master Janinet.
Descourtis was justifiably proud of *Noce de village*, which was published in August 1785 at a
price of 6 livres, and he probably produced the
set of proofs at the time of publication.

The series begins with a simple line etching
of the whole composition (cat. 55a), which would
have been used to transfer the basic image to
each of the other copperplates. The rest of the set
consists of impressions from each individual
plate in its proper color—one each for yellow,
red, blue, and black, the classic color separations,
plus one additional plate for carmine accents—
and combination proofs featuring two, three,
and four colors printed together. Thus the order
in which the colors had to be printed to arrive at

the final print is clearly demonstrated. The set
concludes with a brilliant impression of the finished print from all five plates.

The first plate, in its first state with only the
etched outline of the composition, served as the
key plate by which Descourtis transferred the
image to the four other copperplates that he
needed to produce the final print. All the plates
were cut as closely as possible to the same
dimensions. Descourtis could not print the
etched image directly onto those other plates,
however, for the image would have been reversed
in the printing process. Instead he had to transfer it through the intermediary of paper impressions such as this one. He would first ink the
plate and take an impression on a regular sheet
of paper. While that print was still wet, he immediately laid it, face down, on a fresh copperplate
and passed the plate and the paper together
through the press. He thus obtained a counterproof of the image on the plate in the same
direction as it appeared on the first one. After

repeating this process three more times, Descourtis had the same image on all five copperplates and was ready to begin.

From this first lightly etched plate Descourtis had to take only a few impressions—the four
that would be counterproofed onto the copperplates and perhaps some extra trial impressions.
These impressions were strictly utilitarian—how
they looked once they had served their purpose
was not a concern. Indeed, the sheet in the
National Gallery, which bears impressions of
the line etching on both sides, is in rather poor
condition.

Once the etched design had been transferred
to all the plates, the job of this first state was
done. Then, using the etched lines as his guide,
Descourtis reworked the first plate completely in
mezzotint to turn it into a black-only version of
the entire composition (cat. 55i). Even though it
would be printed last, the black plate was very

55b (left). Plate 2, printed in greenish-ochre ink

55c (right). Plate 3, printed in red-pink ink

55d (left). Plates 2 and 3, printed in ochre and red-pink inks

55e (right). Plate 4, printed in blue ink

55f (left). Plates 2, 3, and 4, printed in ochre, red, and blue inks

55g (right). Plate 5, printed in carmine ink

55h (left). Plates 2, 3, 4, and 5, printed in ochre, red-pink, blue, and carmine inks

55i (right). Plate 1 (2d state before letters), printed in black ink

NOCE DE VILLAGE

Tiré du Cabinet de Monsieur Godefroy
Ancien Controleur Général de la Marine

55j. Plates 1 (3d state with
letters), 2, 3, 4, and 5,
printed in ochre, red-pink,
blue, carmine, and black
inks

likely completed before the plates for the other
colors, for it would have helped guide Descourtis
in his work on them.

The proofs printed in single colors from the
yellow, red, and blue plates (cats. 55b, 55c, 55e) are
surprisingly ghostly in appearance, looking to
some extent like photographic negatives. These
impressions show how much of each color was
actually used to achieve the final print—much
more, actually, than one might expect (cat. 55j).
Surprisingly, blue is the most pervasive color in
the composition, even though in the final impression it mainly asserts itself only in the sky.

The combination proofs (cats. 55d, 55f, 55h)
show how the three basic colors combine to form
a complete palette. Red-pink and yellow-ochre
together (cat. 55d) create a surprising range of
pinks and oranges and even some greens. The
addition of the blue plate (cat. 55f) yields browns
and greens while also toning down the reds; the
blue is also responsible for creating the silver-
gray tones throughout the composition. At this
stage, the pinks and oranges are now visible only
in the foreground and in the delicate glow of
sunset in the sky. The carmine plate (cat. 55g)
was used quite sparingly to deepen some of the
reds in the clothing of selected figures and to add
a healthy glow to the faces of several of the principal figures. The carmine pinks also meld
together with the other three colors to tone
down the blues and greens. With all four color
plates printed together (cat. 55h), the image is
quite garish and still seems unresolved. Printing
the black plate on top of the other four (cat. 55j),
however, clarifies the image and not only adds
details of expression and contour lacking in the
previous proofs, but also unifies the composition
and modulates the colors.

56

Alexandre Briceau
active 1770–after 1788

Study Revealing Anatomy to Medicine and Art
1786
wash manner, printed in green, red, blue, violet, yellow,
brown, and orange inks
sheet: 514 × 356 (trimmed at or just within platemark)
IFF 3:16

Very little is known about Briceau, except that
his first signed prints in chalk manner were
announced in 1770.[1] By 1774 he had added color
wash-manner prints to his repertoire, and his
last dated print was made in 1788.[2] At some
point Briceau must have traveled to Russia,
for his portrait of the Russian actress Ekaterina
Ivanovna Prachinsky includes the inscription
"drawn in Moscow by Briceau and engraved by
the same."[3]

This elaborate allegory served as the frontispiece to an important medical text, *Traité
d'anatomie et de physiologie* by Félix Vicq d'Azyr
(1748–1794), published by Didot in Paris in 1786
and dedicated to the king. In the allegory, Time
(at upper left) and Intellect (at upper right) lift a
curtain to reveal Apollo, god of medicine, ges-
turing to a bas-relief of King Louis XVI held up
by two putti. Apollo hovers above the figure of
Study, who leads Medicine toward new anatomical observations in the form of a cadaver that is
ready for dissection. Painting (at right) is ready
to record Medicine's new discoveries in illustrations much like the seventy that appear on the
thirty-five plates in Vicq d'Azyr's book. Young
medical students stand in the background, ready
to observe and learn from the procedure.

Briceau's print looks very different from the
ones produced by Janinet, Descourtis, and
Debucourt at approximately the same moment
(cats. 55, 57–61). Briceau used a very fine tonal
technique usually described as stipple, but actually consisting of a complex combination of stipple, tool work (including rockers and roulettes),
and very probably aquatint. His colors are

unusually delicate and translucent — more water-
color-like than the weightier, more opaque
colors generally used by his contemporaries.

1. An allegory on the marriage of the dauphin and Marie-
Antoinette was announced in the *Avant-Coureur* on 28
May 1770; two gallant subjects and a head of a child were
announced in the *Mercure* in October of the same year.
See *IFF* 3:1–4.
2. *IFF* 3:6–7, 18.
3. *IFF* 3:15.

57

Philibert-Louis Debucourt
1755–1832

Les Deux Baisers (The Two Kisses)

1786

wash manner, printed in black, blue, red, orange,
and yellow inks

framing line: 276 × 369; plate: 363 × 425 (trimmed within
platemark at lower edge)

watermark: FIN DE / D TAMIZIER / AVUERGNE / 1783

Fenaille 7 ii/iii; IFF 6:4

NATIONAL GALLERY OF ART,
WIDENER COLLECTION 1942.9.2255

Debucourt was not only the last great color
printmaker of the eighteenth century, but also
the only one who regularly used his own paintings and drawings as models for his prints. He
had trained first as a painter and been elected an
associate member of the French Academy in 1781
when he was just twenty-six years old. He exhibited his pictures in several Salons from 1781 to
1785, and then sporadically between 1810 and
1829. After the publication of his first color print
in 1785, he seems to have devoted himself more
to printmaking than to painting. How he
learned his craft is not known, but he quickly
mastered the demands and complexities of the
full-color wash-manner technique that was
already being used with great éclat by both Janinet and Descourtis (see, for example, cats. 47, 55).

From the very beginning of his career, Debucourt tapped into the long-established fashion
for mildly erotic scenes of lust and longing, dalliance and downfall. The generous dose of humor
he always added, however, was peculiarly his
own. Here, in his own version of the centuries-
old subject of the mismatched couple, he showed
the balding, toothless husband admiring the
portrait-in-progress of himself with his young
and beautiful wife. As the wife caresses her husband's cheek, she passes a *billet-doux* behind his
back to the ardent young portraitist who kisses
her ungloved hand. This treatment of the subject
is thoroughly delightful, not only in the composition and the choice of situation, but also in
Debucourt's care in detailing the setting and his
skill in rendering the costumes and expressions
of the protagonists. This work is a remarkable
tour-de-force for an artist who had been a printmaker for little more than a year.[1]

The model for *Les Deux Baisers* was a painting Debucourt had exhibited at the Salon of 1785
under the title *La Feinte Caresse (The Feigned
Caress*, no. 155). Its present location is unknown.

1. Debucourt's first color print was *Suzette mal cachée ou Les
Amants découverts (Suzette Poorly Hidden or The Lovers
Discovered*). See Fénaille 4, reproduced between pages 2
and 3.

58a

Philibert-Louis Debucourt

1755–1832

Le Menuet de la mariée (The Bride's Minuet)

1786

wash manner, printed in black, blue, orange-red, pale pink, and yellow inks

outer framing line: 307 × 234; plate: 386 × 285

watermark: T DUPVY FIN / AUVERGNE 1742

Fenaille 8 iv/vi; IFF 6:5

NATIONAL GALLERY OF ART,
WIDENER COLLECTION 1942.9.2261

58b

Philibert-Louis Debucourt

1755–1832

Le Menuet de la mariée (The Bride's Minuet)

1786

wash manner, printed in black, red, pink, yellow, and blue inks

outer framing line: 307 × 234; sheet: 383 × 270 (trimmed within platemark)

watermark: dovecote

Fenaille 8 v/vi; IFF 6:5 (published state)

NATIONAL GALLERY OF ART,
ROSENWALD COLLECTION 1958.8.87

This print was first announced in the *Gazette de France* on 16 October 1786 as a pendant to Descourtis' *Noce de village* (cat. 55j), published the year before.[1] Still a relative newcomer to the field of color printmaking, Debucourt nevertheless proved himself to be Descourtis' equal — and more. Whereas Descourtis' print was based on a drawing by Taunay, Debucourt's composition was his own invention. He presented a livelier,

busier scene, with many more participants and a greater interest in character and facial expression in the individual figures. He also dressed his players in more elaborate fashions that allowed him to show off his ability to convey the complex folds and frills of women's dresses and hats and the sheen of fancy fabrics, especially the color effects of shot silk.

The two impressions of *Le Menuet de la mariée* in the National Gallery's collection, in the fourth and fifth states, show some marked differences in the colors of the inks. These alterations appear most notably in the skirts of the dancing bride, in the dress of the nurse seated

to her right, and in the dresses of the two women in the lower left corner. The soft rose and peach in the fourth state become bright pink and orange in the fifth state, and the delicate harmonies of the earlier state become generally brighter and more intense. In both impressions, however, the tonalities of the upper half of the composition are virtually identical, suggesting that neither fading nor bleaching altered the colors in the lower half. Rather, Debucourt seems to have made a conscious choice to intensify the colors

1. Charles-Melchior Descourtis, *Foire de village,* 1788, wash manner. National Gallery of Art, Widener Collection 1942.9.2143

2. Philibert-Louis Debucourt, *La Noce au château,* 1789, wash manner. National Gallery of Art, Widener Collection 1942.9.2262

in the crowd of figures, perhaps to better differentiate between them and to highlight certain individuals. At the same time, the light is palpably brighter in the earlier impression, and the overall definition of every contour is more crisp, presumably because it was printed when the plates were fresh and had not yet been passed through the press many times.

Although Descourtis must have agreed to the publication of Debucourt's print as a pendant to his *Noce de village,* he published his own pendant, *Foire de village* (fig. 1), in 1788. Once again, Descourtis based his composition on a gouache by Taunay. (This artist, shortly after completing the design for *Noce de village,* had gone to study in Rome and did not return to Paris until 1787.) In response, Debucourt designed and engraved *La Noce au château* (fig. 2) in 1789 as his own pendant to *Le Menuet de la mariée.* Neither of these afterthoughts approached the brilliance of the first two pieces in the series.

1. The text of the announcement is reprinted in Fenaille 8.

LA· COMPARAISON·

A Paris chez Janinet rue de l'Opera St André des Arts Maison de M.' Dupré·

59

Jean-François Janinet
1752–1814

La Comparaison

1786

after Nicolas Lavreince

wash manner, printed in blue, red, carmine, yellow, and black inks

image: 363 × 286; plate: 484 × 360

watermark: dovecote

Portalis and Béraldi 40; IFF 12:20 ii/ii

NATIONAL GALLERY OF ART,
WIDENER COLLECTION 1942.9.2366

60

Jean-François Janinet
1752–1814

L'Aveu difficile (The Difficult Confession)

1787

after Nicolas Lavreince

wash manner, printed in blue, red, carmine, yellow, and black inks

image: 363 × 286; plate: 487 × 363

watermark: dovecote

Portalis and Béraldi 39; IFF 12:24 i/iii (proof before letters)

NATIONAL GALLERY OF ART,
WIDENER COLLECTION 1942.9.2367

60

Jean-François Janinet
1752–1814

L'Indiscretion

1788
after Nicolas Lavreince
wash manner, printed in blue, red, carmine, yellow, and black inks
image: 362 × 284; plate: 487 × 363
watermark: dovecote
Portalis and Béraldi 41; *IFF* 12:28 ii/iii (proof before letters)

Although these three prints appeared one at a time over a period of more than eighteen months (between December 1786 and July 1788), they were clearly intended to form a suite. Indeed, the advertisement for *L'Indiscretion* in the *Journal de Paris*, 13 July 1788, specifically states that it was a pendant to both *La Comparaison* and *L'Aveu difficile*. Each of the prints was priced at 9 livres. Janinet quite likely intended to add to the set as time went on but was prevented by other projects. *A Woman Playing the Guitar* (cat. 74), which was never published, has been suggested as just such an addition,[1] but considerable differences in composition make it an unlikely part of the series.

The models for all three works were gouaches by the Swedish artist Niklas Lafrensen, known in France as Nicolas Lavreince (1737–1807).[2] He spent considerable time in Paris, including a seventeen-year stretch between 1774 and 1791, and made a specialty of lewd and titillating subjects such as these images. Many were intended to be engraved. In these three compositions, Lavreince focused on pairs of women sharing their secrets in the safety of their boudoirs. The women's casual deshabille and the viewer's role as a

voyeur make the scenes wonderfully provocative. An unexpectedly playful detail that further unites these three prints and adds to their charm is the plumed and beribboned hat featured in each one. Ironically, in *La Comparaison* and *L'Aveu difficile*, the women wearing these elaborate hats are otherwise only half dressed.

As these three prints bear witness, Janinet was a brilliant interpreter of Lavreince's compositions, taking considerable delight in rendering the details of the costumes and the settings, not to mention the women themselves. The two artists collaborated on several other works, including *A Woman Playing the Guitar* (cat. 74), between 1786 and 1791, when Lavreince left Paris for Stockholm.

1. Baltimore 1984, 264, 266, under nos. 93, 94.
2. The model drawing for *L'Aveu difficile* is in the collection of the Albertina, Vienna.

62

Jean-François Janinet
1752–1814

Madame Vestris as Gabrielle de Vergy

from Jean-Charles Le Vacher de Charnois, *Costumes et annales des grands théâtres de Paris* (Costumes and Annals of the Great Theaters in Paris)(Paris, 1786–1789), vol. 1, in-quarto

wash manner, printed in blue, red, yellow, and black inks

image: 128 × 81; plate: 204 × 130

Cohen and Ricci, cols. 226, 227; *IFF* 12:69

NATIONAL GALLERY OF ART,
WIDENER COLLECTION 1942.9.1447

MAD.ᴱ VESTRIS Role de Gabrielle de Vergy.

„Mon cœur est plus heureux, il reste auprès de toi.
Allons-voici la fin de mon affreux suplice.

Beginning in 1786, Janinet undertook a succession of long-term print projects that lasted well into the 1790s. The first was an ambitious record of Parisian theater in the late 1780s, for which he made almost all of the 176 illustrations of actors in some of their most famous roles. It was published as a periodical in weekly installments from 15 April 1786 to 8 November 1789, with forty-eight *livraisons* (deliveries) each year. (Only thirty-three were produced in the last year.) For the price of 30 livres (for the octavo size) or 36 livres (for the quarto size), a subscriber received annually twenty-four plates printed in colors; twenty-four plates printed in black and white; and thirty-six sheets of music as well as commentaries about the actors and their roles, theater news, and announcements of upcoming productions.

First conceived by Hilliard d'Auberteuil, the series was soon taken over by Jean-Charles Le Vacher de Charnois, who had a particular interest in costumes and the theater. In 1790, he published another book that was also partially illustrated in color: *Recherches sur les costumes et sur les théâtres de toutes les nations, tant anciennes que modernes* (Research on the Costumes and Theaters of All Nations, Both Ancient and Modern).

Many of Janinet's illustrations were executed with his characteristic skill, though the speed with which he was expected to produce them— one each week—led to some careless printing and some rather uninspired compositions. Several, however, were every bit as fine as his large, finished prints. Illustrated here is one of the most lyrical images from quite early in the project. Delivered on 21 July 1786, it shows Mme Vestris in her most triumphant role, the title character in *Gabrielle de Vergy* by Pierre-Laurent Buirette, called De Belloy (1727–1775). The chosen scene is the most famous from the play, whose theme is the doomed love affair

between the married Dame de Fayel and Raoul, lord de Coucy. She has been imprisoned by her jealous husband, who has just left after bringing her a vase and a letter from Raoul. As she reads, "My heart is happier, it remains near you. Let us go, here is the end of my frightful torment," she does not realize that her lover's heart is indeed close by, for it is in the vase on the table. The innocent pause before she looks in the vase and the shriek she utters at her realization of the truth apparently provided one of the most chilling moments in French theater of the time.

The Palais Royal-gallery's Walk.   Promenade de la gallerie du Palais Royal.

A Paris Cour du vieux Louvre la 5me porte
a gauche en entrant par la Colonade au premier.

63

Philibert-Louis Debucourt
1755–1832

The Palais Royal—Gallery's Walk / Promenade de la Galerie du Palais Royal

1787

wash manner, printed in blue, red, carmine, yellow, and black inks

outer framing line: 292 × 559; sheet: 365 × 571 (trimmed at or within platemark)

watermark: T DUPVY / AUVERGNE 1742

Fenaille 11 ii-iii/iv; IFF 6:7

NATIONAL GALLERY OF ART,
WIDENER COLLECTION 1942.9.2264

Debucourt's special talent for caricature emerged fully developed in this remarkable print, which was announced on 30 June 1787 in the *Mercure* at a price of 12 livres. The print is described there as "of the grotesque genre, [with] some spice and originality. The figures in it are numerous, varied and diverting."[1] The inspiration for this work came from an even more harshly humorous composition by Thomas Rowlandson, *Vauxhall Gardens* (fig. 1), which had been translated into a hand-colored print by Francis Jukes and Robert Pollard in 1785, just a couple of years before Debucourt made his.

Like Rowlandson, Debucourt chose a popular gathering place for his subject, in this case the Galerie de bois (Wood Gallery) at the Palais-Royal in the center of Paris. In order to earn money to support his expensive lifestyle, the owner of the palace, the duc d'Orléans (cat. 77), had fitted out parts of it with enclosed arcades, stalls, and boutiques that were rented out to shopkeepers, modistes, artisans, and tradesmen. Closed to policemen, the palace galleries were frequented by people from all walks of life, from aristocrats to pickpockets and prostitutes.

In his print Debucourt singled out some wonderfully affected characters for visual ridicule, reserving his sharpest digs for some of the men who strut and preen like pouter pigeons. No one escaped his wickedly observant eye, however, as he found as much humor in a family with three daughters who are but smaller and younger versions of their tall, rail-thin mother,

as he did in the three young women who blatantly flirt with the viewer. Whether some of the characters in Debucourt's print, such as the odd couple at right, represent actual people is not clear, but the marked individuality of many of the faces suggests that they could well have been easily identifiable to his contemporaries. Even if they were invented types, however, the subject matter and the representation of them were apparently scandalous enough for Debucourt to decide not to sign the piece. He did, however, include his own address at the bottom so that interested buyers would be able to find him.

1. The text of the announcement is quoted in Fenaille 11.

1. Robert Pollard and Francis Jukes after Thomas Rowlandson, *Vauxhall Gardens*, 1785, etching and aquatint with hand coloring. National Gallery of Art, Gift of Ruth B. Benedict 1994.60.55

The Palais Royal Garden Walk   *Promenade du Jardin du Palais Royal.*

A Paris, Rue St. Jacques, No. 55.

Imprimé par Jannin.

64

Louis Le Coeur
active 1784–1825

*The Palais Royal — Garden's Walk / Promenade
du Jardin du Palais Royal*
1787
after Claude-Louis Desrais
wash manner, printed in blue, red, yellow, and black inks
plate: 377 × 565; inner framing line: 279 × 539
watermark: FIN DE / D TAMIZIER / AUVERGNE / 178[?]
Fenaille, under no. 11; IFF 13:9

NATIONAL GALLERY OF ART,
WIDENER COLLECTION 1942.9.2265

For the refreshment of visitors shopping in the
arcades at the Palais-Royal, the duc d'Orléans
allowed cafés, restaurants, and food stalls in the
large garden at the center of the palace. This setting was chosen for the pendant to Debucourt's
Promenade de la Galerie du Palais Royal (cat. 63),
the *Promenade du Jardin du Palais Royal*,
engraved by Louis Le Coeur after a drawing
probably executed by Claude-Louis Desrais
(1746–1816).[1] Dated 1787 and announced on
8 January 1788 at a price of 12 livres, Le Coeur's
print is quite different in appearance and effect
from Debucourt's. Not only does it present a less
crowded and lively scene, but it also lacks much
of Debucourt's piquant humor and amusing
exaggerations of pose and expression. Whereas

Debucourt's figures prance their way across the
page, Le Coeur's stand solidly on the ground and
interact more quietly. While Debucourt's composition is filled with atmospheric subtleties and
richly nuanced colors, Le Coeur's is set out in a
more prosaic, factual manner with somewhat
bolder splashes of color and strong contours
defining the figures. Only in some of the ladies'
hats did Le Coeur capture some of Debucourt's
sense of fun.

1. A preparatory sketch in pen and brown ink by Desrais,
290 × 356, is in the Musée Carnavalet, Paris; reproduced
in Denys Sutton, *French Drawings of the Eighteenth Century* (London, 1949), pl. XVI. No finished model drawing
by Desrais is currently known.

65

Philibert-Louis Debucourt
1755–1832

L'Escalade ou Les Adieux du matin
(The Climb or The Morning Farewells)
1787
wash manner, printed in blue, red, yellow, and black inks
outer framing line: 308 × 252; plate: 370 × 282
watermark: dovecote
Fenaille 13 iii/iii; *IFF* 6:9

THE IVAN PHILLIPS FAMILY COLLECTION

L'Escalade is one of Debucourt's most overtly
erotic scenes—the sensual farewell kiss, the girl's
casually exposed breasts, the bare legs and feet,
and the tumbled clothes bear witness to a night
of stolen pleasure and passion. Neither discovery
nor punishment appears to be imminent, suggesting that no moral message is attached to this
image. However, in the pendant print *Heur et
malheur ou La Cruche cassée* (*Happiness and
Unhappiness or The Broken Pitcher*, fig. 1), the
aftermath of a roll in the hay is depicted with
tears and regret.

 Debucourt rendered the exhibited print with
his customary precision and close attention to
detail. He took special delight in portraying
the inhabitants of the farmyard, especially the
chicken at right and the watchdog at center
whose attention is fixed entirely on the small
piece of meat being dangled in front of its nose.
These anecdotal details, which are also sly
sexual references, add both charm and zest to
the composition.

1. Philibert-Louis
Debucourt, *Heur et
malheur*, 1787, wash
manner. National
Gallery of Art, Widener
Collection 1942.9.2257

66

Jean-François Janinet
1752–1814

Nina, ou La Folle par amour
(Nina, or The Woman Maddened by Love)

1787

after Claude Hoin

wash manner, printed in blue, yellow, red, and black inks

image: 321 × 238; sheet: 423 × 296
(trimmed to or within platemark)

watermark: dovecote

IFF 12:70; Portalis and Béraldi 2:35

NATIONAL GALLERY OF ART,
WIDENER COLLECTION 1942.9.2375

Announced in the *Gazette de France* on 11 September 1787 and in the *Journal de Paris* three days later at a price of 6 livres, the print depicts the actress Rose Lefèvre Dugazon in the highly successful one-act musical play *Nina, ou La Folle par amour*, which premiered at the Comédie italienne in Paris on 15 May 1786. The actress is shown in the most famous scene: driven mad by the supposed murder of her beloved fiancé, Germeuil, Nina goes each day to the sylvan grove where they first declared their love. Holding a bouquet for him, she sings, "When the beloved returns/ to his languishing friend/ Spring will be reborn,/ the grass will always be in bloom. But I look, alas! Alas!/ The beloved returns not." When he does not come, she places the bouquet

on the bench and leaves. Fortunately, her lover is actually alive and when he is restored to her, Nina regains her sanity.

The original gouache by Claude Hoin (1750–1817), in the same direction as the print and dated 1786, was in the collection of M. Arthur Veil-Picard when it was last exhibited in 1934.[1] Baron Roger Portalis explained Janinet's unusual concern for maintaining the composition in the same direction as the drawing by noting that the public was accustomed to seeing the actress on the left side of the stage in this particular scene.[2]

Janinet executed another color print of Dugazon in the role of Nina for the seventh delivery of *Costumes et annales des grands théâtres de Paris* on 10 June 1786 (fig. 1). (For information about this publication, see cat. 62.) The scene is the same, the costume is almost identical, but the pose and gesture are slightly different.

1. *Claude Hoin* [exh. cat., Galerie André Weil] (Paris, 1934), no. 21.
2. Roger Portalis, "Claude Hoin," *Gazette des Beaux-Arts* 23, no. 3 (1900), 14.

MAD.ᵉ DUGAZON. Rôle de Nina.

Paix....il.appelle...hélas! hélas!
Le bien aimé n'appelle pas.

1. Jean-François Janinet, *Mme Dugazon in the Role of Nina*, 1786, wash manner. National Gallery of Art, Widener Collection 1942.9.1447

67

Philibert-Louis Debucourt
1755–1832

Le Compliment ou La Matinée du jour de l'an
(*The Compliment or New Year's Morning*)

1787

wash manner, printed in black, blue, red, yellow,
and carmine inks

sheet: 367 × 286 (trimmed at or just within platemark);
outer framing line: 300 × 251

watermark: dovecote

Fenaille 15 iii/v; *IFF* 6:11

NATIONAL GALLERY OF ART,
WIDENER COLLECTION 1942.9.2253

68

Philibert-Louis Debucourt
1755–1832

Les Bouquets ou La Fête de la grand-maman
(*The Bouquets or Grandmother's Party*)

1788

wash manner, printed in two shades of blue, red, brown,
pink, yellow, and black inks

outer framing line: 302 × 251; plate: 386 × 289

Fenaille 16 ii/iv; *IFF* 6:12

THE IVAN PHILLIPS FAMILY COLLECTION

LE COMPLIMENT
ou
LA MATINÉE DU JOUR DE L'AN
Dédiée aux Pères de famille

Clearly timed to coincide with the day celebrated in the print—New Year's Day—the publication of *Le Compliment* was announced in the *Gazette de France* on 25 December 1787 and in both the *Journal de Paris* and the *Mercure de France* on 29 December 1787. In an unusual move, Debucourt dedicated his print to fathers—"Pères de famille"—probably in the hope of encouraging people to buy the print as a gift for their fathers.[1] The pendant piece, *Les Bouquets*, announced eight months later on 16 August 1788, was correspondingly dedicated to mothers. Each print sold for 6 livres.

Images of tranquil domesticity had long been a commonplace in art, but scenes of familial bliss focusing on happy interaction between parents and children became popular only toward the second half of the eighteenth century.

LES BOUQUETS
ou
À
LA FÊTE DE LA GRAND-MAMAN.
Dédiés aux Mères de Famille.

A Paris, chez l'Auteur, Cour du Louvre, la 2ème porte à gauche, en entrant par la Colonade au 1er.

by Greuze: *The Well-Loved Mother* on the left and *Filial Piety* on the right.[2] Debucourt's choice of these particular works is an obvious reinforcement of his own message about happy families and the rewards of good parenting.

A small gouache by Debucourt entitled *La Fête de la grand-maman* was sold at Sotheby's, London, on 10 June 1959, no. 27. It was slightly smaller than the print (273×222) and in reverse to it. Judging from the reproduction in the sale catalogue, it was not in very good condition.

1. For a list of some of the purchasers of this print, see page 21.
2. Both paintings are reproduced in *Greuze the Draftsman* [exh. cat., The Frick Collection] (New York, 2002), figs. 14, 24.

Jean-Baptiste-Siméon Chardin (1699–1779), Jean-Baptiste Greuze, Jean-Honoré Fragonard, and Louis-Léopold Boilly (1761–1845) are perhaps among the best-known French artists who took up such themes in their pictures. Debucourt's two prints are paradigms of these kinds of works, celebrating the continuity of generations and the ties that make families strong.

Debucourt always took considerable delight in enlivening his scenes with anecdotal details that also allowed him to show off his virtuosity as a printmaker. One of his most miraculous passages, for example, is his rendering of the thin strand of wool trailing from the table onto the floor at right in *Les Bouquets*. In *Le Compliment* the two framed prints hanging on the wall were engraved with such accuracy that they are easily identifiable as representing compositions

69

Le Campion family and others
active last quarter 18th century

Hôtel Thélusson and *Interior of the Church*
of Sainte-Geneviève

from *Vues pittoresques des principaux édifices de Paris*
(Picturesque Views of the Principal Edifices of Paris)
(Paris, Les Campions, [1787]), vol 1., in-octavo
wash manner, printed in blue, red, yellow, and black inks
image diams.: 110 (approximate)

The 105 color plates in this publication offer an invaluable look at the major public and private buildings of late eighteenth-century Paris, particularly since many have been destroyed or considerably altered. Presented in small round compositions, each structure was etched with remarkable precision and a delightfully pictorial sense of color and design. Drawings by Pierre-Antoine Demachy (1723–1807), Antoine-François Sergent (cats. 75, 76), Jean Testard (c. 1740–?), and Jean-Henry Alexandre Pernet (cats. 70–72) served as models for the plates, which were engraved by Laurent Guyot (cats. 70–72), Charles-Melchior Descourtis, an artist known only as L. Roger, and members of the Le Campion family. In 1792, Jean-François Janinet published a similar set of 73 color plates under the same title with many of the same buildings. This set was more likely a rival production than a complement to the Le Campion suite.

Reproduced here is one of the most compositionally pleasing plates in the series: a view of the Hôtel Thélusson, by Guyot after a drawing by Testard. The mansion was designed and built by Claude-Nicolas Ledoux between 1779 and 1782 for Mme de Thélusson, who died very shortly after it was completed. Her sons leased the hotel

N.° 3.

MAISON DE M.ᴿ LE Cᵀᴱ DE PONT Sᵀ.
MAURICE, VUE DE FACE.

Testard del.   *Guyot sculp.*

D'après les Dessins de M. le Doux Architecte.

A Paris chez les Campion freres, rue S.ᵗ Jacques, à la Ville de Rouen.
Avec Priv. du Roi.

VUE DE L'INTÉRIEUR DE LA NOUVELLE
EGLISE DE Sᵗᵉ GENEVIEVE DE PARIS.

A Paris Chez les Campions, freres rue St. Jacques, à la Ville de Rouen.
Avec Pri. du Roi.

to the comte, later marquis de Pons-Saint-Mau-rice, who was its occupant at the time the print was made. After becoming a gambling casino during the Directoire, the building was the town house of Napoleon's sister Caroline, then the residence of the Russian ambassador. The house was razed circa 1826. Its most distinctive features were the massive triumphal arch that served as the entrance to the property and the semi-circular pavilion in the center of the main façade. The harmonious curves in the composition of Guyot's print make the most of both.

Also shown here is one of the rare interiors included in the series, that of the church of Sainte-Geneviève, executed by Le Campion *fils* after a drawing by Sergent. Designed and built by Jacques-Germain Soufflot, the church was begun in 1757 and completed by his students after his death. Dedicated to the patron saint of Paris, it was nearing completion when this print was made. During the Revolution, the church was converted to a pantheon of great men that was intended to house the remains of France's most famous citizens and patriots (see cat. 87). Temporarily converted back to a church twice thereafter, it has remained a pantheon since Victor Hugo was buried there with great pomp in 1885. The building, still an important Parisian landmark, is famed for its huge dome, the 360-foot-long façade featuring twenty-two colossal Corinthian columns, and the spacious airiness of the interior.

70

Laurent Guyot
1756–1806 or 1808

Le Temple de Mars

c. 1788

after Jean-Henry-Alexandre Pernet

wash manner, printed in blue, red, yellow, and black inks

image: 182 × 171; plate: 205 × 178

IFF 11:197; Portalis and Béraldi 1:33

THE IVAN PHILLIPS FAMILY COLLECTION

71

Laurent Guyot
1756–1806 or 1808

Le Temple de la Philosophie

c. 1788

after Jean-Henry-Alexandre Pernet

etching and wash manner, printed in blue, red, yellow, and black inks

image: 183 × 167; plate: 220 × 178

IFF 11:196; Portalis and Béraldi 1:33

THE IVAN PHILLIPS FAMILY COLLECTION

Le Temple de Mars

Laurent Guyot's reputation as an artist scarcely survived his own lifetime, but he was quite a skillful printmaker. He was certainly prolific, turning out hundreds of prints in a wide variety of subjects and techniques; his best works were his multiple-plate color prints. One of his first major projects was his collaboration with the Le Campion family on *Vues pittoresques des principaux édifices de Paris* of 1787, to which he contributed twenty-four prints (see cat. 69). This project seems to have revealed Guyot's special affinity for landscapes, for thereafter they became a favorite subject for him.

This remarkably fresh and charming pair of classical landscapes after watercolors by Pernet (c. 1763–?), executed in about 1788, shows Guyot at his best. *Le Temple de Mars*, in particular, is one of his most beautifully rendered prints, with a wonderfully subtle blending of the colors and a delicate sense of light and atmosphere. Here Guyot proved that he was a worthy rival for such master color printmakers as Jean-François

Pernet delineat.

Guyot Sculpt.

Le Temple de la Philosophie.

à Paris chez Guyot Graveur; rue Jacques, N.º 9..

but in many others, more than one hundred impressions of individual prints accompanied the plates.[3] These numbers suggest that color prints were often produced in very large runs and that many of them remained in stock for long periods of time.

1. F.-L. Regnault-Delalande, *Catalogue de tableaux, gouaches, et dessins…après le décès de Mr Guyot* (Paris, 1808). *IFF*, vol. 11, includes relevant information from this sale catalogue in the entries on Guyot's prints.
2. Two plates for chalk-manner prints of hands and feet were accompanied by sixteen impressions of the prints (lot 240; *IFF* 11:35–36); twelve impressions of *Adam and Eve* after Bounieu were included with the copperplates in lot 243 of Guyot's estate sale (*IFF* 11:254).
3. The eight plates used to make two prints of views near Rome after Hubert Robert, for example, were accompanied by 215 color prints (lot 286; *IFF* 11:383); the four plates used to make a color print after a holy family by Rembrandt were accompanied by 345 impressions (lot 293; *IFF* 11:391).

Janinet and Charles-Melchior Descourtis. Rarely did Guyot work in such a finely nuanced manner, however. In the pendant piece *Le Temple de la Philosophie* and in most of his other prints, he preferred a slightly sketchier, less carefully finished manner that combined penlike etched lines with somewhat simplified fields of bright colors. In spite of the differences in execution, the pendants are otherwise perfectly balanced in the organization of the compositions and in the size of the images (but not in the size of the copperplates).

After Guyot's death, the contents of his studio, including many of his copperplates, were sold in Paris on 14 November 1808.[1] The eight plates used in the production of these two views after Pernet, for example, were sold under lot 287. Interestingly, many of the lots of copperplates (but not lot 287) included impressions of the corresponding prints. In some lots, relatively few copies of the prints were included in the sale,[2]

72

Laurent Guyot
1756–1806 or 1808

Twelve Roundels with Landscape Designs

c. 1788

after Jean-Henry-Alexandre Pernet

etching and wash manner, printed in blue, red, yellow, and black inks

image: 167 × 231 (trimmed within platemark); roundel diams.: 42

IFF 11:293

NATIONAL GALLERY OF ART, GIFT OF
MR. AND MRS. PAUL S. MORGAN IN HONOR
OF MARGARET MORGAN GRASSELLI 2003.72.1

This delightful sheet was the fourteenth in a series of sixteen by Guyot bearing a total of 101 landscape designs, cameos, and fantasy subjects set within small inscribed circles.[1] These roundels were apparently intended to be cut out and pasted either on the large buttons that were in fashion toward the end of the 1780s (see, for example, page 20, fig. 9) or on the tops of small boxes. Alternatively, they could have been set into pieces of jewelry or other small personal ornaments, or used for a host of other decorative purposes. In essence, they served as cheap imitations of more expensive hand-painted designs on ivory, glass, porcelain, or bone. (For a discussion of the market and uses for such "populuxe" prints — affordable imitations of luxury items — see pages 9, 18–21.)

As he had in the preceding pair of classical landscapes (cats. 70, 71), Guyot based these roundels on watercolors by Pernet. In contrast to those brightly colored, fully worked prints, these designs are quite sketchy, giving the effect of quick pen jottings lightly tinted with watercolor. The models provided by Pernet, now lost, were probably not much more finished. Still, Guyot took care in arranging the individual medallions in a pleasing manner on the page. He even went to the trouble of creating a printed background that sets off the images and presents them as if they were miniatures displayed on light blue velvet.

Since sheets of medallions such as this one were produced for the specific purpose of being cut apart, relatively few survive intact. Of the sixteen such sheets produced by Guyot, for example, only three are in the collection of the Bibliothèque nationale in Paris, including an impression of the one presented here.[2]

1. *IFF* 11:280–295. Nos. 294 and 295, which are mistakenly referred to as the fourteenth and fifteenth sheets, are the fifteenth and sixteenth in the series.
2. The Bibliothèque nationale owns the eighth, tenth, and fourteenth sheets in the series. *IFF* 11:87, 289, 293.

73

Gilles-Antoine Demarteau
1750–1802

Head of a Woman Looking Down

c. 1788

after François-André Vincent

chalk manner and tool work, printed in red, black, and blue inks

sheet: 640 × 476 (trimmed within platemark); image: 508 × 374 (without the "mat")

Leymarie 662; IFF 6:74

As is the case with all Demarteau prints that appear to have white highlights, the whites here are actually created by reserves of untouched paper. In his prints of this type, the elder Demarteau had simulated the appearance of colored or prepared papers heightened with white (cats. 35, 38), but his nephew here used a more subtle, pale gray background tone that hardly colors the paper at all. The visual effect is the same, however, with the face and clothing of the figure appearing to be heightened with white and giving the appearance of a drawing executed in red, black, and white chalks. The large blue "mat" that surrounds the central "drawing" is also printed, creating the effect of a mounted sheet that is ready to be framed and hung. The price for this elaborate work was 3 livres, quite high for a chalk-manner print but undoubtedly justified by its large scale and the use of three colors. It is one of the very last prints (no. 662 of 664) included on Demarteau's price list of 1788.[1]

François-André Vincent (1746–1816) made a number of large chalk studies of women's heads over the course of his career.[2] Three others were also copied by Demarteau in chalk-manner prints (Leymarie 648, 649, 663); the last served as the pendant to the exhibited sheet.

By the time Demarteau made this imposing piece, the market for chalk-manner prints was already in sharp decline. The taste for these prints had actually started to wane in the 1770s, but Demarteau and Bonnet and a few other printmakers continued to produce them into the 1790s. With the invention of lithography in the late 1790s,[3] however, the more complex, labor-intensive chalk-manner technique was quickly rendered obsolete.

1. Leymarie catalogues 729 numbered prints by the Demarteau workshop in all, followed by 70 *cahiers* and some miscellaneous suites and individual prints that had appeared, unnumbered, at the beginning of Demarteau's price list.
2. See Jean-Pierre Cuzin, *François-André Vincent, 1746–1816*, Cahiers du dessin français, no. 4 (Paris, n.d.), especially nos. 36, 37. The location of the drawing that served as Demarteau's model for the exhibited print is not known.
3. The lithographic technique, invented in Germany between 1796 and 1798 by Alois Senefelder, allowed artists to draw their compositions directly on the surface of smooth, finely grained limestones with special, greasy lithographic crayons and inks. When printed, the lithographed images looked exactly like the drawings made on the stones, but in reverse.

74

Jean-François Janinet
1752–1814

A Woman Playing the Guitar

1788/1789

after Nicolas Lavreince

wash manner, printed in red, blue, yellow, and black inks

image: 354 × 278; sheet: 485 × 365
(trimmed to or just within platemark)

watermark: dovecote

Portalis and Béraldi 2:481; *IFF* 12:25

This print is certainly one of the greatest of Janinet's oeuvre—and the rarest. Only a handful of impressions is known: two in the Bibliothèque nationale, Paris, one in black and one in color; one in color in the Cincinnati Art Museum; and the present one in the National Gallery of Art. All are proofs without inscriptions and none were marketed during his lifetime. Indeed, the print was completely unknown until five proofs were discovered in 1878 in a portfolio of Janinet's prints belonging to a Mlle Ufel in Haguenau, Alsace. Apparently she had inherited the portfolio from a lady who had been either a relation or a friend of Janinet's.[1] The location of the fifth impression is now unknown.

One can only speculate why Janinet chose never to publish this print, which can easily be regarded as his masterpiece. (The treatment of the *changeant* silk of the guitarist's dress is particularly exquisite.) The most likely cause was the onset of the French Revolution. Indeed, from the end of 1789 to the beginning of 1791, Janinet was fully occupied publishing in fifty-six weekly installments a series of brief pamphlets, each one illustrated with a single print documenting the main events and decrees of the National Assembly.[2] *A Woman Playing the Guitar* may well have been Janinet's last foray into the gallant and often titillating society subjects that occupied him in the 1780s.

Like the earlier trio of boudoir subjects by Janinet (cats. 59–61), this one was based on a gouache (now lost) by Nicolas Lavreince. However, this print was probably not intended to be part of the same series, for its composition is markedly different from the others. Whereas those each show two women conversing and interacting, this guitarist is alone, calmly and perhaps regretfully playing her instrument with no audience but the two dogs perched on the chair at right. An overturned chair at left intro-duces a jarring note, as does the jumble of objects on her dressing table. What caused the turmoil? Given the gallant and erotic subjects that were the theme of so many prints in the 1780s, a likely guess is that either a lover has left in a hurry or the young woman is waiting for a faithless lover who has failed to come.

1. See Charles E. Russell, *French Colour-Prints of the XVIIIth Century, The Art of Debucourt, Janinet & Descourtis* (London, 1927), v.
2. *Gravures historiques des principaux événements depuis l'ouverture des États-Généraux* (Historic Prints of the Principal Events from the Opening of the Estates General); see *IFF* 12:93–148.

75

Antoine-François Sergent
1751–1847

Monsieur Frère du Roi (The King's Brother)
1789
after Joseph-Siffred Duplessis
wash manner, printed in blue, red, carmine,
yellow, orange, green, and black inks
image: 203 × 142; sheet: 209 × 147
Portalis and Béraldi 34

Trained as an engraver by Augustin de Saint-Aubin (1736–1807), Sergent quickly turned to color printmaking as his métier and portraiture as his specialty. His major work was the monumental *Portraits des grands hommes, femmes illustres, et sujets mémorables de France*, which he produced in collaboration with several other artists beginning in 1786 (cat. 76).

Sergent's color portrait print of Louis Stanislas Xavier, comte de Provence (1755–1824) and younger brother of Louis XVI, is one of the most striking of the eighteenth century, a true miniature masterpiece. Sergent himself never produced anything else as fine. The likeness is beautifully rendered, with wonderfully subtle modulation of the planes and flesh tones of the face. Even more impressive is the exquisite handling of the embroidered white satin coat and the blue watered-silk sash. The frame around it and the faux bronze bas-relief below are also executed with amazing precision.

The third grandson of Louis XV, the comte de Provence was devoted to both food and learning, and was especially proud of his fluency in Latin. Ambitious for power, he often worked in opposition to his brother, King Louis XVI, by supporting to a certain extent the political

reforms that led up to the Revolution. When the king and his family were arrested in 1791, the count escaped France on an English passport and spent the next twenty-three years in exile. Following the deaths of his brother and his nephew, he was regarded as the true king by French royalists, but did not assume the throne as Louis XVIII until 1814, when Napoleon was exiled to Elba. Louis' hold on the crown was not finally secured until Napoleon's defeat at Waterloo, after which Louis reigned for nine years.

The books in the frieze make symbolic allusion to the count's erudition and his support for the law. The inclusion of a volume of Plato may even allude to his sympathies — at least at the

time the print was made in 1789 — with the incipient movement toward a French republic. Surmounting the coat of arms of France is a laurel wreath rather than the traditional crown, which lies instead on the ground beside it. This choice may well reflect Sergent's ardent Revolutionary sentiments more than those of the king's brother.

The original painting by Joseph-Siffred Duplessis (1725–1802), or a very good replica after it, is in the collection of the Musée Condé at the château de Chantilly, France.[1] Duplessis' portrait was exhibited at the Salon of 1779 (as no. 124), ten years before Sergent made his print after it.

1. Inv. 387, oil on canvas, 80 × 64 cm. Reproduced in Nicole Garnier-Pelle, *Chantilly, musée Condé, Peintures du XVIIIe siècle* (Paris, 1995), no. 14.

76

Antoine-François Sergent and others
1751–1847

Hermann-Maurice, Comte de Saxe and
Fontenelle méditant sur la pluralité des mondes
(Fontenelle Meditating on the Plurality
of Worlds)

from *Portraits des grands hommes, femmes illustres, et sujets*
mémorables de France (Portraits of Great Men, Illustrious
Women, and Memorable French Subjects) (Paris, Blin,
[c. 1789–1792]), vol. 1, in-quarto

wash manner, printed in blue, red, yellow, and black inks

portrait, outer framing line: 149 × 130; plate: 245 × 164

scene, outer framing line: 118 × 142; plate: 246 × 165

NATIONAL GALLERY OF ART,
WIDENER COLLECTION 1942.9.1826

This grand historical compendium of 192 prints
pairs portraits of ninety-six illustrious Frenchmen and women with scenes showing the most
memorable event of each individual's life.
Antoine-François Sergent (see also cat. 75),
was the principal contributor to the project. He
produced most of the model drawings—with
some assistance from Jacques-François-Joseph
Swebach-Desfontaines (cat. 82) and Duplessis—and many of the prints. Other printmakers
involved were Jean-Baptiste Morret (cat. 84);
Mme Émira de Cernel (1753–1804) who later
married Sergent; and virtually unknown jour-
neymen whose full names remain unknown—
L. Roger and Ridé (or Ridet). The prints, which
are dated variously from 1786 to 1792, were delivered by subscription in forty-eight installments
of four prints each. The mixture of dates within
the deliveries, however, indicates that a large
number of the plates were completed before the
first installments were made.

MAURICE, COMTE DE SAXE,

DUC DE CURLANDE ET DE SÉMIGALLE,

Maréchal Général

des Camps et Armées Françaises;

né à Dresde le 19 Oct.^{bre} 1696; mort au Château Chambor le 30 Nov.^{bre} 1750.

A Paris, chez Blin, Imprimeur en Taille-Douce, Place Maubert, N.º 17. vis-à-vis la rue des 3 Portes. A.P.D.R.

B.   N.° 16.

Desfontaines del.   *1791*   *Moret Sculp.*

FONTENELLE MÉDITANT SUR LA PLURALITÉ DES MONDES.

Bernard le Bovier de Fontenelle, *né à Rouen en 1657, montra, dès sa plus tendre jeunesse, de grands talens. Peu de tems après son admission au Barreau, il le quitta pour la littérature et la philosophie, et vint à Paris en 1679, où la célébrité de son nom l'avoit précédé; plusieurs pièces de vers l'annoncèrent comme un Poète délicat. A peine avoit-il vingt ans lorsqu'il fit une grande partie des Opéras de Psiché et de Bellérophon, qui parurent en 1678 et 1679, sous le nom de Thomas Corneille son oncle. La tragédie d'Aspar, qu'il fit jouer en 1681, ne réussit pas, et il la jeta au feu. Ses Dialogues des Morts, publiés en 1683, furent bien accueillis; ils offrent un grand fonds de littérature, de la philosophie, et une morale agréable. Les Lettres du Chevalier d'Her.... que Fontenelle fit paroître en 1685, confirmèrent sa réputation, qui étoit déjà très brillante. Il publia, en 1686, un ouvrage important, sous le titre d'Entretiens sur la pluralité des mondes: c'est celui de ses travaux qui a eu le plus de célébrité; on y reconnoît Fontenelle tel qu'il étoit, philosophe clair et profond, bel esprit, fin, enjoué, galant, &c. Cet écrit fut le premier exemple de l'art délicat de répandre des graces sur la philosophie. L'histoire des Oracles parut en 1687, et soutint la gloire de son auteur. Cet ouvrage instructif, agréable, précis, méthodique, très-bien raisonné, et écrit avec moins de recherches que les autres productions de Fontenelle, réunit les suffrages des philosophes et des gens de goût. Le même Écrivain publia, en 1688, des Pastorales avec un discours sur l'Eglogue, et une digression sur les Anciens et les Modernes. On reproche à ses Pastorales de se trop ressentir du bel esprit, et c'est en général le défaut des Ouvrages de Fontenelle, mais ce défaut est racheté par de grandes beautés. Il est l'auteur de plusieurs volumes des Mémoires de l'Académie des Sciences, dont il avoit été nommé Secrétaire en 1699, et dont il remplit les fonctions pendant 42 ans. La Préface générale de cette histoire est un de ces écrits qui suffiroient pour immortaliser un auteur. Ses autres ouvrages sont l'Histoire du Théâtre François jusqu'à Corneille, avec la vie de ce célèbre Dramatique, des réflexions sur la poëtique du Théâtre et du Théâtre tragique, des élémens de géométrie, de l'infini; une théorie des tourbillons cartésiens, des discours moraux et philosophiques, des Lettres, &c. Cet homme prodigieux et digne de toutes les Académies, fut de celle des Sciences, des Belles-Lettres, et de l'Académie Françoise. Peu de savans ont eu plus de gloire, et en ont joui plus long-tems. Il mourut le 9 Janvier 1757, avec cette sérénité d'ame qu'il avoit montrée pendant toute sa vie.*

A Paris, chez Blin, Imprimeur en Taille Douce, Place Maubert, N.° 17, vis-à-vis la Rue des 3 Portes. A. P. D. R.

Many of the plates are rather crude in comparison to some of the independent prints produced at about the same time (cats. 74, 75, 77–80): the colors are bold and brassy, and relatively little attempt was made to model the forms and blend the tones. One exception is quite a refined engraving by Ridet after a drawing by Sergent: the 1787 portrait of Hermann-Maurice, comte de Saxe (1696–1750), from group "B," one of the first deliveries. The illegitimate son of Augustus II of Poland and Saxony, Maurice of Saxony entered the military at the age of twelve and there achieved a brilliant career. In 1720, he entered the service of Louis XV of France, who eventually bestowed on him the highest military honor, the rank of marshal general. Apart from his military exploits, the marshal was also famous for amorous escapades with many ladies of the court and several actresses.

Like the portraits, most of the accompanying scenes exhibit a rather naïve simplicity in both the execution and the coloration. Many of these plates are consequently rather wooden in effect, but some are quite charming: for instance, the moonlit *Fontenelle méditant sur la pluralité des mondes*, engraved in 1791 by Morret after a drawing by Swebach-Desfontaines. In it, the poet and philosopher Bernard le Bovier (or Bouyer) de Fontenelle (1657–1757) observes the night sky and reflects on his favorite subject, the nature of the universe and the possible existence of other worlds.

77

Philibert-Louis Debucourt
1755–1832

Mgr. Le Duc d'Orléans

1789
wash manner, printed in black, red, yellow, and blue inks
plate: 245 × 190
Fenaille 20 iii/iii; *IFF* 6:16

The striking similarities between this portrait and the one of the king's brother made by Sergent (cat. 75) in the same year suggest that they might have been linked in some way. Both the format of the portraits and the treatment of the frames around them are closely comparable, though the plate sizes are somewhat different. Perhaps they were part of an aborted project that would have portrayed illustrious personages of the day—this genre was certainly enjoying a certain vogue at the time (see cat. 76). Or perhaps the similarities were merely coincidental and resulted from the new fashion for such printed portrait miniatures.

Louis-Philippe-Joseph, fifth duc d'Orléans (1747–1793), was a distant cousin of King Louis XVI and one of the wealthiest men in France. He lived an extravagant, libertine lifestyle and was perpetually at odds with leading members of the court who thought he had ambitions to become king. The duke was one of the most liberal-minded nobles of his time and had earned the appreciation of the lower classes through open-handed gifts of charity. In addition, he had turned the gardens of the Palais-Royal into a popular gathering spot for Parisians from all levels of society (see cats. 63, 64, 83). Soon after

this print was announced (7 April 1789, for 3 livres), the duke was elected to the Estates General and in June led the group of noble deputies who abandoned the aristocrats to join the Third Estate. He changed his name to Philippe Égalité (equality) and after being elected to the National Convention in 1792, he voted for the death of his cousin, the king. When his son, the duc de Chartres, fled Paris in 1793, all the members of the Bourbon family remaining in France were arrested, including Philippe Égalité. He became an early victim of the Reign of Terror, facing the guillotine on 6 November 1793.

The allegorical bas-relief below the portrait celebrates the duke's legendary generosity and

his patriotic fervor. As Debucourt himself wrote in the accompanying inscription: "Charity, in the form of Minerva, stretches out a helping hand to Indigence and covers her with an Aegis bearing the Orléans arms; near her some children spread abundance and comfort: farther on the Genius of Patriotism meditates on projects for the public good fortune and felicity."

78

Philibert-Louis Debucourt
1755–1832

Annette et Lubin

1789

wash manner, printed in blue, dark pink, bright pink,
yellow, orange, brown, and black inks

outer framing line: 270 × 230; sheet: 394 × 294
(trimmed within platemark)

watermark: T DUPVY FIN / AUVERGNE 1742

Fenaille 22 ii/v; *IFF* 6:18

NATIONAL GALLERY OF ART,
WIDENER COLLECTION 1942.9.2252

The real-life story of Annette and Lubin was
popularized in the *Contes moraux* by Jean-
François Marmontel, first published in 1761, and
then in a musical play by Mme Favart in 1762.
Annette and Lubin were orphaned first cousins
who grew up tending sheep together. Complete
innocents, they knew nothing of the world or
the facts of life. Annette became pregnant by
Lubin, but did not realize it until it was explained
to her. She was told that it was a crime for an
unmarried woman to bring a child into the
world, that her child would reject her because
of her sin, and that she could not marry Lubin
because he was her first cousin. Annette was so
distressed that she started wasting away, wishing
only to die once her child was born and no longer needed her. Desperate, Lubin sought the help
of the local lord, who obtained a papal dispensa-
tion allowing the couple to marry.

Below the color print, Debucourt included
portraits of the actual Annette and Lubin, then
in their seventies and living in conjugal harmony
in Cormeille-en-Parisis. In the published state,
he also included a long inscription that explains
the print's purpose: Though Annette and Lubin
had survived many difficulties "some unhappy

circumstances together with the rigor of the last
winter having reduced them to more dire neces-
sity, people who knew of their misfortune have
invited sensitive souls to come to their aid; the
interest that their youth had inspired has been
reawakened in their favor and everyone hastens
to participate in their comfort. On their behalf,
messieurs the Italian Comedians have assured
them a pension of 300 livres." Debucourt also
intended that half of the proceeds of the sale of
this print would go to support the old couple.
With that in mind, he offered the print on a subscription basis, first advertising it in the *Journal
de Paris* on 7 April 1789 at a prepublication price
of three livres.[1] The subscription was apparently
so successful that by 30 April, Debucourt had
turned over 450 livres to the *Journal de Paris* for

the benefit of the old couple. The subscription
price was then raised to 4 livres and by 19 June
1789, the nonsubscription price was announced
as 6 livres.

Debucourt's presentation of the figures
clearly evokes a scene from the theater. Indeed,
he himself noted in the announcement of 7 April
that his print "represents the instant when
Annette and her lover beg their lord to allow his
heart to be softened and Lubin sings, 'My lord,
see her tears, etc.'"[2] In a footnote, Debucourt
added that this print would be the first in a series
of "the prettiest tableaux from the Italian theater." He appears to have abandoned the project,
however, for no other theater subjects by him
are known.

1. All the announcements and advertisements cited here are
   transcribed in their entirety in Fenaille 22.
2. Fenaille 22.

Charles-Melchior Descourtis
1753–1820

Le Tambourin

c. 1789

after Nicolas-Antoine Taunay

wash manner, printed in blue, red, yellow, white,
and black inks

outer framing line: 310 × 235; plate: 392 × 290

watermark: G. de R. Im-Hof

IFF 7:12

NATIONAL GALLERY OF ART,
WIDENER COLLECTION 1942.9.2129

80

Charles-Melchior Descourtis
1753–1820

La Rixe (The Brawl)

c. 1792

after Nicolas-Antoine Taunay

wash manner, printed in blue, red, yellow, white, green,
and black inks

outer framing line: 310 × 235; plate: 392 × 290

IFF 7:13

NATIONAL GALLERY OF ART,
WIDENER COLLECTION 1942.9.2146

The publication dates for these two prints are
not known, but Marcel Roux described them as
being part of the same series as *Noce de village*
(cat. 55), published in 1785, and *Foire de village*
(page 115, fig. 1), published in 1788.[1] Certainly all
four prints are nearly the same size and were
made after designs by the same artist, Nicolas-
Antoine Taunay. *Le Tambourin*, however, does
have some affinities of subject and style with the
previous two, whereas *La Rixe* is markedly different from the others in these respects. Even as

Le Tambourin

80

Tounsy Pinx.   Descourtis Sculp.

La Rixe

A Paris chez Moret Rue de la Bucherie, N.º 5.

a pendant only to *Le Tambourin*, *La Rixe* makes a strange pairing. The graceful group of ladies and gentlemen entertained by dancing dogs in *Le Tambourin* seems to have nothing in common with the rowdy soldiers quarreling over a woman in *La Rixe*. One still belongs to the old order of the ancien régime; the other seems to evoke the changing social fabric of the Revolution. Indeed, the skintight pantaloons and the short, unpowdered haircuts worn by some of the figures in *La Rixe* indicate a date in the early-to-mid 1790s, placing this print well after the other three. The style of execution, too, is markedly different from the others, with a boldness of form and color that suits the brashness of the subject. In many ways *La Rixe* is closer in its rich tonalities and well-defined forms to Descourtis' *Les Espiègles* (cat. 94), executed about 1798, than to his works from the 1780s.

1. *IFF* 7:8.

81

Pierre-Michel Alix
1762–1817

Queen Marie-Antoinette
c. 1789
after Élisabeth Vigée-Lebrun
wash manner, printed in blue, red, yellow, and black inks
plate: 233 × 179
IFF 1:1; Portalis and Béraldi 1:25

NATIONAL GALLERY OF ART,
WIDENER COLLECTION 1942.9.2430

Having trained with the venerable black-and-white printmaker Jacques-Philippe Le Bas (1707–1783), Alix quickly made his mark in the realm of color printmaking. He chose to specialize in portraiture, executing close to one hundred prints of contemporary and historical figures over the course of his career. Remarkably, he was able to adapt his subject matter to the shifting political climate: from the ancien régime (this *Marie-Antoinette* is his undisputed chef d'oeuvre), through the Revolution (see cat. 87) and the Napoleonic years, and finally to the first moments of the reign of Louis XVIII.

As Richard Campbell remarked in 1984, Alix's prints are generally catalogued as color aquatints, but magnification clearly shows that the tonal areas were created with rockers, roulettes, and other tools not used in the aquatint method.[1] In addition, although Marcel Roux noted that the rectangular frame of the impression of *Marie-Antoinette* in the Bibliothèque nationale, Paris, was colored by hand,[2] close examination of the National Gallery's impression reveals that all of its colors were printed, both in the central image and in the surrounding frame.

The model for Alix's print was one of the many replicas of the full-length portrait of the queen painted by Élisabeth Vigée-Lebrun (1755–1842); the original, dated 1788, is now in the Musée national de Versailles (inv. 2097).[3] Alix's translation, suitably refined for a royal portrait, takes exceptional care in all aspects of the execution, especially in the handling of the colors. The print is extremely rare, presumably because the fall of the royal family forced Alix to destroy the plate and any unsold impressions still in his possession.

1. Baltimore 1984, 111.
2. *IFF* 1:1.
3. For one of the replicas and a discussion of the portrait, see *Élisabeth Louise Vigée Le Brun 1755–1842* [exh. cat., Kimbell Art Museum] (Fort Worth, 1982), no. 27.

82

Louis Le Coeur
active 1784–1825

Bal de la Bastille
1790
after Jacques-François-Joseph Swebach-Desfontaines
wash manner, printed in blue, red, and black inks
plate: 402 × 319; sheet: 520 × 388
IFF 13:16

BAL DE LA BASTILLE.

On 14 July 1790, exactly one year after the fall of the Bastille, grand celebrations were held throughout France. In Paris, two major events marked this key anniversary: the Fête de la Fédération, a demonstration of national unity on the Champs-de-Mars, attended by a multitude of citizens and the royal family; and a large outdoor ball held on the very site where the old prison had stood. Both were recorded in pendant color prints by Louis Le Coeur, *Serment fédératif du 14 Juillet 1790* (fig. 1) and *Bal de la Bastille*, after drawings by Swebach-Desfontaines (1769–1823).[1] The first records the symbolic moment when the marquis de Lafayette, on behalf of the entire French National Guard, swore to remain faithful to the nation, the law, and the king. The print's actual focus, however, falls on the activities of the crowd, in particular the figures in the foreground. The second, illuminated by strings of fairy lights and decorated with arbors and a pavilion, offers an even more charming image that is reminiscent of some of the court balls recorded in black-and-white prints by Jean-Michel Moreau the Younger (1741–1814) and Charles-Nicolas Cochin the Younger (1715–1790). Here, however, citizens from all walks of life take part. The importance of the event is indicated to

some extent by the inscription on Le Coeur's print: "It was precisely on the ruins of despotism that the French celebrated the first anniversary of liberty. The speed of the preparations for this festival should doubtless astonish, but how else to express the sentiments one feels in reading this inscription: Here we dance." This was perhaps one of the happiest days of the Revolution, as many Frenchmen were encouraged to think that the country was moving toward important social, economic, and legal reforms.

1. A drawing of the *Bal de la Bastille* by Swebach-Desfontaine—very likely the one he made in preparation for the print—was sold at Drouot, Paris, 19 March 1906, no. 55. It was executed in pen and black ink with gray wash, heightened with white gouache, and measured 20 × 27 cm. Sweback-Desfontaine's watercolor for the *Serment fédératif* is in the Musée Carnavalet, Paris (inv. D.7107).

1. Louis Le Coeur after Jacques-François-Joseph Swebach-Desfontaines, *Serment fédératif du 14 Juillet 1790*, 1790, wash manner. Musée Carnavalet, Paris

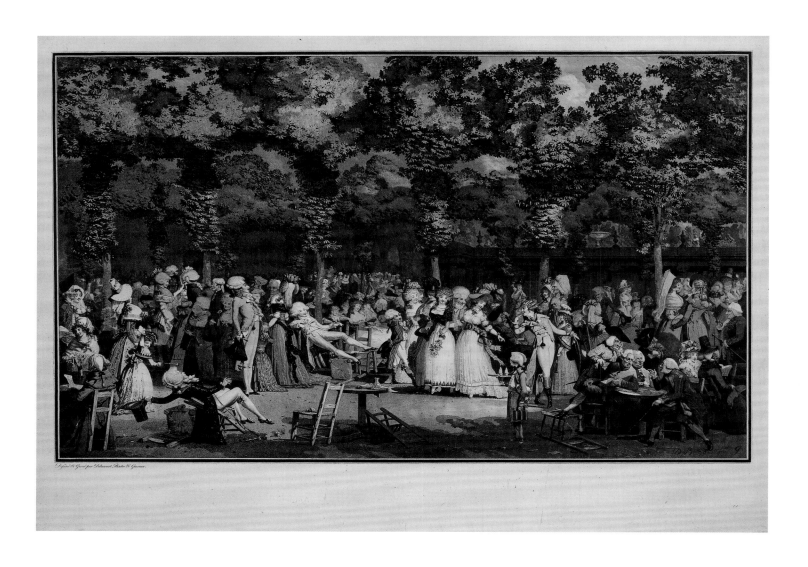

83

Philibert-Louis Debucourt
1755–1832

La Promenade publique

1792

wash manner with aquatint, printed in blue, carmine, dark pink, yellow, and black inks

outer framing line: 366 × 600; sheet: 452 × 637 (trimmed within platemark)

Fenaille 33 ii/iii; *IFF* 6:26; Baltimore 1984, no. 103 ii/iv

NATIONAL GALLERY OF ART,
WIDENER COLLECTION 1942.9.2266

Returning to the subject matter, format, and even the locale (the Palais-Royal) that had been so successful for him five years earlier (cat. 63), Debucourt produced this, his most famous color print, at a time when the political turmoil in France was nearing its height. The exact publication date of the print is not known, for Debucourt chose not to advertise it. However, the declaration of the Republic on 21 September 1792 and the arrest of Louis XVI could not have been far off, and the political mood leading up to those events must have made Debucourt well aware that a society piece would not be well received. Nevertheless, he published *La Promenade publique*, but considerably toned down

the elements of caricature and fun that had made the earlier *Promenade de la Galerie du Palais Royal* so delightfully witty. Still, touches of humor remain—the foreground figure of the man whose chair is breaking under him, for example—and Debucourt's contemporaries would surely have recognized inside jokes and prominent individuals in the crowd. Among the suggested identities are the young duc de Chartres,[1] who is blowing a kiss to the group of ladies, and the duc d'Aumont, who lounges in a chair at center. The rather serious group of older men seated at the table at lower right supposedly portrays close friends of the artist.[2]

Given the timing of the project, one cannot help wondering whether the print is indeed the society piece it appears to be on the surface, or whether it may carry a political subtext directed against the very members of society who are depicted in it. The chair breaking under the elegantly dressed man in the foreground then becomes an obvious reference to the hoped-for, even imminent, downfall of the upper classes, and the foppish poses of the two young dukes can be seen as an indictment of indolence and privilege. Such underlying meanings give the print a broader appeal and make Debucourt's decision to publish it when he did more understandable.

This print has been described as the one great multiple-plate color print made with aquatint.[3] However, as Judith Walsh has discovered, aquatint seems to have been a staple of the color printmakers' technical arsenal and was surely in regular use for wash-manner prints before 1792 (see page 29). This print is the only one, however, in which aquatint can be identified so clearly.

Debucourt's original model drawing in gouache, in reverse, is in the Metropolitan Museum of Art, New York.[4]

1. Pierrette Jean-Richard, in *Graveurs français de la seconde moitié du XVIIIe siècle* [exh. cat., Musée du Louvre] (Paris, 1985), under no. 146, notes that the duc de Chartres was actually absent from Paris in the summers of 1791 and 1792. However, since Debucourt was probably depicting an imaginary gathering rather than an actual one, he still could have included the young duke (then in his late teens) in his print.
2. Edmond and Jules de Goncourt, "Debucourt," in *L'Art du XVIIIe siècle* (Paris, 1882), 2:271, note 1.
3. In Baltimore 1984: 290, under no. 103.
4. 580 × 350. Reproduced very poorly in *Exposition Debucourt* [exh. cat., Palais du Louvre] (Paris, 1920), 53, no. XXXI.

Caffée des Patriotes. *a Patriot's Coffée House.*

84

Jean-Baptiste Morret
active 1789–1820

*Caffée des Patriotes — A Patriot's
Coffée House*

1792
after Jacques-François-Joseph Swebach-Desfontaines
wash manner, printed in blue, red, yellow, and black inks
outer framing line: 281 × 540; plate: 413 × 618
watermark: double-headed eagle
Portalis and Béraldi 2: page 207

Little more than a journeyman printmaker, Jean-Baptiste Morret first made his living by turning out mediocre color prints of gallant subjects after the likes of Augustin de Saint-Aubin and Antoine Borel (1743–1810 or after). He also made some of the prints for the *Portraits des grands hommes, femmes illustres, et sujets mémorables de France*, in which the small-scale format suited his somewhat simplified execution (one is illustrated under cat. 76). The one color print that earned him a lasting reputation, however, is *Caffée des Patriotes* of 1792, based on a drawing by Jacques-François-Joseph Swebach-Desfontaines. Executed on an ambitious scale and in a format that recalls the great promenade prints of Debucourt and Le Coeur (cats. 63, 64, 83), *Caffée des Patriotes* is a bold but rather coarse work. In spite of its rather cartoonish character (the result of strong contours combined with relatively unmodulated fields of color), Morret's print brings to life with a certain naïve charm one of the less public sides of the Revolution.

The Café des Patriotes is said to have been situated next to the headquarters of the Jacobin club on the rue Saint-Honoré, where such leaders as Robespierre, Marat, and Mirabeau gathered to formulate policies and to lead the Revolution.[1] Republicans who were interested in keeping abreast of the news gathered at the neighboring coffee house, which also then served as a headquarters of sorts for the police responsible for the security of the Jacobin revolutionaries. When Robespierre fell victim to the guillotine in 1794 and the Jacobin club was dissolved, the café's political role ceased.

In the second state of Morret's print, the English part of the title is burnished out and replaced by "Grande nouvelle du Nord" (Great news from the North), thus giving a general indication of what the man at center is reading aloud to the crowd around him. Also changed in the second state are the towering bearskin busbies worn by the two guards at left: one became a flat helmet and the other a Phrygian cap, one of the symbols of the Revolution. Several of the figures depicted by Morret were quite possibly intended to be recognizable portraits, but their identities are no longer known.

1. See Edward Clayton, *French Engravings of the Eighteenth Century in the Collection of Joseph Widener, Lynnewood Hall* (London, 1933), 3:462–463.

85

Frédéric Cazenave
active 1793–1843

L'Optique (The Optical Viewer)

c. 1793

after Louis-Léopold Boilly

wash manner, inked *à la poupée* in black, brown, and green
with hand coloring

plate: 550 × 450

watermark: double-headed eagle

IFF 4:4; Portalis and Béraldi 1: page 346
(proof before letters)

NATIONAL GALLERY OF ART, GIFT OF
IVAN E. AND WINIFRED PHILLIPS IN
HONOR OF MARGARET MORGAN GRASSELLI
AND ANDREW ROBISON 2002.125.1

Little is known about Cazenave (also called
Cazeneuve) except that he made several wash-
manner prints in the 1790s and turned to lithography some years later. This handsome print
after a painting by Louis-Léopold Boilly that had
been exhibited in the Salon of 1793 is universally
regarded as Cazenave's masterpiece.[1] His handling of the shimmering fabric of the woman's
white skirt is especially beautiful. As was his
usual practice, Cazenave worked the entire print
on a single plate and printed many of the earliest
impressions only in black. In order to get the
most out of his work, he would often switch to
color when the plate began to show some wear,
inking it with several colors *à la poupée*.[2] The
National Gallery's impression, however, shows
no signs of wear in the lines; indeed, it is a proof
before letters that must have been pulled at an
early stage of the print's manufacture. It was
possibly one of Cazenave's first trials with colored inks, for the considerable amount of hand
touching with watercolor, especially in the
blues and light browns, seems to indicate that

Cazenave was still working out the color scheme
for the final print.

The young woman depicted here is Louise-
Sébastienne Gély (1776–1856), who married the
Revolutionary leader Georges-Jacques Danton in
July 1793. Looking at images through the optical
viewer with her is most likely Antoine, Danton's
oldest son from his previous marriage. Danton
was guillotined less than a year after his marriage to Gély, who then married Baron Claude
Dupin in 1794.

1. The painting, now in a French private collection, is reproduced in *Louis Boilly, 1761–1845* [exh. cat., Musée Mar-
mottan] (Paris, 1984), no. 7.
2. For an explanation of *à la poupée* inking see pages 6, 7.

86

Nicolas Colibert
c. 1750–after 1810

Cain Fleeing in Shame after Murdering Abel

from Salomon Gessner, *La Mort d'Abel* (The Death of Abel)
(Paris, Defer de Maisonneuve, 1793), in-quarto

etching and stipple, inked *à la poupée* in blue, red, green,
and brown

image: 213 × 144

NATIONAL GALLERY OF ART,
WIDENER COLLECTION 1942.9.1554

Amidst the turmoil of the French Revolution,
several impressive books illustrated with color
prints were published. The house of Defer de
Maisonneuve seems to have made a specialty of
sorts of these works, bringing out four between
1792 and 1796: John Milton, *Le Paradis perdu*,
1792; Florian, *Galatée, Roman pastoral*, 1793;
Salomon Gessner, *La Mort d'Abel*, 1793; and Jean-
Joseph Vadé, *Oeuvres poissardes*, 1796. The first
was illustrated with twelve prints after paintings
by Jean-Frédéric Schall; the illustrations of the
other three were all drawn by Nicolas-André
Monsiau (1754–1837), a painter who had been
admitted to the French Academy in 1789 but had
soon thereafter begun an active side career as
an illustrator. Among the printmakers involved
in these projects were A. S. Clément, Frédéric
Cazenave, and Nicolas Colibert; all three worked
on *La Mort d'Abel*. Colibert was responsible for
four of the plates; Clément and Cazenave each
made one. All the prints were executed in stipple
and printed from single plates inked *à la poupée*
in an unusually delicate and remarkably subtle
range of colors.

One of the best illustrations in *La Mort
d'Abel* is the print by Colibert that introduces

chant IV: Cain, having killed his brother Abel by
striking him on the head with a massive cudgel,
flees in horror and shame. On the altar at center
is his offering of fruit, which had been rejected
by the Lord and was at the root of his jealousy
for his brother, whose sacrificial lamb had
been accepted.

The drawings by Monsiau for the illustrations to *La Mort d'Abel* were formerly in the
collection of Henri Béraldi.[1]

1. See Cohen and Ricci, col. 436.

87

Pierre-Michel Alix
1762–1817

Michel Lepelletier

1794
after Jean-François Garneray
wash manner, printed in yellow, blue, red, and black inks
sheet: 353 × 280 (trimmed to platemark);
framing line: 246 × 218
watermark: AUVERGNE 1742
IFF 1:45; Portalis and Béraldi 1:17

NATIONAL GALLERY OF ART, GIFT OF
JACOB KAINEN 2002.98.370

Michel Lepelletier

Before the Revolution, Louis-Michel Lepelletier de Saint-Fargeau (1760–1793) was controller general of finances under Louis XVI. A very rich man in his own right, this moderate royalist served as president of the Parlement of Paris and was a delegate representing the nobility to the Estates General in 1789. Radicalized by the events of July 1789, however, he became an ardent revolutionary and as a deputy at the National Convention in 1792, he voted to send the king to the guillotine. On the evening before the king's execution, Lepelletier was angrily accosted by a former royal guardsman named Pâris, who killed him with a saber thrust to the chest. Lepelletier's dying words were inscribed on his tomb: "I am satisfied to shed my blood for my country. I hope that it will serve to consolidate Liberty and Equality and to make its enemies known."[1] The state funeral of this "martyr of liberty" was orchestrated by the great neoclassical artist Jacques-Louis David (1748–1825), from the dramatic lying-in-state on the place Vendôme, with the fatal wound left visible for all to see, to the final burial in the Panthéon (see cat. 69).

The print by Alix, announced in the *Journal de Paris* on 1 March 1794, was part of the *Collection des grands hommes*, a long series of color portrait prints of great Frenchmen. Inaugurated in 1791 with a portrait of Voltaire,[2] the project was a collaborative effort between Alix and the publisher Drouhin, with most of the model drawings produced by Jean-François Garneray (1755–1837). By the time the last one was published in 1797, about one hundred portrait prints had been produced; all present the sitters in bust-length within an inscribed oval. The best are generally considered to be the contemporary heroes of the Revolution, for they, like the portrait of Lepelletier, are distinguished by an exceptional vitality of expression and bold richness of color.

1. A useful source of information about the murder of Lepelletier and its aftermath is Claudette Hould, *L'Image de la Révolution française* [exh. cat., Musée du Québec] (Quebec, 1989), nos. 105–108.
2. *IFF* 1:25.

88

Anne Allen
active 1790s

Chinese Arabesque with a Double Parasol

c. 1795

after Jean-Baptiste Pillement

etching, inked *à la poupée* in gray, black, blue, green-blue, olive green, pink, and yellow-brown

plate: 195 × 140

IFF 1:1

NATIONAL GALLERY OF ART,
AILSA MELLON BRUCE FUND 1991.186.2

89

Anne Allen
active 1790s

Chinese Arabesque with a Tightrope Walker

c. 1795

after Jean-Baptiste Pillement

etching, inked *à la poupée* in black, gray, blue, green, golden-brown, pink, and olive green

plate: 193 × 138

IFF 1:1

NATIONAL GALLERY OF ART,
AILSA MELLON BRUCE FUND 1991.186.5

90

Anne Allen
active 1790s

Fantastic Flowers with Peapod Leaves

c. 1795

after Jean-Baptiste Pillement

etching, inked *à la poupée* in green, red, blue, purple, and golden-brown on pale green paper

plate: 194 × 139

watermark: sun

IFF 1:2

NATIONAL GALLERY OF ART,
AILSA MELLON BRUCE FUND 1985.60.1

91

Anne Allen
active 1790s

Fantastic Flowers with Oyster-Shell Blossoms

c. 1795

after Jean-Baptiste Pillement

etching, inked *à la poupée* in green, blue, purple, red, golden-brown, and yellow on pale green paper

plate: 196 × 138

IFF 1:2

NATIONAL GALLERY OF ART,
AILSA MELLON BRUCE FUND 1985.60.2

Very little is known about Anne Allen: she was the second wife of Jean-Baptiste Pillement (1728–1808), she may have been English, and she made utterly charming color prints after her husband's whimsical designs. She published nine *cahiers* (notebooks) of prints, five after Pillement's highly inventive fantasy flowers and four after his Chinese-inspired ornamental designs. Each *cahier* consisted of a title page and

four prints, each pulled from two plates inked *à la poupée* in a profusion of bright colors. The two chinoiserie prints exhibited here are from the *Nouvelle suite de cahiers de desseins chinois à l'usage des dessinateurs et des peintres* (New Suite of Notebooks of Chinese Designs for the Use of Designers and Painters), of which the National Gallery owns the complete set (1991.186.1–5). The two prints of flowers are the only examples in the collection from the *Nouvelle suite de cahiers de fleurs idéales à l'usage des dessinateurs et des peintres* (New Suite of Notebooks of Ideal Flowers for the Use of Designers and Painters).

These highly ornamental prints evoke the spirit and taste of the 1770s, but a date of 1796 on one of Pillement's flower designs and a date of 1798 on one of Allen's chinoiserie prints indicate a surprisingly late date for them all.[1] Born in 1728, Pillement was apparently so deeply steeped in the rococo style of his youth and maturity that neither the neoclassical movement nor the French Revolution had any obvious effects on his art in his later years. One has to wonder, then, if these delightful prints served their intended purpose as models for artists and craftsmen, or whether they fell quickly into oblivion because they were so out of step with their time.

1. The dated drawing and print were contained in an album sold at Christie's, London, on 8 December 1981, lot 130. The lot included a number of Pillement's drawings and a slightly incomplete set of Allen's prints after them.

92

Philibert-Louis Debucourt
1755–1832

Les Plaisirs paternels (Paternal Pleasures)

c. 1797

wash manner, printed in orange-red, blue, yellow, and black inks

outer framing line: 466 × 366; plate: 517 × 383

Fenaille 63 i/ii; *IFF* 6:56

After *La Promenade publique* in 1792, Debucourt made very few large-scale multiple-plate color prints, following instead a general trend toward the cheaper and less time-consuming production of compositions on single plates inked *à la poupée*. One great exception is his print *Les Plaisirs paternels*, based on his own drawing, which was surprisingly enough executed only in black chalk heightened with white (Collection of Jeffrey Horvitz, Boston).[1] This brilliant impression

shows yet again what a supremely gifted printmaker Debucourt was, and how much was lost when he gave up this type of printmaking in favor of other less demanding techniques.

Debucourt returns here to a subject he had first treated about a decade earlier in *Le Compliment* and *Les Bouquets* (cats. 67, 68): the joys and virtues of a happy family life. *Les Plaisirs paternels* is one of several prints he made about 1795 on the same theme,[2] including a pendant piece,

Joies maternelles (*Maternal Joys*) (fig. 1), which was unknown to Fenaille.[3] As Victor Carlson observed, Debucourt may have been responding to the then-new concern that strong family units could serve as the foundation for a newly stabilized, post-Revolutionary society.[4] The French constitution of 1795 even articulated the specific desire "to naturalize the family spirit in France" and declared flatly, "No one is a good citizen if he is not a good son, good father, good husband."[5]

Just as he had dedicated the two earlier prints to fathers and mothers, Debucourt dedicated this one to "Bons Papa[s]" (grandfathers). The one impression of *Joies maternelles* is trimmed to the image (and therefore now bears no inscriptions), but very likely, in its turn, it was dedicated to grandmothers. The establishment

in 1794 of a Fête à la Vieillesse (festival honoring the aged) suggests that Debucourt may have been following a current vogue for celebrating the older generations.[6]

1. 455 × 365 mm. Reproduced in *Mastery & Elegance, Two Centuries of French Drawings from the Collection of Jeffrey Horvitz* [exh. cat., Harvard University Art Museums] (Cambridge, Mass., 1998), 349, no. 113b.
2. Fenaille 58–63.
3. The drawing for *Joies maternelles* is also in the Horvitz collection (reproduced in Cambridge 1998, no. 113a).
4. Cambridge 1998, 347, under nos. 113a, 113b.
5. Quoted by Carlson in Cambridge 1998, 347.
6. See for example the drawing *Fête à la vieillesse* by Pierre-Alexandre Wille (1748–1821), reproduced in Aileen Ribeiro, *Fashion in the French Revolution* (London, 1988), 91, fig. 58.

1. Philibert-Louis Debucourt, *Joies maternelles*, c. 1797, wash manner. Private collection, Philadelphia

93

Philibert-Louis Debucourt
1755–1832

Le Couronnement (The Crowning)

from Le Chevalier de Querelles, trans. *Héro et Léandre*
(Paris, Pierre Didot the Elder, 1801), in-quarto

wash manner, printed in red, blue, green, yellow, brown,
and black inks

image: 195 × 154

Fenaille 124 iii/iii

NATIONAL GALLERY OF ART,
WIDENER COLLECTION 1942.9.1808

Debucourt's first foray into book illustration was *Héro et Léandre*, which was translated from the original Greek by his friend Le Chevalier de Querelles and published in 1801. Debucourt designed and executed eight text illustrations printed in color, as well as a frontispiece, dated 1797, which was printed only in black ink.[1]

Hero and Leander is a famous love story, best known for Leander's nightly swim across the straits of the Hellespont to be with his love, Hero. Debucourt's most successful illustrations, however, belong to the earlier part of the story, in which Hero, a priestess of Venus, carries out her duties during the annual festival honoring her deity. Particularly handsome is *Le Couronnement*, in which she crowns Leander, whom she secretly loves, as the winner of the palm of the arts for his sculpture of Venus and Adonis.

The book's publication was mentioned in the *Journal typographique et bibliographique* on 1 November 1801; Debucourt's contribution was noted with considerable approbation: "The prints that ornament the poem appear to us to be the best one can do in this genre. The drawing is very correct and the engraving is of a color tone that is very difficult to obtain in these sorts of prints. We can therefore assure amateurs that this beautiful work can only augment very much the reputation of citizen Debucourt."[2] To modern eyes, however, the compositions and poses in *Héro et Léandre* are rather self-consciously stiff and contrived when compared to the liveliness and wit of Debucourt's earlier works. Clearly the artist had tried to adapt his style and tone to a restrained classicism that would be suited to an ancient tale of tragic love, but the story did not seem to unleash his imagination in the same way that the foibles and manners of contemporary society did throughout his career. On the other hand, the extraordinarily rich and saturated colors in these prints are among the most beautiful in Debucourt's oeuvre.

1. The nine model drawings in pen and wash were formerly in the collection of comtesse Henry de Gontaut-Biron. See Paris 1920, under no. XXXVI, where all nine are reproduced. Five of the drawings (for the frontispiece and plates 1,3, 6, and 8 in the book) were engraved in the same direction; the four others were reversed in the prints.
2. The advertisement is transcribed in Fenaille 123.

P. L. Debucourt.

LE COURONNEMENT.

94

Charles-Melchior Descourtis
1753–1820

Les Espiègles (The Pranksters)

c. 1798

after Jean-Frédéric Schall

wash manner, printed in blue, red, yellow, and black inks

outer framing line: 466 × 376; sheet: 545 × 442 (trimmed within platemark)

THE IVAN PHILLIPS FAMILY COLLECTION

95

Charles-Melchior Descourtis
1753–1820

L'Amant surpris (The Lover Surprised)

c. 1798

after Jean-Frédéric Schall

wash manner, printed in blue, red, yellow, and black inks

outer framing line: 462 × 372; plate: 559 × 430

watermark: sun

THE IVAN PHILLIPS FAMILY COLLECTION

The gallant and mildly salacious subjects that had enjoyed so much popularity prior to the Revolution had been condemned as immoral during the Terror (1793–1794) and the Directoire (1795–1799). Toward the end of the Directoire, however, such works were again received with a certain amount of enthusiasm. Descourtis had produced very few prints during that turbulent period, but these two masterly works show that he had lost none of his skill in the interim. He worked the plates with extreme care to produce remarkably rich and velvety effects of tone and color; he also matched the size of the plates to the dimensions of the original paintings by Jean-Frédéric Schall, thus replicating as closely as possible their appearance.[1]

Fine multiple-plate color prints like these two were already becoming rare by the time they were published. The acknowledged masters, Descourtis, Janinet, and Debucourt, each pro-

L.ͤ Amant Surpris

Paris chez Descourtis, Rue du Grands Degris N. 12.

The market for expensive, finely crafted "printed paintings" in France had collapsed during the Revolution and was only partially revived under Napoleon. The color printing phenomenon of the eighteenth century in France was so fundamentally a part of its own time and was so deeply connected to the taste, culture, and exquisite craftsmanship of the ancien régime that it could not endure much beyond it. Other than aquatint, the complex techniques that were invented specifically for chalk-manner and full-color, multiple-plate printmaking quickly and quietly fell by the wayside as lithography took hold and printmaking moved in new and different directions.

1. The painting *Les Espiègles*, formerly in the collection of Baron Fernand de Christiani, is now in the Musée du Louvre, Paris. *L'Amant surpris* was formerly in the collection of Franklyn Laws Hutton, New York, and its current location is unknown. See Girodie 1927, 21, 63.
2. See Baltimore 1984, no. 123.

duced very few thereafter, and only a handful of lesser-known artists such as Alix and Sergent carried on the genre into the nineteenth century. This time-consuming, demanding, and expensive process was already being replaced by the simpler, faster method of *à la poupée* inking on a single plate (cats. 85, 86, 88–91). However, that, too, required considerable technical expertise in the inking and wiping of the plate. The last great color print project using that technique—plus some hand coloring—was the long series of

illustrations of Empress Josephine's collection of flowers, *Les Liliacées* (1802–1816), by Pierre-Joseph Redouté (1759–1840).[2] By the time it was completed, *à la poupée* inking had been replaced by an even cheaper, more expedient method of adding color to prints—good, old-fashioned hand coloring, which could be applied by moderately skilled specialists following approved models, often with the aid of stencils.

Paper Used in the Prints

Watermarks and Observations

Lehua Fisher and Judith C. Walsh

Tonal printing from multiple plates presented new requirements for the printing paper. The ideal sheet had to be smooth to render the details in texture and tone. It had to be absorbent to pull the ink out of the copperplate, and it had to be strong to withstand multiple runs through the press. Finally, the sheet could expand only a little when damp so that the printing would be kept in register.

Only one type of sheet appears to have been acceptable for this use: the moderately thick, cream-colored laid paper[1] known as the "fine" or "middle quality" paper made in the mills of Auvergne. Of the twenty-four sheets in the exhibition that can be associated with a particular papermaker through the watermarks, twenty-two are associated with papermakers from Auvergne, specifically from the town of Ambert.

Joseph Jérôme de Lalande described the state of French papermaking in 1761: "Of all the provinces in France, Auvergne produces the favorite paper for writing and for plate printing" in the towns of Thiers and Ambert.[2] Angoumois came in a close second, with papers "good for plate printing, superior to those of the same type from Limoges but a large part of the paper is sold at Bordeaux for export to Holland."[3]

Throughout the eighteenth century, Auvergnat paper-makers relied on antiquated wooden stampers in their paper-making.[4] Water-powered wooden stampers had been used in Europe since the twelfth century to crush the retted rags against stone, but were quickly supplanted by the more effi-cient Hollander beaters after 1680. Hollander beaters use a series of metal blades that strike a metal plate to cut the rags apart. The cutting action makes a shorter fibered pulp that forms a dense sheet more typical of Dutch, English, and Ger-man papers of the era.[5] Although stampers took longer to render the pulp, they made a soft, durable sheet.

French papermakers also used a lighter style of gelatin sizing on their sheets than did Northern papermakers,[6] and the French sent their sheets to market right after they were made. Such sheets would lose a considerable portion of their sizing when dampened for printing. By contrast, in Holland and England the gelatin sizing used on sheets incorporated excess alum as a hardener, and sheets were aged in the lofts of the papermakers for up to a year before they were offered for sale. When dampened for printing, such papers retained this hardened, aged, less soluble gelatin sizing. The French combi-nation of stamped fiber and light, unaged sizing made a paper that was well suited to plate printing. These sheets would dampen easily, expand little, absorb ink, and ride through the press without breaking at the platemark.

These French print papers were also in demand outside France. Despite the history of hostility between the countries and the British Crown's increasingly punishing duties against imported paper, printers in Britain also relied upon French sheets.[7] Francis Spilsbury advised them that "French paper above all others takes the best impressions."[8] From as early as 1757, British mezzotints were consistently printed on sheets bearing the same watermarks found in the French colored prints.[9] Also, "considerable stocks" of French papers suitable for use in copperplate printing could be found in London.[10] But even as these stocks were used, the Society for the Encour-agement of Arts, Manufacturers, and Commerce mounted a competition to devise a replacement plate paper in England.[11] Perhaps paper shipments were finally interrupted by the Napoleonic blockade of 1793, although as late as 1804 some French sheets were still available to English printers.[12] Indeed, Joseph Mallord William Turner used them for early impres-sions of the *Liber Studiorum*.[13]

By this time, forgers of the papers were pirating the water-marks found in the French sheets (see cats. 16b, 44, 45, 57). For example, the true watermark "FIN / D TAMIZIER / AUVERGNE 1742" (cat. 36) was counterfeited as "FIN DE / D TAMIZYER / AVUERGNE" (cat. 45). In the prints exhibited here, false sheets were used in 1769 and from 1783 to 1786, which suggests either periodic domestic shortages of authentic paper or breakdowns of official controls.

One other anomaly found in the watermarks is worth commenting upon. The date 1742 found in many of the water-marks does not indicate the date of their manufacture. Rather, it indicates compliance with an edict from Paris regulating paper manufacture and trade. In 1739 regulations were issued to improve the consistency and quality of French paper by setting standards for the manufacture and sale of the sheets. The regulations demanded that the watermark text denote the quality of the sheet, the papermaker's first initial and surname, and the location of the mill. In 1741 the edict was clarified and amended: paper was to be made in standard weights and sizes; it also had to include the date 1742 in the watermark as an indication of compliance with the act, which went into effect on 1 January 1742.[14] Certain papermakers used 1742 in their watermarks for many years; some, well into the 1780s.[15]

Fifty-nine standard sizes and weights of sheets were named and described by the regulations of 1741, thus assigning specifications to many of the watermark devices traditionally used by French papermakers. For example, among the sheets used for color prints are several *soleil* or sun watermarks (cats. 6, 90, and 95). The sun watermark had been used in French paper at least since the late fifteenth century, but starting in 1742 only three specific sheets were allowed to use the symbol: the *petit soleil, soleil,* and *grand soleil* papers. The last was standardized at about thirty-six by twenty-four inches; a ream was to weigh between 112 and 120 pounds (but never less than 105 pounds).[16]

The watermarks illustrated here were taken from prints in the exhibition by beta-radiography, effectively making an X-ray of the sheet.[17] These watermarks are described using the terminology and methodology set out in Nancy Ash and Shelley Fletcher's study *Watermarks in Rembrandt's Prints.*[18] Their protocol requires overlapping similar beta-radiographs for direct comparison of the many revealed details in the watermarks before describing them as "identical" or "closely related." "Identical" watermarks agree in all details, thus indicating that the sheets were made from the same mould at about the same time. Moulds for papermaking were made in pairs and used alternately in sheet forming; thus sheets made at the same time are not always "identical." Sheets that were likely cast at the same time from two such moulds are called "twins."[19] Published references to similar watermarks have been included,[20] but most of the watermarks found in the sheets are as yet unpublished.

CAT. 4

1757

Dovecote

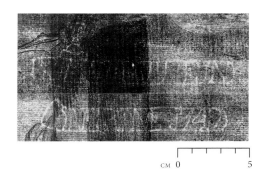

CAT. 4

1757

T DUPVY FIN /
AUVERGNE 1742

CAT. 5

1759

Dovecote

Heawood 1233, 1234

Related to cats. 14, 19,
and 37a

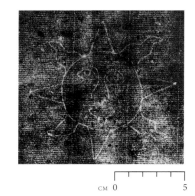

CAT. 6

c. 1760

Sun

CAT. 7

before 1764

Chaplet with Maltese cross

Gaudriault 300

Possible countermark:
T DUPUY

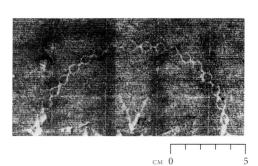

CAT. 9b

1773 or later

Chaplet (partial)

Heawood 238

CAT. 10

1766

T DUPVY FIN /
AUVERGNE 1742

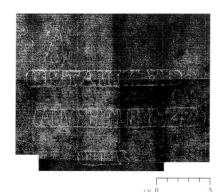

CAT. 11

1766

D TAMIZIER /
AUVERGNE 1742 / FIN

Heawood 1237

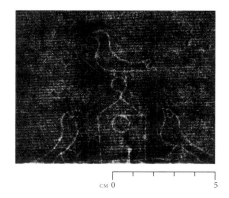

CAT. 14

1767

Dovecote (partial)

Heawood 1233

Identical to cat. 19; related to cats. 5 and 37a

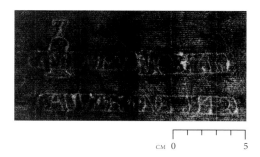

CAT. 15

1767

T DUPVY MOYEN / AUVERGNE 1742

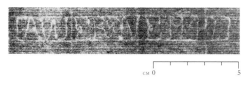

CAT. 16b

c. 1769

AVUERNE 1742

Counterfeit: see also cats. 44, 45, and 57; compare cat. 37b

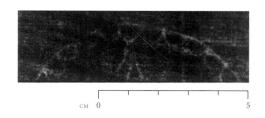

CAT. 17b

c. 1769

Unknown fragment

CAT. 19

1769

Dovecote

Gaudriault 369

Heawood 1233

Identical to cat. 14; related to cats. 5 and 37a

CAT. 20

1769

Dovecote

Heawood 1233 (similar)

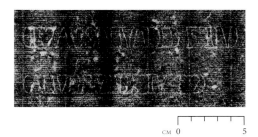

CAT. 20

1769

I A SAUVADE FIN / AUVERGNE 1742

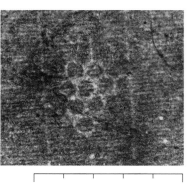

CAT. 24

1773

Grapes

Heawood 3302, 3407, 3416

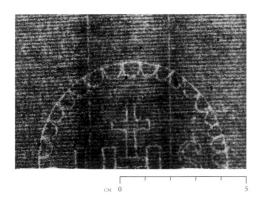

CAT. 25

1773

IHS in a circle (partial)

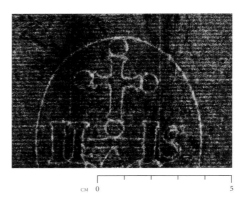

CAT. 26

1774

IHS with cross in a circle

Gaudriault 735

Heawood 2952, 2981,
2997, 3310

Closely related to cat. 55a

CAT. 27b

c. 1773

T DUPVY MOYEN

CAT. 29

c. 1774

T DUPVY FIN /
AUVERGNE 1742

Heawood 1234

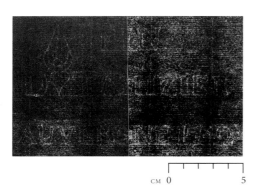

CAT. 36

1775

FIN / D TAMIZIER /
AUVERGNE 1742

Closely related to cat. 37b

CAT. 37a

c. 1776

Dovecote

Heawood 1234

Related to cats. 5, 14, and 19

CAT. 37b

c. 1776

AUVERGNE 1742

Closely related to cat. 36

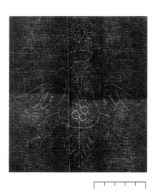

CAT. 40

1778

Double-headed eagle

Heawood 1316

Possible twin of cat. 41

CAT. 41

1778

Double-headed eagle

Heawood 1316

Possible twin of cat. 40

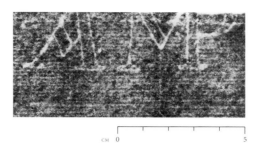

CAT. 43

c. 1784

AMP

Identical to cat. 48: could be Antoine and Meynard Perrot, papermakers of Angoulême, c. 1771

CAT. 44

1783

FIN DE / D TAMIZ ER / AVUERGNE

Counterfeit: see also cats. 16b, 45, and 57; compare to cats. 36 or 45

CAT. 45

1783

FIN DE / D TAMIZYER / AVUERGNE / 1742

Counterfeit: see also cats. 16b, 44, and 57; compare to cats. 36 or 44

CAT. 47b

1783

FIN DE / D TAMIZIER / AUVERGNE / 1781

Heawood 3430

CAT. 48

1783

AMP

Identical to cat. 43: could be Antoine and Meynard Perrot, papermakers of Angoulême, c. 1771

CAT. 49b

1785

Dovecote

Identical to cat 52b; closely related to cat. 65

CAT. 52b

1785

Dovecote

Identical to cat. 49b; closely related to cat. 65

CAT. 54

c. 1785

AUVERGNE 1742

Possible twin of cat. 63

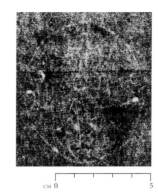

CAT. 55a

1785

IHS in a circle

Gaudriault 735

Heawood 2952, 2981, 2997, 3310

Closely related to cat. 26

CAT. 55d

1785

FIN / T DUPVY / AUVERGNE 1742

Identical to cat. 55h; closely related to cat. 55f

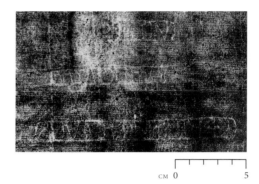

CAT. 55f

1785

FIN / T DUPVY / AUVERGNE 1742

Closely related to cats. 55d and 55h

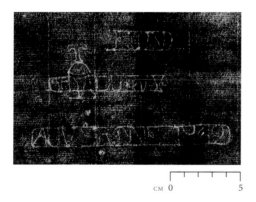

CAT. 55h

1785

FIN / T DUPVY / AUVERGNE 1742

Identical to cat. 55d; closely related to cat. 55f

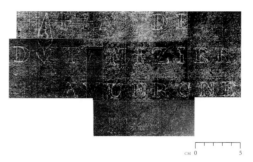

CAT. 57

1786

FIN DE / D TAMIZIER / AVUERGNE / 1783

Counterfeit: see also cats. 16b, 44, and 45; compare to cat. 36

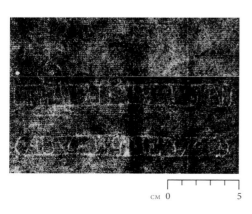

CAT. 58a

1786

T DUPVY FIN / AUVERGNE 1742

Heawood 1233, 1234, 1317

Identical to cat. 78

CAT. 58b

1786

Dovecote

Identical to cat. 67

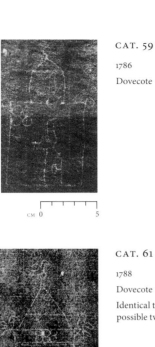

CAT. 59

1786

Dovecote

CAT. 60

1787

Dovecote

Possible twin of
cats. 61 and 66

CAT. 61

1788

Dovecote

Identical to cat. 66;
possible twin of cat. 60

CAT. 63

1787

T DUPVY / AUVERGNE
1742

Possible twin of cat. 54

CAT. 64

1787

FIN DE / D TAMIZIER /
AUVERGNE / 178[?]

Heawood 1320A, 1314

CAT. 65

1787

Dovecote

Heawood 1237

Closely related to
cats. 49b and 52b

CAT. 66

1787

Dovecote

Identical to cat. 61;
possible twin of cat. 60

CAT. 67

1787

Dovecote

Identical to cat. 58b

CAT. 74

1788/1789

Dovecote

Heawood 1233

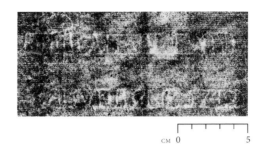

CAT. 78

1789

T DUPVY FIN /
AUVERGNE 1742

Heawood 1233, 1234, 1317

Identical to cat. 58a

CAT. 79

c. 1789

G. de R. IM-HOF

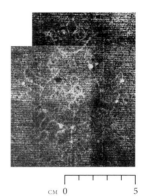

CAT. 84

1792

Double-headed eagle

CAT. 85

c. 1793

Double-headed eagle

Heawood 1317

Possible countermark:
T DUPUY FIN

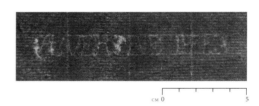

CAT. 87

1794

AUVERGNE 1742

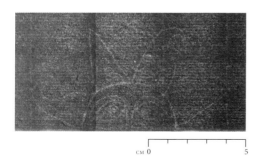

CAT. 90

c. 1795

Sun

CAT. 95

c. 1798

Sun

Essay Notes

Color Printmaking before 1730

1. For some reproductions of uncolored fifteenth-century woodcuts, see Richard S. Field, *Fifteenth Century Woodcuts and Metalcuts from the National Gallery of Art* (Washington, [1965]), pls. 51–53, 55, 62, 122, 158, 207, 227.

2. See Susan Dackerman in *Painted Prints, The Revelation of Color in Northern Renaissance & Baroque Engravings, Etchings & Woodcuts* [exh. cat., The Baltimore Museum of Art](Baltimore, 2002), 11, 19, 29, 30.

3. For several very elaborately colored engravings from the sixteenth century, see Baltimore 2002, figs. 5, 9, 10, 12–14, and nos. 26–28.

4. For other examples of colored metalcuts, see Field [1965], nos. 296–365, most of which have at least a touch of color. Field, in Baltimore 2002, 92, articulates the different roles that color plays in woodcuts and metalcuts: in woodcuts, color stands out as a prominent part of the composition and maintains a substantial, physical presence within the image; in metalcuts, color usually enhances the decorative aspects of the design and tends to merge into the background.

5. The practice of hand coloring black-and-white prints never died out completely and is still used by artists today. It returned to favor periodically over the years, as tastes changed and innovations in printing techniques warranted—toward the end of the color print phenomenon of the eighteenth century, for example. For the most recent research on hand coloring in northern prints of the Renaissance and baroque, see Baltimore 2002.

6. For a discussion of the first woodcuts with printed color, see Arthur M. Hind, *An Introduction to a History of Woodcut*, 2 vols. (Boston and New York, 1935), 2:274, 275, 299–302 462, fig. 110; Andrew Robison in *Paper in Prints* [exh. cat., National Gallery of Art](Washington, 1977), 50, note 43; David Landau and Peter Parshall, *The Renaissance Print, 1470–1550* (New Haven and London, 1994), 180. An unpublished manuscript by Albert Haemmerle, *Der Farbstich—Seine Anfaenge und seine Entwicklung bis zum Iahre MDCCLXV* (1937), includes a brief but useful summary of early multicolored woodcuts, page 1, note 1. My thanks go to Armin Kunz for giving a copy of this manuscript to the National Gallery.

7. Field [1965], no. 248, was inclined to believe the 1494 woodcut by Burgkmair was hand colored with the aid of stencils, but careful examination under a microscope shows the color was printed from multiple blocks. Walter Strauss, in *Chiaroscuro, The Clair-Obscur Woodcuts by the German and Netherlandish Masters of the XVIth and XVIIth Centuries* (Greenwich, Conn., 1973), page VII, likens the use of color in Ratdolt's illustrations to stained glass.

8. Diam. 106, National Gallery of Art, New Century Gift Committee 1999.27.1. Reproduced in *Art for the Nation: Collecting for a New Century* [exh. cat., National Gallery of Art](Washington, 2000), 129.

9. Suzanne Boorsch has kindly brought to my attention four prints in red ink by Antonio Fantuzzi and Léon Davent in the collection of the Metropolitan Museum of Art (personal communication, 18 May 2003). According to Boorsch, two of the Metropolitan Museum's prints, *Psyche* by Davent and *God Seated on the World* by Fantuzzi, bear watermarks that indicate that these red impressions were pulled at Fontainebleau in the mid-sixteenth century. Although such color prints from the Fontainebleau School must be authentic, similar red-ink impressions of prints by Rembrandt and Callot were probably pulled well after the deaths of the artists, perhaps even in the eighteenth century. Such "false rarities" were then sold at premium prices to print collectors. For some years, Andrew Robison has collected research on these and other impostures in printmaking, and I am grateful to him for sharing his knowledge on the subject with me. See Robison in Washington 1977, 51, and Margaret Morgan Grasselli, "Rococo and Neoclassicism," in Andrew Robison, ed., *Dürer to Diebenkorn: Recent Acquisitions of Art on Paper* [exh. cat., National Gallery of Art](Washington, 1992), 28, 29.

    The Fontainebleau prints may have been preceded in Italy by some earlier experimental engravings in colored inks: Boorsch has pointed out an impression in blue ink of a print by Nicoletto da Modena, *The Fate of an Evil Tongue* in the Metropolitan Museum, New York. Black-ink impressions of that print date from c. 1507; the blue-ink impression may well have been published at about the same time, though the date must remain in question until the paper on which it is printed can be carefully studied.

10. I am indebted to Arthur Vershbow for pointing out the use of color in this publication. According to Ruth Mortimer, *Harvard College Library Department of Printing and Graphic Arts, Catalogue of Books and Manuscripts: Italian 16th Century Books* , 2 vols. (Cambridge, 1974), 1: 319, one of the Houghton Library's two copies of Gualterotti's festival book has five of the sixteen images printed in red ink and eight printed in green ink. (The second copy is printed only in black ink.) The Library of Congress in Washington also has two copies, both of which were recently examined by Andrew Robison. One of those copies is also printed only in black ink, but the other is even more colorful than the one in the Houghton Library: seven of the plates are printed in red ink and four are printed in green, while two others are printed in blue and three are print in bluish-green ink. A copy formerly in the Otto Schafer collection also had all sixteen plates printed in color.

11. One of the earliest drawings in the collection of the National Gallery of Art is on prepared paper: Franco-Flemish, *Death of the Virgin*, c. 1390, silverpoint on blue-green prepared paper, 291 × 400, Rosenwald Collection 1950.20.2.

12. Mair's technique continued to be used by a few printmakers who wished to individualize some impressions of their prints, especially in the circle of Parmigianino in the 1520s and 1530s. An etching printed on prepared paper and heightened with white by Schiavone, *Christ Healing the Sick*, 1543–1546, is reproduced in *Italian Etchers of the Renaissance & Baroque* [exh. cat., Museum of Fine Arts](Boston, 1989), no. 13.

13. For a detailed discussion of these prints and the origins of chiaroscuro woodcuts, see Landau and Parshall 1994, 184–190, figs. 195, 197–199 (all in color).

14. An excellent reference on late sixteenth- and early seventeenth-century chiaroscuro prints by Netherlandish artists is *Chiaroscuro Woodcuts, Hendrick Goltzius and His Time* [exh. cat., Rijksmuseum Rijksprentenkabinet](Amsterdam, 1992), by Nancy Bialler. Thirty-four chiaroscuro prints by and attributed to Goltzius, many in two or more impressions with different color schemes, are reproduced (nos. 22–55). Examples by Büsinck and Jegher are also reproduced, figs. 143, 147, 148.

15. For Jackson's chiaroscuro woodcuts, see Jacob Kainen, *John Baptist Jackson, 18th-Century Master of the Color Woodcut* (Washington, 1962). For Zanetti's, see Caroline Karpinski, ed., *The Illustrated Bartsch: Italian Chiaroscuro Woodcuts, 48 (Formerly Vol. 12)* (New York, 1983), 271–342.

16. Hand-colored woodcut on blue paper, 293 × 212, National Gallery of Art, Print Purchase Fund (Mr. and Mrs. J. Watson Webb) 1979.63.1. I am grateful to Andrew Robison for calling my attention to this print, which constitutes an important revision to his essay in Washington 1977. As early as 1514, a few books were printed on blue paper by Aldus Manutius, but the first illustrated book printed on blue paper was not published until 1540. See Robison in Washington 1977, 33. As Robison points out, colored or dyed papers (other than buffs and light browns) were always blue prior to the eighteenth century because indigo appears to have been the only dye that could hold up to the chemicals used in the papermaking process. Blue-dyed work clothing was apparently the main source for the color in old blue papers.

17. The National Gallery owns two prints on blue paper by Master F.P., *Endymion* and *Woman Carrying a Tray* (inv. nos. 1979.24.3, 1977.46.1). Another print on blue paper by Master F.P., *Hercules and Cerberus*, is illustrated in Boston 1989, no. 11.

18. Among the impressions on blue paper in the collection of the National Gallery are the Fontainebleau School *Dance of the Dryades*, which may have been made as early as 1550 (inv no. 1976.80.1); an etching by Angiolo Falconetto, *Decorative Panel with Mythological Figures*

(1978.97.7; reproduced in Boston 1989, no. 22); and two woodcuts by or attributed to Goltzius, *Cliff on the Seashore* (with hand-applied white highlights; 1981.24.2) and *Arcadian Landscape* (1950.1.70). For reproductions of several blue-paper prints by Goltzius, see Amsterdam 1992, under nos. 22–24, 49–55, 57, 60–62. Also illustrated in that catalogue are some earlier prints on blue paper by Dirck Volkertsz. Coornheert from 1553 and 1556 (173, 174, figs. 93–95) and an etching on blue paper by Esaias van de Velde from the early years of the seventeenth century (192, fig. 110).

19. Etching and woodblock, 276 x 407, Museum of Fine Arts, Boston, inv. no. 61.1211 (reproduced in Boston 1989, no. 10).

20. Prints of this type by Beccafumi are reproduced in color in Landau and Parshall 1994, figs. 291, 293, 297, 299.

21. Several chiaroscuro prints in this combination of intaglio and woodcut by Goltzius, Van den Broeck, and a member of the school of Frans Floris are illustrated in Amsterdam 1992, nos. 2, 9–14, 17–21. Prints in the same technique by or after Abraham and Frederick Bloemaert are illustrated in Strauss 1973, nos. 143, 165–170, 172–173.

22. At about the same time in England, Arthur Pond used the same technique to make prints after drawings. One after Parmigianino is reproduced in color in Bamber Gascoigne, *How to Identify Prints* (London, 1986), pl. 81. In Italy several years later, also in color reproductions of drawings, Andrea Scacciati and Stefano Mulinari replaced the woodblocks with intaglio tone plates, worked with either sulphur tint or aquatint and then burnished to create highlights. One example by Scacciati is reproduced in Evelina Borea, "Per i primi cataloghi figurati delle raccolte d'arte nel Settecento," in *Il segno che dipinge* (Bologna, 2002), 85, fig. 9. Borea reproduces five others by Mulinari in "Per la fortuna dei primitivi: La *Istoria Pratica* di Stefano Mulinari e la *Venezia Pittrice* di Gian Maria Sasso,"in *Hommage à Michel Laclotte, Études sur la peinture du Moyen Age et de la Renaissance* (Milan, 1994), 504–506, figs. 576–580.

23. These prints are reproduced in *L'Anatomie de la couleur: L'Invention de l'estampe en couleurs* [exh. cat., Bibliothèque nationale de France and Musée Olympique] (Paris and Lausanne, 1996), nos. 35, 36. Alvin L. Clark discusses Perrier's prints in *François Perrier, Reflections on the Earlier Works from Lanfranco to Vouet* [exh. cat., Galerie Eric Coatelem](Paris, 2001), 21–23, 39.

24. Three are reproduced in Paris and Lausanne 1996, no. 37. Bosse explained the process used in these prints *en camayeux* (in the style of cameos) in his treatise *De la Manière de graver a l'eau forte et de la gravure en manière noire* (Paris, 1745), 74, 75. The text is transcribed in Paris and Lausanne 1996, 41, note 4.

25. For Seghers' prints, see Egbert Haverkamp Begemann, *Hercules Seghers* (Amsterdam, 1968).

26. 265 × 215, Rijksprentenkabinet, Amsterdam, inv. no. H. 361 (reproduced in Paris and Lausanne 1996, 45, no. 38). For information on the development of aquatint in the eighteenth century, see Antony Griffiths, "Notes on Early Aquatint in England and France," *Print Quarterly* 4, no. 3 (September 1987), 255–270.

27. Fifty-two color prints from Teyler's workshop are reproduced in *Farbige Graphik* [exh. cat., C. G. Boerner](Düsseldorf, 1999), nos. 11–62.

28. See *Mary Cassatt: The Color Prints* [exh. cat., Williams College Museum] (Williamstown, Mass., 1989).

"An Exact Imitation Acquired at Little Expense"

1. "La Gravure supplée à l'inégalité des fortunes en satisfaisant les amateurs de toutes les classes. Les souverains, les grands, les hommes opulens, possedent les tableaux, et le public en jouit à son tour par une imitation exacte, et acquise à peu de frais." Charles-François Joullain, *Réflexions sur la peinture et la gravure* (Paris, 1786), 31. Unless otherwise noted, all translations are my own. I would like to thank Jane Boyd, Paul Cohen, Margaret Morgan Grasselli, Rena Hoisington, Graham Larkin, Karen Sherry, John Shovlin, Perrin Stein, and Pamela Warner for their advice and assistance in the preparation of this essay.

2. There is a vast literature on the subject of eighteenth-century journals. For a succinct summary, see Jean Sgard, "La Multiplication des périodiques," in Roger Chartier and Henri-Jean Martin, *Histoire de l'édition française: Le Livre triomphant, 1660–1830* (Paris, 1989), 246–255. For discussions of individual journals, see the entries in Jean Sgard et al., *Dictionnaire des journaux, 1600–1789*, 2 vols. (Paris, 1991).

3. Christopher Todd, "French Advertising in the Eighteenth Century," *Studies in Voltaire and the Eighteenth Century* 266 (1989): 532 and 546.

4. Cissie Fairchilds, "Populuxe Goods in Eighteenth-Century Paris," in *Consumption and the World of Goods*, eds. John Brewer and Roy Porter (London and New York, 1993), 228–248; for her definition of populuxe, see 228–231.

5. "Plusieurs personnes venues d'Angleterre depuis peu de temps parlent d'un habile Peintre nommé le Blond, qui a imaginé & trouvé l'Art admirable d'imprimer des portraits & des tableaux peints à l'huile, avec la même précision, la même regularité, la même exactitude que s'ils étoient faits au pinceau." *Mercure de France* (June/July 1721): 115–116.

6. John Lord Percival, first earl of Egmont, to his brother, 2 November 1721, cited in Otto Lilien, *Jacob Christoph Le Blon, 1667–1741: Inventor of Three- and Four-Colour Printing* (Stuttgart, 1985), 40.

7. Lilien 1985, 40–43.

8. "Le Burin est ici déguisé si parfaitement, & le tout paroît si bien être l'ouvrage du Pinceau, que plusieurs personnes s'y sont méprisés en ma présence." *Le Pour et contre* 17 (1739): 265–266.

9. "Son utilité fut constatée par les Copies des Tableaux les plus recherchés, qu'on pouvoit désormais avoir presque pour rien, & par les *Portraits* des Souverains & Hommes Célèbres qu'on pourroit dans la suite facilement transmettre à la Posterité, & répandre par tout le Monde, non avec cet air efacé & simplement blanc & noir de la *Gravure ordinaire*, qui n'immortalise, en quelque sorte, que des morts; mais avec leurs traits les plus animés, la *nouvelle Gravure* pouvant aussi bien que le Pinceau des Peintres donner de la Vie à ses Figures." *Le Pour et contre* 17 (1739): 268.

10. "Un amour peut-être trop tendre pour les beaux Arts, ne nous aveugle point; comme Portrait, ce morceau ne peut être pas entierement parfait, quoique tout le monde en paroisse content, mais il s'agit du nouvel Art, de l'Art de peindre avec trois couleurs, sans pinceau, par le moyen du Burin & de l'impression, & de l'avantage qu'il y aura desormais, 1º. de multiplier les Tableaux & les Portraits, 2º. de les avoir à des prix très-modiques; 3º. d'avoir, par ce moyen, quelque chose d'assés fini, qui

puisse décorer & faire quelque plaisir à la vûë." *Mercure de France* (September 1739): 2,214.

11. The price was announced in the *Observations sur les écrits modernes* 19 (1739): 70, where it is implied, perhaps in comparison with the prices readers were led to expect, that 15 livres is rather high: "Ces sortes d'estampes ne peuvent produire que 200 exemplaires; ce qui fait qu'on les vend 15 liv." This price would put the print well out of reach of the laboring poor in France, who, according to Jean Sgard's estimates for the period 1726 to 1790, earned 100 to 300 livres annually, and of most manual laborers, whose annual income is estimated by Sgard to range between 300 and 1,000 livres. See Jean Sgard, "L'Échelle des revenus," *Dix-huitième siècle* 14 (1982): 425–433.

12. *Mercure de France* (August 1737): 1803–1804. See also, *Observations sur les écrits modernes* 14 (1738): 309.

13. Compare a varnished color mezzotint after Raphael by Le Blon reproduced in Carol Wax, *The Mezzotint: History and Technique* (New York, 1996), 163, with an unvarnished version of the same print reproduced in Florian Rodari et al., *L'Anatomie de la couleur: L'Invention de l'estampe en couleurs* [exh. cat., Bibliothèque nationale de France and Musée Olympique] (Paris and Lausanne, 1996), 69. Line engravings were frequently varnished as well. Such a protective measure obviated the need to frame prints under glass.

14. Lilien remarks that these color separations are the most frequently encountered prints by Le Blon today, and suggests that this high rate of survival attests to their popularity with eighteenth-century consumers. Lilien 1985, 71.

15. *Mercure de France* (August 1737): 1803–1804; *Observations sur les écrits modernes* 14 (1738): 309.

16. See Corinne Le Bitouzé, "Une entreprise familiale," in Paris and Lausanne 1996, 100–105. The printmaker Jacques-Fabien Gautier Dagoty was initially known by the surname Gautier. Early in his career, he added his mother's surname, Dagoty, in part to distinguish himself from his contemporary Antoine Gautier de Montdorge. However, Jacques-Fabien is commonly referred to (in this essay and in other sources) by the shorter form of Gautier.

17. *Mercure de France* (December 1741): 2,926–2,927. An impression of the shell is reproduced in Paris and Lausanne 1996, 109.

18. *Mercure de France* (December 1741): 2,926–2,927. Since 1 sol was equivalent to ¹⁄₂₀ of a livre, the price of 10 sols for a "printed painting" was low indeed. The exact dimensions of Gautier's "canvases" are taken from a subsequent advertisement in the *Mercure de France* (August 1742): 1,841–1,842.

19. In 1748, the French connoisseur Louis Petit de Bachaumont explained that paintings executed on *toiles de measures* were preferable because ready-made frames could easily be purchased for them: "A l'égard des tableaux des peintres vivants qu'on rassembleroit ou qu'on leur commanderoit, il faudroit toujours leur commander de les faire sur des toiles que les peintres appellent toiles de mesures, parce que on trouve des bordures de ces mesures toutes faites. Ainsi, on jouiroit plus tôt que s'il falloit les faire exprès et de fausses mesures." Louis Petit de Bachaumont, "Conseils d'un ami des arts au roi de Prusse, Frédéric II," *Revue universelle des arts* 3 (1856): 355.

20. "les coller sur toile, les tendre sur un Chassis, & les vernir." *Mercure de France* (December 1741): 2,927.

21. *Mercure de France* (December 1741): 2,927.

22. This was not Gautier's innovation. Line engravers throughout the century marketed their prints as pendants as well.

23. See Colin B. Bailey, "Conventions of the Eighteenth-Century *Cabinet de tableaux*: Blondel d'Azincourt's *La Première idée de la curiosité*," *Art Bulletin* 69 (1987): 441–443.

24. *Mercure de France* (January 1743): 149–150.

25. "Ces estampes de nouvelle invention sortent de la presse avec toutes leurs couleurs, representant le vrai tableau peint à l'huile; elles sont à l'épreuve du tems." *Observations sur les écrits modernes* 29 (1742): 359–360.

26. "[Les Tableaux] ont non seulement le coloris de chaque Peintre dont les Tableaux sont gravés, mais ils ont la force & le moëlleux de ces mêmes Tableaux. Il n'y paroît aucun coup de burin; ils sont exactement conformes aux Tableaux d'après lesquels ils ont été gravés, en un mot ils trompent le premier coup d'oeil des Connoisseurs." *Mercure de France* (March 1745): 144.

27. "Ce sont de fort jolis ornemens pour des cabinets, surtout dans les maisons de campagne." *Observations sur les écrits modernes* 29 (1742): 359–360.

28. *Mercure de France* (August 1742): 1,843.

29. *Observations sur les écrits modernes* 30 (1742): 238.

30. *Mercure de France* (May 1745): 118.

31. Olivier Bonfait, "Les Collections des parlementaires parisiens du XVIIIe siècle," *Revue de l'art* 73 (1986): 30; Annik Pardailhé-Galabrun, *The Birth of Intimacy: Privacy and Domestic Life in Early Modern Paris* (Philadelphia, 1991), 153–164.

32. Jean Chatelus, "Thèmes picturaux dans les appartements de marchands et artisans parisiens au XVIIIe siècle," *Dix-huitième siècle* 6 (1974): 322; Pardailhé-Galabrun 1991, 162–163. It is not impossible that some of Gautier's framed and varnished color mezzotints were mistaken for paintings in eighteenth-century estate inventories.

33. "Je vous en fait mon compliment [de l'empressement du Public à acheter vos ouvrages], & je souhaite de tout mon coeur qu'elle soit bien fondée sur la vérité. Ce qui pourroit la rendre douteuse, c'est l'activité que vous avez à réveiller le Public, apparemment endormi, par des annonces récidivées." *Mercure de France* (March 1756): 200.

34. Though Gautier Dagoty *père* announced no new printed paintings, he did continue to sell impressions of them. In an announcement in 1762 for a new set of anatomical prints, he noted that in his shop "on y trouvera aussi les tableaux imprimées en couleurs d'après les plus grands maîtres, par le même auteur." *L'Avant-Coureur* (10 January 1762): 20.

35. "le corps humain y est enfin représenté d'après nature; sans l'horreur qu'inspire ordinairement la présence du sujet, ni l'odeur pestilentielle qu'il exhale, on a l'avantage de le posséder tel qu'il est." *Mercure de France* (July 1751): 164.

36. "Cette édition est faite pour les Hôpitaux, les Amphithéâtres, les Académies & Sales de Démonstrations publiques.... L'Auteur, qui veut rendre son ouvrages à la portée de tout le monde, à cause de son utilité presque générale, distribue en même tems aux souscripteurs... sa moyenne édition." *L'Avant-Coureur* (5 March 1770): 145–146.

37. "On sçait qu' Albertdure & Marc-Antoine, ces Graveurs si célèbres, s'attachoient à contrefaire parfaitement le crayon, en gravant les Desseins de Raphaël & d'autres grands hommes. Mais quelques efforts qu'ils fissent, ils ne pouvoient éviter la sécheresse du travail de la gravûre.

Le coup de crayon laisse comme des traces légères & imparfaites occasionnées par le grain du papier qui en émousse la pointe; c'est là sur-tout ce qu'il étoit difficile d'imiter.... Vous pouvez juger vous-même, Monsieur, du succès de son entreprise par l'inspection du premier Recueil qu'il vient de publier, composé de six estampes, ou plutôt de six Desseins; car l'illusion est parfaite, & vous croiriez qu'ils ont été faits au crayon." *L'Année litteraire* (24 September 1757): 191.

38. "La gravure en Taille-douce n'étant pas suffisante par elle-même pour rendre le doux, le gras & le moëlleux de l'Estampe, qui décèle si merveilleusement l'esprit & les finesses d'un Original.... Par ce nouvel art, un habile Dessinateur peut rendre entierement la franchise du trait & de toutes les parties d'un Original de Grand-Maître: objet si précieux & si intéressant pour les Eléves! Au lieu que par la méthode ordinaire, il n'est pas possible de rendre la franchise entiere du trait, quelqu'habile que l'on suppose l'Artiste: il ne peut éviter de répandre dans son ouvrage, une molesse dans l'expression & un froid sur l'esprit de l'Original." *Mercure de France* (December 1761): 155 and 157.

39. "Cette découverte est en effet d'une grande utilité pour perpétuer les desseins des grands Maîtres, & mettre aux mains des élèves, tant à Paris que dans les provinces, les meilleurs originaux, rendus d'une manière beaucoup plus propre à les former au bon goût du dessein, qu'ils ne le pourroient être par la gravure ordinaire." *Mercure de France* (October 1757), 2:185.

40. The free drawing schools were founded on the premise that educating craftsmen in drawing would help to maintain the high standards of the French luxury trades. Unlike academic students, pupils of the *écoles gratuites* were restricted to copying and not permitted to draw from the live model. See Ulrich Leben, "New Light on the École Royale Gratuite de Dessin: The Years 1766–1815," *Studies in the Decorative Arts* 1 (1993): 101, and Reed Benhamou, "Private and Public Art Education in France, 1648–1793," *Studies on Voltaire and the Eighteenth Century* 308 (1993): 38–39.

41. "Pour apprendre à dessiner, il est nécessaire de copier les Desseins des grands maîtres; mais ces Desseins sont fort rares, fort chers, & ceux qui en possèdent ont beaucoup de répugnance à les prêter, parce que les élèves les gâtent, les usent, & les perdent souvent. De combien de morceaux précieux, d'excellens originaux, dignes d'être conservés à la Posterité, ne sommes-nous pas privés, faute de quelque invention heureuse qui pût imiter & multiplier les chefs-d'oeuvres du crayon!" *L'Année litteraire* (24 September 1757): 190–191.

42. As Demarteau noted, an additional advantage of chalk-manner prints over drawings was that prints could not be erased: "ces estampes ne s'effacent point, expérience faite avec la mie de pain." *L'Avant-Coureur* (25 May 1767): 323.

43. Diderot held this opinion: "Those who draw after regular engravings [as opposed to chalk-manner] develop styles that are hard, dry, and overly systematic." *Diderot on Art. I. The Salon of 1765 and Notes on Painting*, trans. John Goodman (New Haven and London, 1995), 181.

44. *La Feuille nécessaire* (14 May 1759): 214.

45. *L'Avant-Coureur* (25 May 1767): 323.

46. *L'Avant-Coureur* (23 March 1761): 184.

47. *Mercure de France* (January 1762): 131–132; *L'Avant-Coureur* (13 September 1762): 589.

48. "Elles...conviennent aux personnes du beau Sexe qui s'adonnent au dessein." *Mercure de France* (February

1762): 157. This rare example of a print advertisement directed explicitly toward women suggests Magny perceived there to be a market of draftswomen substantial enough to merit niche marketing.

49. "La plûpart de ceux qui l'ont tenté n'ont produit que des copies informes & mêmes dangereuses pour les élèves qui en auroient fait l'objet de leurs études; mais ce que je viens d'observer ne regarde nullement Madame Lingée." *L'Année littéraire* 1 (1777): 284. Lingée's heads were also announced in the *Affiches, annonces et avis divers* (*Affiches de province*) (23 April 1777): 67, hereafter *Affiches de province*.

50. "Les artistes peuvent se procurer ces gravures à très bon compte, & prendre le goût du grand & du beau, c'est une voie de communication ouverte entr'eux & les grands hommes qui sont à la tête des arts." *L'Avant-Coureur* (4 May 1761): 284–285.

51. Demarteau's print after François Boucher's *Education of Cupid* was described as "fait pour plaire également aux jeunes artistes & aux amateurs." *L'Avant-Coureur* (23 March 1761): 184. For the print, see Jean-Richard 604.

52. "Ces nouvelles estampes forment les numéros 344 & 345 de l'oeuvre de cet artiste." *Mercure de France* (November 1772): 175; *L'Avant-Coureur* (12 October 1772): 641. The prints represented a group of angels (see *IFF* 6:344) and a Leda with cupids (Jean-Richard 820).

53. See Joachim Wasserschlebe to Johann Georg Wille, Copenhagen, 26 January 1762, in *Johann Georg Wille (1715–1808): Briefwechsel*, eds. Elisabeth Decultot, Michel Espagne, and Michael Werner (Tübingen, 1999), 258.

54. On Boucher's drawings for the market see Beverly Schreiber Jacoby, "François Boucher's Stylistic Development as a Draftsman: The Evolution of his Autonomous Drawings," in *Drawings Defined*, eds. Walter Strauss and Tracie Felker (New York, 1987), 259–279.

55. "Elles se vendent aussi collées comme les desseins." *L'Avant-Coureur* (25 May 1767): 323.

56. "Elle représente une jeune personne, qui, la tête légerement appuyée sur une de ses mains, goûte les douceurs du sommeil; mais rien n'indique que ce soit Vénus; on n'apperçoit ni ses colombes, ni l'Amour qui sert ordinairement à désigner la Déesse de la Beauté." *L'Avant-Coureur* (16 December 1771): 785. For the print, see Jacques Hérold, *Louis-Marin Bonnet (1736–1793), Catalogue de l'oeuvre gravé* (Paris, 1935), 89, no. 62.

57. Bonfait 1986, 28–42. Bonfait's study charts the rise of drawings and pastels, after midcentury, in the homes of socially prominent, though not always affluent, parliamentarians. By contrast, as Chatelus' study of inventories from 1726 to 1759 shows, drawings were completely absent from the homes of Parisian wholesale merchants and artisans though pastels became increasingly prevalent. Chatelus 1974, 316 and 324. It would be interesting to know if drawings began to appear in such homes after 1759. For pastels as interior decoration, see also Pardailhé-Galabrun 1991, 160.

58. "C'est en même temps un Dessein d'étude & une Estampe qui fait tableau." *Mercure de France* (April 1758): 163.

59. "Ce n'est pas un dessin, une estampe: c'est un tableau des mieux composés & des plus agréables." *L'Année litteraire* (20 December 1766): 212. See also *Mercure de France* (January 1767): 164–165, and especially *L'Avant-Coureur* (5 January 1767): 3–5, where a set of rhetorical questions—"Est-ce une estampe? Est-ce une dessein?"—emphasizes the illusionism of the print. For the print, see *IFF* 6:380, no. 141.

60. The term "wall power" was used by Beverly Schreiber Jacoby to describe Boucher's adaptation of his drawing style to the formal requirements of display. See Schreiber Jacoby 1987, 271.

61. "La Tête est d'une grandeur suffisante, pour être vue & bien démêlé, même parmi des Tableaux ou de grands morceaux de Gravûre, dans quelque lieu que ce soit.... une espece de Tableau colorié qui a de l'effet." *Affiches de province* (5 August 1767): 123.

62. Earlier in the century, Le Blon's color mezzotint portrait of Louis XV was deemed suitable for interior decoration because of its finish. See note 10.

63. See Regina Shoolman Slatkin, "Some Boucher Drawings and Related Prints," *Master Drawings* 10 (1972): 264–283, and Schreiber Jacoby 1987, 277.

64. Antony Griffiths, "The Search for the Facsimile," in Michel Melot et al., *Prints: History of an Art* (Geneva and New York, 1981), 164–165. See Victor Carlson et al., *Regency to Empire: French Printmaking, 1715–1814* [exh. cat., Baltimore Museum of Art] (Baltimore, 1984), 136, where the modifications are attributed to Boucher.

65. "Ce dessein avoit paru dans le dernier Sallon, où il avait fait l'admiration de tous les connoisseurs." *Mercure de France* (April 1758): 163.

66. On François and Varin's early experiments, see Hérold 1935, 6.

67. "Cette estampe, ou plutôt ce dessein." *L'Avant-Coureur* (18 May 1767): 305.

68. See note 57.

69. "Ces deux têtes sont...dignes d'interesser les amateurs." *Mercure de France* (November 1767): 184. See also *Affiches de province* (7 October 1767): 159, and *L'Avant-Coureur* (12 October 1767): 642. For the prints, see Hérold 1935, 60, no. 9, 2d state, and 61, no. 10.

70. "Cette imitation du Pastel entier avec toutes ses teintes claires & obscures, fait illusion & ne le céde point aux tableaux pour la fraîcheur, ni pour la vivacité des couleurs. Un agrément que les amateurs y trouveront de plus, c'est que cette fraîcheur ne peut être altérée, soit en roulant l'estampe, soit en la transportant dans un porte-feuille, puisque ce qui est d'impression ne peut s'effacer." *L'Avant-Coureur* (3 July 1769): 419–420. The prevalence of advertisements for pastel fixatives in the French press, particularly after midcentury, testifies to the increasing popularity of pastels and suggests that the durability of the medium was a pressing issue.

71. Framed and glazed pastel-manner prints could even deceive more experienced eyes: when the framed impression of Bonnet's *Tête de Flore* (fig. 5) entered the collection of the Victoria and Albert Museum in 1882, it was initially catalogued as a pastel. I am very grateful to Liz Miller and Katharine Donaldson of the Victoria and Albert Museum for examining the print and for sharing this information.

72. Printing a pastel-manner print in two colors, and therefore with only two of the original five or so plates, was an ingenious way for Bonnet to compensate for wear in the more lightly worked plates. See cats. 9a, 9b, 19 and Baltimore 1984, 198.

73. *Mercure de France* (March 1768):170; *L'Avant-Coureur* (1 February 1768): 66; Hérold 1935, 63–64, no. 16.

74. Hérold 1935, 26–27.

75. See Carol Sargentson, *Merchants and Luxury Markets: The Marchands Merciers of Eighteenth-Century Paris* (London, 1996), 113–142.

76. Hérold 1935, 26–27; Baltimore 1984, 201–202.

77. The abrupt disappearance, in 1777, of works printed in gold from Bonnet's oeuvre suggests that he was eventually threatened with legal action. See Baltimore 1984, 201–202 and 202, n. 5.

78. Sgard et al. 1991, 2:628.

79. "Le sieur Marin, Graveur à Londres, vient d'inventer un nouveau genre d'Estampes qui imite la miniature, & qui produit l'effet le plus agréable. Il en fait actuellement paroître deux, représentant l'une, une jeune Laitière dans une attitude & un desordre que sa fraîcheur rend très-piquants; l'autre une jeune personne qui prend du caffé.... Ce sont des ovales renfermés dans une bordure qui fait partie de l'Estampe, & qui est enrichie d'or, ainsi que l'Estampe elle-même. On les trouve à Paris, chez Bonnet." *Journal de politique et de littérature* (24 December 1774): 279–280.

80. *Mercure de France* (January 1775): 196. As Antony Griffiths has suggested, it is possible that Bonnet did have an arrangement with Vivares to sell prints in England. See Antony Griffiths, "French Prints for the English Market," *Print Quarterly* 4 (1987): 423.

81. *Mercure de France* (January 1770): 167. The portrait was also announced in *L'Avant-Coureur* (15 January 1770): 34–35. It sold for 3 livres. A few months later, the portrait was also made available in two colors. See *L'Avant-Coureur* (2 April 1770): 209–210. See also Hérold 1935, 79, no. 37².

82. John Gage has pointed out that Claude Boutet's *Traité de la peinture en mignature* (The Hague, 1708) was the first text, in the context of specialist art literature, to clearly expound the idea of three primary colors that formed the basis for Le Blon's theories. See John Gage, "Jacob Christoph Le Blon," *Print Quarterly* 3 (1996): 66. Though it is more likely that Liotard was responding to news of Le Blon's color mezzotints, it is tempting nonetheless to speculate that Liotard, a miniaturist himself, may have been prompted in his experimentation by Boutet's treatise.

83. "Le sieur Liotard, Peintre et Graveur en taille-douce, dont on a vû divers Portraits en Email, qui lui ont acquis de la réputation, vient de trouver un moyen fort ingénieux de multiplier ses Ouvrages en Peinture, par le moyen de trois couleurs et de trois Planches gravées, dont les premiers Essais ont satisfait les Curieux. Ce genre de Peinture peut avoir la fraîcheur du Pastel et la force et la durée de la Peinture à l'huile. Il vient de finir deux Portraits de Mrs. Fontenelle et de Voltaire, de la grandeur de l'ongle, à pouvoir être mis en Bague, qui sont très ressemblans, malgré la petitesse." *Mercure de France* (June 1735): 2:1,392–1,393.

84. In 1775, Hester Thrale, a visiting Englishwoman, was surprised to see "a Sawyer working thro' a Block of Marble with his Muff and Snuff Box lying by him & his Dog to guard them." Hester Lynch Piozzi, *The French Journals of Mrs. Thrale and Dr. Johnson*, eds. Moses Tyson and Henry Guppy (Manchester, 1932), 148. Thrale's observation is also discussed by Fairchilds 1993, 228.

85. Henri Bouchot, "Les Graveurs Demarteau, Gilles et Gilles-Antoine (1722–1802) d'après des documents inédits," *Revue de l'art ancien et moderne* 18 (1905): 100 and 102.

86. "Ce portrait est une jolie miniature que l'on peut placer dans une boîte ou sur un bracelet. Ce portrait peut être aussi mis dans une bordure quarrée en conservant le cartel qui le renferme." *L'Avant-Coureur* (30 April 1770): 274. A second advertisement announced that the medallion could be placed on a large or small box, presumably depending on how closely to the head one trimmed it. *Mercure de France* (May 1770): 187. The portrait sold for 3 livres. For the print see Hérold 1935, 75, no. 34³.

87. *IFF* 12:20, no. 31. It is possible that the very small print in the center of Janinet's sheet was meant for a ring or a bracelet. For the portrait of Bertin, see *IFF* 12:31, no. 61.

88. "La composition de ces Médaillons est neuve, & l'Auteur a tiré la parti le plus avantageux des sujets, de manière qu'ils peuvent servir pour boutons patriotiques, éventails, tabatières, souvenirs et encadremens." *Journal de Paris* (9 July 1790), supplement.

89. See the buttons on the coat of the standing male figure clad in red, at the right of Debucourt's 1792 *La Promenade publique* (cat. 83).

90. Henriette Louise von Waldner Oberkirch, *Mémoires de la Baronne d'Oberkirch*, ed. Léonce de Montbrison (Paris, 1869), 2:310.

91. I have found no evidence of who these purchasers were. It is possible that Janinet, like other color printmakers such as A.-B. Duhamel, produced his prints for the fashion press. See *Modes et révolutions, 1780–1804* [exh. cat., Musée de la Mode et du Costume, Palais Galliera] (Paris, 1989), 110–111, and *IFF* 8:168, no. 267. For Bonnet, see Hérold 1935, 79, no. 37², and 75, no. 34³.

92. Fairchilds 1993, 229. One can also speculate that the purchase of color prints for use on accessories would be a quick and inexpensive way for modish men and women to keep up with changing fashions.

93. The École Royale Gratuite in Paris purchased prints from Demarteau, as well as a chalk-manner printing machine invented by Alexis Magny. See Leben 1993, 118, n. 14, and Jacques Hérold, *Jean-Charles François (1717–1769), Catalogue de l'oeuvre gravé* (Paris, 1931), 45.

94. See Pierre-François Basan, *Catalogue raisonné des différens objets de curiosités dans les sciences et les arts qui composoient le cabinet de feu M. Mariette* (Paris, 1775), print section, lots 894, 974, 984, 996, and 1,100.

95. Pierre Casselle, "Le Commerce des estampes à Paris dans la seconde moitié du XVIIIe siècle" (Ph.D. diss., École nationale des chartes, 1976), 171. Debucourt's print sold for 6 livres. See *Journal de Paris* (29 December 1787): 1,571.

96. Casselle 1976, 172. See also Anne L. Schroder, "Genre Prints in Eighteenth-Century France: Production, Market, and Audience," in Richard Rand et al., *Intimate Encounters: Love and Domesticity in Eighteenth-Century France* [exh. cat., Hood Museum of Art] (Dartmouth, 1997), 82–83.

97. In 1794, Athanase Détournelle deplored the fact that the poor were unable to acquire quality prints of Revolutionary scenes or martyrs, and that instead the "laboureur et le vigneron" had to live with hideously colored woodcuts. He called on legislators to rectify the situation. Athanase Détournelle, "Réflexions sur la gravure," *Aux Armes et aux arts! Journal de la société républicaine des arts* 1 (1794): 289–302.

Ink and Inspiration

1. See the appendix "Paper Used in the Prints: Water-marks and Observations," pages 162–163.

2. Jacques-Fabien Gautier Dagoty, *Lettres concernant le nouvel art de graver et imprimer les tableaux* (Paris, 1749).

3. Antoine Gautier de Montdorge, *L'Art d'imprimer les tableaux* (1756; reprint, Geneva, 1973).

4. Eau-de-vie is a strong clear brandy, such as cognac or Poire William, distilled from fruit or cereal. Immediately after distilling, it has an alcohol content of 70 percent. During aging, about half of that is lost to evaporation (Prosper Montagné, *The New Larousse Gastronomique* [New York, 1977], 894–895). It pleases me that so often in the French manuals, foodstuffs are cited as necessary for printmaking. Strong red wine, vinegar, olive oil, walnut oil, garlic, sea salt, and sugar all appear in the "recipes" for ink, varnish, and grounds. One imagines the French printer sitting down to a long lunch, discussing his technical problems with all gathered around, until finally—after dessert—it occurs to him that eau-de-vie will solve the problem!

5. Alternately, copies of the drawing could be traced on paper with sanguine, and then dampened and offset onto the plate. Because new tracings were required for each plate, good registration was even less likely in this method than in the veil method Montdorge describes (Montdorge 1756, 96–97). Robert Dossi, *Handmaid to the Arts* (London, 1758), 100, offers further criticism of the sanguine method, "it is very difficult to find [chalk] such as is very soft and fat, and will not score or scratch the varnish."

6. Montdorge to the *Journal de Trévoux*, August 1737, in Dagoty 1749, 27–30.

7. Baltimore 1984, pages 100–101.

8. Mouffle writes: "dans le portrait du Roi, il y avait une quatrième planche qui portoit un second bleu pour finier le cordon bleu de ce portrait et quel ques autres teints bleues" (Dagoty 1749, 29). Dagoty describes the overprinting as "glazing," which was needed because the blue of the first plate was too pale (Dagoty 1749, 12). Although the texts do not clearly indicate whether the blue was the same as the first inking, both inks appear to be Prussian blue in our example.

9. Lisha Glinsman and Michael Palmer, conservation scientists in the scientific research department at the National Gallery of Art, very kindly identified the pigments in the prints for this project. Non-destructive elemental analysis was conducted by energy dispersive X-ray fluorescence (XRF). Glinsman did the XRF analysis using a Kevex 0750A spectrophotometer equipped with 6 mm collimators and BaCl₂ target. Data were collected for 100 live-time seconds at a 60 kV anode voltage and 0.4 mA anode current. This data coupled with microscopic examination of the printed areas and their years of experience allowed Palmer and Glinsman to identify pigments found in the prints. All the named pigments described as being in the prints in this essay were determined by them. As in so many other projects undertaken by the conservators at the National Gallery of Art, their analytical contributions were important and graciously rendered.

10. "Stil-de-grain" is a bright yellow color made by laking vegetable tinctures on a white. Strangely, it is known as "brown pink" in English. A high amount of calcium appeared in the red and yellow areas of this print. Chalk white or calcium carbonate is a possible substrate for laked colorants, and is transparent in oil (an additional desirable characteristic). Le Blon also mentions adding a little massicot, a lead-based yellow pigment, to the brown-pink. We found a small amount of lead mixed in with the yellow.

11. Le Blon also recommends the use of ochre and vermilion in his text (Montdorge 1756, 40, 116, 117). These we did not find in this print.

12. Dagoty 1749, 26.

13. Abraham Bosse, *De la manière de graver à l'eau forte et au burin et de la gravûre en manière noire*, ed. Charles-Nicholas Cochin (Paris, 1745), 125.

14. Denis Diderot and Jean-le-Rond d'Alembert, *Encyclopédie, ou dictionnaire raisonné des Sciences, des Arts et des Métiers*, vol. 7 (Paris, 1757), 877–890.

15. The two methods had been shown together previously in Abraham Bosse's etching of 1642, *Engravers* (National Gallery of Art, Washington, Rosenwald Collection 1948.11.35).

16. Diderot 1757, 881.

17. The text was most likely by Benoît-Louis Prévost (c. 1735–1804), an etcher-engraver in Paris.

18. [Benoît-Louis] Prévost, "Gravure, en taille-douce, en manière noire, manière de crayon & etc," in *Recueil de Planches, sur les sciences, les arts libéraux, et les arts mechaniques avec leur explications, quatrième livraison* (4th delivery) (Paris, 1767).

19. Antony Griffiths, "Notes on Early Aquatint in England and France," *Print Quarterly* 4, no. 3 (September 1987), 255. I am grateful to Peter Parshall for sharing this reference with me, and for offering helpful suggestions on an earlier version of this text.

20. Baltimore 1984, pages 195–196.

21. Don Paver and Peter Staple, *Artists' Colourmen's Story* (Middlesex, 1984), 30.

22. "23 roulettes et 157 champignons pour le lavis et le pointillé," from Albert Vuaflart and Jacques Hérold, "Les Procédés de gravure," in *Exposition Debucourt* [exh. cat., Palais du Louvre] (Paris, 1920), 67.

23. William Gilpin, *An Essay on Prints* (London, 1792), 35.

24. Gilpin 1792, 39.

25. Montdorge 1756, 112.

26. The printed areas of the paper seem calendered to a high polish, a phenomenon caused by printing under heavy pressure. Although British mezzotint printers used the same paper, they could not print mezzotints under the same pressure without damaging their plates. Consequently, British mezzotints now show a common damage of ink abrasion on the raised knots of fiber.

27. See "Monsieur Perrier's New Invention," in William Faithorne, *The Art of Graveing and Etching* (London, 1662), n.p., and Dossi 1758, 212.

28. Montdorge 1756, 111–112.

29. Vuaflart and Hérold in Paris 1920, 74.

30. William Savage, *On the Preparation of Printing Inks both Black and Coloured* (London, 1832), 144–145.

31. Savage 1832, 113–114. Some ink recipes call for the oil to be stored in "leaden vessels"—perhaps as another way to introduce lead driers into the oil used for the inks.

32. Griffiths 1987, 255–270.

33. Jules Hédou, *Jean Le Prince et son oeuvre* (Paris, 1879), 179–188.

34. Some authors have not identified aquatint in prints before 1790, but I believe it was used well before that date in the full-spectrum prints. Part of the confusion may come from the effect of the materials used in early aquatints. During the eighteenth century, powdered mastic varnish was sometimes used to create the finest possible ground, which is rarely seen in later prints. T. H. Fielding, *Art of Engraving* (London, 1844), 40, 41, has examples of printed aquatints made from a series of grounds, including mastic. One can hardly credit that the mastic example is really aquatint, it is so even and fine. The telltale aquatint grain is not revealed unless the passage is quite dark and examined under high magnification (100x) with a microscope. The texture might be mistaken for that created by brushing acid etching fluid directly on the plate, a method later known as *lavis*. Such might have been used in these prints but for its extreme fragility; only a very few impressions can be made from brushed acid etches. I did not see any areas that appeared to be direct acid washes in the exhibited prints.

35. M. Stapart, *L'Art de graver au pinceau* (Paris, 1773), 50, 51, 55, 56. His new method was touted as being the "fastest now in use, that can be easily used by those who are not habituated to the burin nor the (etching) needle." Stapart also notes that "salt is cubic, sugar is round, and can be used. If one used sugar rather than sea salt, you avoid the pains of dissolution, filtration and evaporation necessary for sea salt."

36. A proof from the partially worked plate for Philibert-Louis Debucourt's *Le Menuet de la mariée* (cat. 58a) is illustrated in Vuaflart and Hérold in Paris 1920, 73. All the work within the etched outline appears to be engraved with hand tools.

37. Ittmann cites Bonnet as the first to use registration points in 1769 (Baltimore 1984, page 195). Two points are actually sufficient for registration, but most often four were used and they were usually hidden by the engraved black line bordering the images. Debucourt used twenty points in his print *Le Menuet de la mariée* (cat. 58a), proving that additional registration points do not actually improve registration.

38. Dossi 1758, 98–100.

39. For mezzotint, the copperplate was completely roughed up by rocking its surface with a grooved, curved chisel blade, known as a rocker. Working back and forth, with moderate pressure, each sweep of the rocker left a series of small bite marks that was slightly offset from the line just made. The rocking followed a set pattern of four passes: the first two passes were up and down, then across the plate, the second two passes were at diagonals across the plate. The four passes were repeated, rotating the orientation of the plate by one-third for each set. This series of twelve rockings made a "turn." The plate was given twenty turns, or two hundred and forty passes of the rocker. This method was calculated to create a plate that when inked would print completely black. Dossi 1758, 170–178 admits, "The forming of the ground on the plate, which is part of the necessary work, is indeed laborious and tedious: but it may be thrown upon those who are used to such mechanical employments; as it requires little or no skill or judgement…and therefore no proper part of the business of the artist."

40. Dossi 1758, 184.

41. Savage 1832, 145.

42. Dossi 1758, 390–391, suggests isinglass as a mordant for gold leaf on paper. Oil staining in the prints indicates an oil mordant, which mimics contemporary framing techniques. Stephan Wilcox, senior frames conservator at the National Gallery, generously looked at the prints and discussed their gilding with me. His knowledge of the techniques used in eighteenth-century French frame manufacture was invaluable.

43. Dossi 1758, 205, suggests adding a small amount of ox gall, vinegar, and salt to the boiled oil used in inks that were to be printed on gold leaf.
44. The gold in the jug is a different formulation than the gold found in the frame; in the jug, it has more silver and nickel admixed, making it a "whiter" gold.
45. Serge Roche, *Cadres français et étrangers du XVe siècle au XVIIIe siècle: Allemagne, Angleterre, Espagne, France, Italie, Pays-Bas* (Paris, [c. 1931]). I am grateful to Stephan Wilcox for sharing this reference with me.

A Collector's Perspective

1. Leymarie 346, Jean-Richard 821.
2. Leymarie 69, Jean-Richard 636 (*A Young Peasant Woman Seen from Behind*, after Boucher); Leymarie 446, 447 (*The Painter* and *The Sculptor*, after Clermont).
3. Sotheby Parke Bernet, New York, 5–7 December 1974, lot 568.
4. My late brother Neil participated in the purchase of five drawings and watercolors, whose ownership is designated as The Phillips Family Collection in the exhibition and the catalogue.
5. As Campbell Dodgson, a curator at the British Museum, observes in *Old French Colour-Prints* (London, 1924), 2, "The total number of really fine French colour-prints—I am not speaking now of the extant impressions, but of the separate subjects engraved in this manner—is quite small. To state it at fifty is, perhaps, to exaggerate. Outside the number of the really fine things there are many that are negligible, many that are acceptable *faute de mieux*. And nearly all the really fine things were produced in a very limited period—from about 1775 to the Revolution."
6. *IFF* 3:19.
7. Highly deceptive reproductions of the prints were generally made by color gravure and color collotype. Since these are both printing processes, the prints produced with them closely imitate the appearance of the originals. For discussions of these processes, see Bamber Gascoigne, *How to Identify Prints* (New York, 1986), sections 39, 40, 43b–c, 44a; Felix Brunner, *A Handbook of Graphic Reproduction Processes* (New York, 1962), 357; Antony Griffiths, *Prints and Printmaking, Introduction to the History and Techniques* (Berkeley, 1996).
8. The catalogue is cited throughout this volume as Baltimore 1984.
9. *Exposition Debucourt* [exh. cat., Palais du Louvre](Paris, 1920), 5.

Paper Used in the Prints

1. Papers examined for this study have been described using the terminology suggested by Roy Perkinson and Elizabeth Lunning's *Paper Sample Book*, published by the Print Council of America in 1999. Except where noted in the object entries, the sheets were "moderately textured," "moderately thick," "cream or dark cream" laid paper.
2. Joseph Jérôme Le Français de Lalande, *L'Art de faire le papier* (Paris, 1761; reprint, The Scholar Press, privately distributed), 85, paragraph 136.
3. Lalande 1761.
4. A papermill of the Auvergne is illustrated in Lalande 1761, pl. II. The mill is clearly using stampers. The illustration was repeatedly used in other editions until 1791. See *Descriptions des Artes et Métiers, faites approuvèes par MM. le Academie des Sciences* (Paris, 1761; 1762; 1778; 1791).
5. Dard Hunter, *Papermaking; the History and Technique of an Ancient Craft*. 2d ed. (New York, 1947), 115–121.
6. Lalande notes that the quality of the water had much to do with the quality of the sizing in the sheets. Two towns in the Auvergne were noted for paper production, Thiers and Ambert. Thiers sat on a river that contained impurities that allowed more glue to dissolve in it, making a heavier size. Ambert's water came directly from the mountain and was so pure it would not dissolve gelatinous material as readily, making a lighter size. Although Ambert made better, whiter paper, Lalande indicates that Thiers got the better part: the heavier sized writing papers were more marketable and produced a greater profit than the printing papers of Ambert (Lalande 1761, 85).
7. H. Dagnall, *The Taxation of Paper in Great Britain 1643–1861*, The British Association of Paper Historians (Middlesex, 1998), 8–38.
8. Francis Spilsbury, *The Art of Etching and Aqua Tinting* (London, 1794), 27.
9. See C. G. Boerner, Inc., *English Mezzotints from the Lennox-Boyd Collection* (New York, 2002).
10. Peter Bower, *Turner's Papers: A Study of the Manufacture, Selection and Use of His Drawing Paper 1787–1820* (London, 1990), 56–57.
11. John Krill, *English Artists' Paper: Renaissance to Regency* (Winterthur, Del., 2002), 79–92.
12. See the print *The Alpine Traveller* by James Ward after James Northcote. Illustrated in Boerner 2002, 168, no. 77.
13. Bower 1990, 56–57.
14. Lalande 1761, 89–102 (paragraph 146) reprints both the regulations of 1737 and 1741. In Britain the duty on papers changed from year to year. Although paid at the time of use or export, the levy was charged based on the year of manufacture. The dates in British sheets, therefore, had to indicate the calendar year in which the sheets were made (Dagnall 1998).
15. Raymond Gaudriault, *Filigranes et autres caractéristiques des papiers fabriqués en France aux XVII and XVIII siècles* (Paris, 1995), 27.
16. Lalande 1761, 99.
17. Of the fifty-seven watermarks on fifty-five sheets, we were able to obtain images of all but one (cat. 1). For more information on beta-radiography, see Stephen Spector, *Essays in Paper Analysis* (Washington, 1987), 157–159.
18. Nancy Ash and Shelley Fletcher, *Watermarks in Rembrandt's Prints* (Washington, 1998), 13–14.
19. We thank Shelley Fletcher, who looked at some of the watermarks with us and helped in determining their relationship.
20. Edward Heawood, *Watermarks* (Amsterdam, 1970) and Gaudriault 1995.

Glossary

À LA POUPÉE is a method of inking intaglio prints. Two or more inks of different colors are selectively applied to different parts of a single plate so that all the colors can be printed in one pass through the press. The method takes its name from the small ball-shaped wad of fabric, called a *poupée* (doll), that is used to ink the plate. (See cats. 85, 86, 88–91.)

AQUATINT is a tonal printing process. The preparation for aquatint consists of a porous ground, usually created by sprinkling powdered resin liberally and evenly over the plate and then heating the plate from below to liquefy the powder and fuse it to the copper. When this prepared copperplate is dipped into the acid etching bath, the minute irregularities in the ground allow the acid to bite into the plate in an overall pattern that, when inked, prints as tone. (See cats 10, 11, 20, 21.)

BOLE is a very fine gesso or clay mixed with glue that, in gilding, is used to adhere gold leaf to the surface being decorated. Bole can be various colors, including yellow, red, black, or white. In printmaking, Louis-Marin Bonnet invented a kind of liquid bole, either red or white, that could be printed directly onto paper and then gilded by hand. (See cats. 30–34.)

BURNISHING or scraping is a reductive printmaking technique in which work on the copperplate is removed partially (so that the burnished area will print more lightly) or completely (so that no ink will be held by the plate and the area will not print).

CHALK MANNER (also called crayon manner) is a print-making process that imitates the appearance of chalk lines. Chalk-manner prints were made in as many as three colors—black, red, and white—from one or more copperplates worked either in etching or engraving, or in a combination of the two. Toothed tools — roulettes, *mattoirs,* and the like—were used to create dotted patterns on the plate that suggest the grainy appearance of chalk strokes on paper. (For an illustration of some of the tools, see page 25, fig. 2. For some examples of chalk-manner prints, see cats. 5–9b, 13, 14.)

CHIAROSCURO (literally, light-dark) woodcuts are multiple-block relief prints in which one woodblock carries the linear design and one or more others add color and tone. Highlights are reserves of untouched white paper that are created by strategic cutting of the tone block(s).

ENGRAVING is an intaglio printmaking process in which the design is incised directly into the surface of a metal plate, usually copper. The ink is held by the incisions and is transferred to the sheet of paper by means of a printing press.

ETCHING is an intaglio printmaking process in which the design is worked onto a copperplate through a protective, acid-resistant ground. Thus, selected areas of the plate's surface are uncovered. The plate is then bitten by acid, creating furrows and troughs in the exposed areas. The etched plate is inked and printed in the same manner as an engraving.

GROUNDS, hard and soft, are acid-resistant waxy or varnish preparations that are applied to copperplates as part of the etching process. The design is worked through the ground to expose the copperplate beneath. With a hard ground, an etching needle is usually used. With a soft ground, which never hardens completely but remains sticky, a variety of tools can be used to create a design on the plate. The entire plate, still covered by the ground, is then dipped into an acid bath, which corrodes the exposed areas of the plate. The ground is removed before the plate is inked and printed.

INTAGLIO is an Italian word that describes any printing process in which the ink is held in furrows below the surface of a metal plate and is transferred to paper through the application of pressure. Aquatint, mezzotint, etching, and engraving are examples of intaglio printmaking methods.

LAVIS (wash, in French) is a tonal etching method in which acid is brushed directly onto a copperplate. This particular method does not stand up well to the pressure of the press and yields relatively few good impressions.

METALCUT is a relief printmaking method in which a metal plate, usually copper, is used.

MEZZOTINT is a tonal engraving process in which the entire copperplate is roughened by repeated rocking with a curved, grooved blade—called a *berceau* or a rocker—in a regular pattern over the surface. When fully rocked, the inked plate prints as a solid dark tone. The image emerges as the artist creates a range of lights by selectively smoothing the rough surface of the plate with scrapers and burnishers. (See cats. 1–3.)

PASTEL MANNER is a printmaking process that imitates the appearance of pastels. Pastel-manner prints were made in many colors from multiple copperplates worked in the same manner as those used for chalk-manner prints. (See cat. 19.)

RELIEF PRINTING describes any printmaking process in which the parts of the design that will be left blank are cut away, leaving a smooth, raised surface that will hold the ink for printing. Woodcuts and metalcuts are examples of relief prints.

STIPPLE is a dotted tonal printmaking technique in which patterns of dots are made by repeatedly impressing pointed or pronged tools into the copperplate or through an etching ground. (See cats. 53, 54, 86.)

TOOL WORK describes any mark made on the copperplate with steel tools (either directly in engraving or through a ground in etching). When inked and printed, some specific tool work can be identified, such as the work of *mattoirs* and roulettes in chalk manner, points in stipple, or work with a *berceau* in mezzotint. However, most of the work done with the hundreds of available tools is given the generic designation "tool work" or "work with tools" because the specific tool used cannot be determined.

WASH MANNER is a printmaking process that employs any tonal intaglio technique or combination of tonal intaglio techniques in order to imitate the appearance of ink, wash, watercolor, gouache, or even oil painting. These techniques may include aquatint, mezzotint, stipple, tool work, and *lavis*. In prints executed in a combination of techniques from multiple plates, it is virtually impossible to identify with confidence the specific techniques used. These prints may also include linear work executed in etching or engraving or both. (For some examples, see cats. 36, 47, 55, 83.)

WOODCUT is a relief printmaking method in which a wooden block is used.

Selected Bibliography

BOOKS AND ARTICLES

Adhémar, Jean. *Graphic Art of the Eighteenth-Century*. Trans. M.I. Martin. New York, 1964.

Ananoff, Alexandre, and Daniel Wildenstein. *François Boucher*. 2 vols. Geneva, 1976.

Clayton, Edward. *French Engravings of the Eighteenth Century in the Collection of Joseph Widener, Lynnewood Hall*. 4 vols. London, 1933 (privately printed).

Cohen, Henri, and Seymour de Ricci. *Guide de l'amateur de livres à gravures du XVIIIe siècle*. 6th ed., rev. and enl. Paris, 1912.

Diderot, Denis, and Jean-le-Rond d'Alembert. *Encyclopédie, ou dictionnaire Raisonné des Sciences, des Arts et des Métiers*. 17 vols. Paris, 1757. See also *Diderot Pictorial Encyclopedia of Trades and Industry: Manufacturing and the Technical Arts in Plates, Selected from l'Encyclopédie; ou dictionnaire Raisonné des Sciences, des Arts et des Métiers of Denis Diderot*. Ed. Charles Coulston Gillispie. 2 vols. New York, 1959.

Dilke, Lady. *French Engravers and Draughtsmen of the XVIIIth Century*. London, 1902.

Dodgson, Campbell. *Old French Colour-Prints*. London, 1924.

Fenaille, Maurice. *L'Oeuvre gravé de P.-L. Debucourt (1755–1832)*. Paris, 1899.

Franklin, Colin and Charlotte. *A Catalogue of Early Colour Printing from Chiaroscuro to Aquatint*. London, 1977.

Gascoigne, Bamber. *How to Identify Prints*. London and New York, 1986.

Gascoigne, Bamber. *Milestones in Colour Printing, 1457–1859*. Cambridge and New York, 1997.

Gaudriault, Raymond. *Filigranes et autres caractéristiques des papiers fabriqués en France aux XVII et XVIII siècles*. Paris, 1995.

Gautier Dagoty, Jacques-Fabien. *Lettres concernant le nouvel art de graver et imprimer les tableaux*. Paris, 1749.

Girodie, André. *Un Peintre de fêtes galantes, Jean-Frédéric Schall (Strasbourg 1752-Paris 1825)*. Strasbourg, 1927.

Goncourt, Edmond and Jules de. *L'Art du XVIIIe siècle*. 2 vols. Paris, 1880–1882.

Griffiths, Antony. "Notes on Early Aquatint in England and France." *Print Quarterly* 4, no. 3 (September, 1987): 255–270.

Griffiths, Antony. *Prints and Printmaking, Introduction to the History and Techniques*. Berkeley, 1996.

Heawood, Edward. *Watermarks*. Amsterdam, 1970.

Hédou, Jules. *Jean Le Prince et son oeuvre*. Paris, 1879.

Hérold, Jacques. *Jean-Charles François (1717–1769), Catalogue de l'oeuvre gravé*. Paris, 1931.

Hérold, Jacques. *Louis-Marin Bonnet (1736–1793), Catalogue de l'oeuvre gravé*. Paris, 1935 (abbreviated as Hérold).

Hind, Arthur M. *A History of Engraving and Etching from the 15th Century to the Year 1914*. 3d ed., rev. New York, 1963.

Hind, Arthur M. *An Introduction to a History of Woodcut*. 2 vols. Boston and New York, 1935.

Hunter, Dard. *Papermaking: The History and Technique of an Ancient Craft*. 3d ed. New York, 1947.

(IFF) *Inventaire du fonds français, Graveurs du XVIIIe siècle*. 14 vols. Bibliothèque nationale de France, Paris, 1930–1977.

Jean-Richard, Pierrette. *L'Oeuvre gravé de François Boucher dans la Collection Edmond de Rothschild. Inventaire général des gravures, École française, I*. Paris, 1978.

Landau, David, and Peter Parshall. *The Renaissance Print, 1470–1550*. New Haven and London, 1994.

Le Blon, J.C. *Coloritto or the Harmony of Colouring in Painting*. London, n.d. [1725]. Facsimile ed., Ed. Faber Birren. New York, 1980.

Leymarie, Louis de. *L'Oeuvre de Gilles Demarteau l'Aîné, graveur du roi, Catalogue déscriptif précedé d'une notice biographique*. Paris, 1896.

Lilien, Otto. *Jacob Christoph Le Blon, 1667–1741: Inventor of Three- and Four-Colour Printing*. Stuttgart, 1985.

Melot, Michel, et al. *Prints: History of an Art*. Geneva and New York, 1981.

Montdorge, Antoine Gautier de. *L'Art d'imprimer les tableaux. Traité d'après les écrits, les opérations et les instructions verbales de J.C. Le Blon*. Paris, 1756. Reprint, Geneva, 1973.

Portalis, Baron Roger, and Henri Béraldi. *Les Graveurs du dix-huitième siècle*. 3 vols. Paris, 1880.

Russell, Charles E. *French Colour-Prints of the XVIIIth Century, The Art of Debucourt, Janinet and Descourtis*. London, 1927.

Salaman, M.C. *French Colour-Prints of the XVIII Century*. London, 1913.

Slatkin, Regina Shoolman. "Some Boucher Drawings and Related Prints." *Master Drawings* 10, no. 3 (1972): 264–283.

Wax, Carol. *The Mezzotint: History and Technique*. New York, 1996.

EXHIBITION CATALOGUES

Amsterdam, 1992. *Chiaroscuro Woodcuts, Hendrick Goltzius and His Time*. Rijksmuseum, Rijksprentenkabinet (Nancy Bialler).

Austin, 1996. *Prints of the Ancien Régime*. Archer M. Huntington Art Gallery, University of Texas (Jonathan Bober).

Baltimore, 1984. *Regency to Empire: French Printmaking 1715–1814*. Baltimore Museum of Art (Victor Carlson, John Ittmann, et al.).

Baltimore, 2002. *Painted Prints, The Revelation of Color in Northern Renaissance and Baroque Engravings, Etchings and Woodcuts*. Baltimore Museum of Art (Susan Dackerman et al.).

Coburg, 1965. *Französische Farbstiche, 1735–1815, aus dem Kupferstichkabinett der Veste Coburg*. Kunstsammlungen der Veste Coburg (Heino Maedebach).

Cologne, 1987. *Rokoko und Revolution, Französische Druckgraphik des späten 18. Jahrhunderts*. Wallraf-Richartz-Museum.

Darmstadt, 1996. *Farbdrucke des 18. Jahrhunderts aus eigenem Bestand*. Hessisches Landesmuseum, Graphische Sammlung.

Düsseldorf, 1999. *Farbige Graphik—Colour Prints*. C.G. Boerner (Armin Kunz).

London, 1974. *French Prints of the XVIII Century*. P. & D. Colnaghi.

New Haven, 1962. *Color in Prints. Catalogue of an Exhibition of European and American Color Prints from 1500 to the Present*. Yale University Art Gallery (Egbert Haverkamp-Begemann).

New Haven, 1978. *Color Printing in England, 1486–1870*. Yale Center for British Art (Joan Friedman).

Nice, 1977. *Carle Vanloo, Premier peintre du roi (Nice, 1705-Paris, 1765)*. Musée Chéret (Marie-Catherine Sahut and Pierre Rosenberg).

Paris, 1920. *Exposition Debucourt*. Palais du Louvre.

Paris, 1985. *Graveurs français de la seconde moitié du XVIIIe siècle*. Musée du Louvre (Pierrette Jean-Richard).

Paris and Lausanne, 1996. *L'Anatomie de la couleur: L'Invention de l'estampe en couleurs*. Bibliothèque nationale de France and Musée Olympique (Florian Rodari et al.).

Quebec, 1989. *L'Image de la Révolution française*. Musée du Québec (Claudette Hould).

Rome, 1990. *J. H. Fragonard e H. Robert a Roma*. Villa Medici.

Roslyn Harbor, N.Y., 1997. *The Age of Elegance, Eighteenth Century French Prints from the Collection of Mr. and Mrs. David P. Tunick*. Nassau County Museum of Art (Beverly Schreiber Jacoby).

Washington, 1973. *François Boucher in North American Collections: 100 Drawings*. National Gallery of Art (Regina Shoolman Slatkin).

Washington, 1977. *Paper in Prints*. National Gallery of Art (Andrew Robison).

Index

ILLUSTRATION DETAILS

half-title page: cat. 55
frontispiece: cat. 22
page vi: cat. 37a
page viii: cat. 89
page xi: cat. 11
page xii: cat. 85
page 8: cat. 9a
page 22: cat. 45
page 34: cat. 47a
page 40: cat. 74
page 160: cat. 25